THE
WINE
LIST
2007

To Nathalie

Also by Matthew Jukes
THE WINE LIST 2002
THE WINE LIST 2003
THE WINE LIST 2004
THE WINE LIST 2005
THE WINE LIST 2006
AND THE WINE BOOK

Acknowledgements

I would like to thank everyone in the UK wine trade and all of those wonderful people abroad who have helped me so much over the past twelve months. I have travelled extensively and tasted more wines than ever before. Your collective encouragement is phenomenal and enormously humbling – I simply couldn't write this book without you. Special thanks must go to my family for their unstinting support and love. I would also like to thank Robert Kirby at PFD and the huge team at Headline. Jo Roberts-Miller, my editor, has worked particularly hard this year on my behalf – thank you all.

THE WINE LIST 2007

THE TOP 250 WINES OF THE YEAR
MATTHEW JUKES

headline

First published in 2006 by
HEADLINE BOOK PUBLISHING

1

Cataloguing in Publication Data is available from the British Library

0 7553 1359 3 (ISBN-10)
978 0 7553 1359 4 (ISBN-13)

Designed by Fiona Pike
Printed and bound in the UK by The Bath Press

Headline's policy is to use papers that are natural, renewable and
recyclable products and made from wood grown in sustainable forests.
The logging and manufacturing processes are expected to conform to
the environmental regulations of the country of origin.

Headline Book Publishing
A division of Hodder Headline
338 Euston Road
London NW1 3BH

www.headline.co.uk
www.hodderheadline.com

CONTENTS

INTRODUCTION

Good day to you and welcome back if you are TWL frequent flyer. If you are new to **THE WINE LIST**, I hope you will find that it's a doddle to navigate around the chapters. This book is designed to help you find all of the wines you need to satiate your thirst, widen your vinous horizons and amaze your taste buds over the coming year. So, come in, pull up a chair and make yourself at home. All you need is a glass and a corkscrew (or a fully functioning hand for screwcaps); leave the rest to me. And remember to enjoy it – wine is fun.

The **Top 250** is the definitive distillation of my entire year's tasting notes – everything from my travels, judging, lecturing and tasting all over the world. Fifty-one and a half weeks of non-stop tasting ends and a few days of frantic typing begins! Bearing in mind I write every word of this book myself and don't use other people's tasting notes or freelance 'researchers' to do the donkeywork, everything you see is mine (and that means any errors, too!). I update the 250 during the editing and proofing stages but every year as soon as the Top 250 is published, wine merchants across the country rush to stock the wines included to sell to their clients. Clearly it is too late to list these shops so, come October, many of the wines will have much wider distribution than is shown here – good news for everyone. Price-wise, some shops may sell a little over my rrp (which I get from the UK agent), equally others can be cheaper – I note the 'official' list price. And remember, just because a shop is not on your doorstep, this shouldn't stop you buying their wines – every single merchant in the Directory delivers nationwide.

So, what trends have shone through in the Top 250 this year? Last year the New World gained a princely 131 listings. This year, bizarrely, this figure has stayed exactly the same. However, the balance within the New World's 131 has shifted. Australia remains omnipotent with a massive 86 entries – this is a thoroughly deserved, awesome performance from the most complete winemaking country in the world at present. New Zealand has slipped back from 22 to a pathetic 5. This is partly to do with my apathy, not yours. There are hundreds of good Kiwi wines out there, but how many are truly jaw-dropping? This is the problem – they need more character and more points of difference to wow me. South Africa hovers under the 20 mark, but still wins new places thanks to an ever-improving attitude and the ageing of their finest vineyards. South America is finally starting to get into its stride. From a combined effort of 7 last year to 18 this year. This is very encouraging; they are finally hearing us when we say we don't like over-oaked whites or alcohol-hot reds! California is starting to make waves again, at all price points, which is good news for everyone. Back to the Old World, France continues its charge up the ladder. Although it sits some twenty or so wines behind Australia, it is still the most important country for fizz and other well-known classics. Australia and France combined equal 147 of the 250. With Italy, Spain, Portugal and Germany on board, we are over 200 and I could, quite honestly, only drink wines from these countries for the rest of my life and have no regrets whatsoever. The other nations make up the last 50 with moments of genius, but life without Italy would be boring, Spanish wines improve ever year and Portuguese wines are going through the biggest transformation in their history. All of these players' wines are fundamental to our wine diets.

A few years ago I began to preach to the world on the benefits of screwcaps. I have also brought your attention to the cost of the wine in the bottle, explaining why you only really start to see true quality above seven pounds. Last year I fired a shot across the bows of supermarket and national chain store wine buyers. I couldn't think of more than a handful of buyers whose palates I thought could be categorised as 'world class'. Luckily a few more people have been drafted in over the past twelve months, so this coming year should not be quite as depressing when you browse the supermarket shelves. But, doom and gloom in the wine trade comes from the agents' side, too. I have never heard so much angst concerning under-qualified tasters and over-zealous accountants slashing agent's margins to boost their own handsome retailer profits. A lot of winemakers around the world say it is just not worth doing business in the UK – there is no support and no money to be made and the damage to their brand is sometimes too risky. I have been asked by winemakers so many times in the past year what is wrong with the UK market. My standard answer is that we are drinking more and better wine than ever (this is true), but we are not able to progress at the pace at which we would all like because of the deep discounting and shoddy selection in the big supermarkets. This is impeding progress and stifling choice. The US, Far East and other European countries are the new targets for these winemakers and we are in danger of missing out. So, how do we, the wine drinker, start to put things right? The answer is – by voting with our palates.

Readers of **THE WINE LIST** should boycott the crap wine on the shelves – full stop. You should also rely more on independent wine merchants who, like your specialist butcher or fishmonger, really know their product and care about what they sell – it is on this that their livelihood depends. With **THE WINE LIST**'s help, spend your money on wine wisely and avoid the dross (remember I only write up around 10% of the wines that I taste each year – by definition that leaves over 25,000 that I consider to be well below par – that's a lot of dross!). Search out other wine lovers and drink great wines together! There's no time like the present – life's too short, as they say.

THE TOP 250

£5.99 **Prosecco La Marca, NV**, Veneto, Italy (**Wai**). It is virtually impossible to find decent fizz under six pounds. Don't even bother trying – you'll lose the will to live. Luckily this Prosecco is a beacon that shines refreshing, effervescent, floral, fruit flavours on all who stumble into its path. It is not only an effortlessly delicious wine to drink straight, it is also perfectly prickly and thirst-quenching when blended with peach juice to make a classic Bellini cocktail.

£6.99 **Cuvée Royale Crémant de Limoux Brut, NV**, South of France (**Wai**). This is one of the tastiest inexpensive sparklers on the shelves. Clean, dry and made with a Chardonnay backbone, it is the perfect aperitif/party wine. At seven pounds it is also not going to break the bank. Waitrose also happens to sell Crème de Framboise, Vedrenne (£5.29, 350ml), which is a thoroughly delicious raspberry liqueur. Normally 'Kir Royale' is made with blackcurrant liqueur (Crème de Cassis) and Champagne – my suggested twist on this classic is a Framboise Royale, made with a dash (to taste) of this liqueur blended with my chosen wine.

£6.99 **Sparkling Pinot Grigio, NV**, Lombardy, Italy (**M&S**). This delightful froth-frenzy combines two immensely popular categories in one. It is a sparkler – giddee up! – and it is also a Pinot Grigio – hoorah! But in this wine's case, it is more than the sum of the two parts. This is a gorgeous, friendly fizz with crunchy pineapple and crisp pear notes running up and down the palate. Before you know it, you'll be red-faced and dancing on the table.

£7.95 **Prosecco di Valdobbiadene, Endrizzi, NV**, Veneto, Italy (**Great Western Wine**). Just two quid more than the La Marca above and you're in very posh territory indeed. This wine is a dreamboat, and it is one of the best Proseccos I have tasted in years. I lined it up on my tasting bench at home alongside a load of Champagnes, including some vintage labels around the thirty-five pound mark, and this wine walked it. Why? All of the others were trying too hard and they seemed coarse, muscular and acidic. Endrizzi's glorious fizz was relaxed, mellow, cheery and, ultimately, very classy indeed. It is a veritable bargain.

£7.99 **Jacob's Creek Sparkling Rosé, NV**, Australia (**Asd**, **Sai**, **Tes**, **Thr** and **Wai**). Since this wine first appeared in last year's 250 it has gone gangbusters in the UK. And the reason is, it is a delightfully cheery little number, bursting with cranberry and raspberry fruit and topped off with loads of refreshing acidity. If you are having a big get together and fancy serving something a little different, this rosé looks the part and does the trick. Also, remember that rosé fizz goes really well with a wide range of canapés including the spicier ones, so it is the perfect wine for a drinks party.

£9.60 **Domaine des Baumard Carte Turquoise, NV**, Crémant de Loire, France (**Jeroboams**). I have tried hard to beat this beautiful fizz over the last twelve months but Baumard's Carte Turquoise is still the reigning champ of Loire Crémants. Baumard is a legend in the Loire, but he specialises in semi-sweet to very sweet whites, so it was a surprise to discover this cheeky sparkler. Once again, it is a Champagne standard that he has set his sights on and he effortlessly bowls over the vast majority of them at twice the price. Well played sir.

£9.99 **Brown Brothers Pinot Noir/ Chardonnay/Pinot Meunier, NV**, Victoria, Australia (**Boo**, **Christopher Piper**, **Noble Rot**, **Peckhams**, **S H Jones** and **Wai**). Truly serious New World sparkling wine under a tenner is a very rare beast indeed. Brown Bros. are masters at this style of wine. By sourcing pristine fruit, they manage to fashion a very chic fizz indeed. I have poured this wine for the cream of UK wine journos and buyers and nobody blinked!

£10.99 **Taltarni Brut Taché, 2004**, Tasmania/ Victoria, Australia (**deFINE**, **Philglas & Swiggot** and **Whitebridge Wines**). This is a joyous, Kir Royale-stained, rosé wine. The nose is the definition of wild strawberries and the palate is seamless and silky. While you could accuse it of being unashamedly tarty, I love it. Taché is a Basque and stockings in a glass. Moulin Rouge is your theme when drinking this wine.

£12.99 **Graham Beck Blanc de Blancs, 2001**, South Africa (**Wai**). Pieter Ferreira is the finest maker of fizz in South Africa. This jaw-dropping Blanc de Blancs is not only a bargain price, but it is one of my favourite sparkling wines in the world. With class, elegance, remarkable persistence on the palate and a scintillating nose, this wine puts inexpensive Champagne to shame.

£12.99 **Green Point by Chandon, 2002**, Australia (**Fortnum & Mason**, **Harvey Nichols**, **Odd**, **Philglas & Swiggot** and **Wai**). Vintage GP gets better and better with every new release. There is true 'vintage' weight and intensity here, and the crisp acidity and stiletto finish balances the decadent palate perfectly. It is this magnificent poise allied to considerable power that typifies this cuvée – it is world class.

£13.99 **Green Point by Chandon, Vintage Brut Rosé, 2002**, Australia (**Odd**). Just to prove that Tony Jordan and his team are not one trick ponies, their 2002 rosé is a sensational wine, too. And, what's more, it is sealed with a crown cap (like a beer bottle). This looks great and is easy to flick off, too. Why do it? Cork taint (which ruins wine, giving it a musty smell) is rife. I see one in ten bottles with some sort of cork-affected problem. No cork – no cork issues! By sealing with a crown cap, Tony has ensured that this wine tastes every bit as good in your home as it did in the winery when he bottled it.

£14.99 **Jansz Tasmania Vintage Cuvée, 2001**, Tasmania, Australia (**Berkmann** and **Odd**). The Jansz NV is a perennial favourite in TWL but the 2001 vintage could possibly be the finest wine ever made at this estate. It swaggers around the glass like Johnny Depp and it kidnaps your olfactory system – the ransom being another bottle! Keep your eyes peeled for an otherworldly NV rosé, too.

£16.95 **Camel Valley Cornwall Brut, 2004**, Cornwall, England (**Camel Valley**, selected **Waitrose** branches in the southwest). I like English wines and support them where and when I can, but there are very few that I really love on a world scale. This is my favourite sparkling wine of the year and it is worth every penny. The Lindo family's wines always do well in my tastings and I know they sell out every year, so don't hang around if you want some of this elegant, classy fizz or the Bacchus in the unoaked section! These are wines that I have shown to very important winemakers all over the world and they marvel at the complexity and precision in the glass. The direct number for the winery is 01208 77959 and you can also access them online at www.camelvalley.com

£19.50 **Dumangin Fils Brut Grande Réserve, NV**, Champagne, France (**Yapp**). This is my favourite sub-twenty Champs of the year. With an extra year of bottle age under its belt than the wine I wrote up last year, this is a more intense, creamy, subtle and all-enveloping style of Champagne.

£22.99 **Saint Gall, Grand Cru, 2000**, Champagne, France (**M&S**). M&S sells buckets of NV Oudinot, its 'house' Champagne (£17.49), and it is a goodly offering. But I would recommend trading up to the 2001 Vintage Oudinot (£19.99) for far more than two and a half pounds' worth of extra flavour. But, better still, climb the ladder further and hurdle the psychological twenty-pound barrier and dive into a glass of this brilliant 2000 Saint Gall. I think this is the finest Champagne I have tasted from M&S in the six years I have been your official taster. It is creamy, smooth, mellow, balanced, refreshing and moreish. It ticks all of the boxes and, in fairness, is remarkably good value in the Champagne scheme of things!

£24.99 **Billecart-Salmon, Brut Réserve, NV**, Champagne, France (£24.99, **Berry Bros. & Rudd, Fortnum & Mason, Harrods, Harvey Nichols, Lay & Wheeler, James Nicholson, Odd, Philglas & Swiggot, Selfridges, Uncorked** and **Valvona & Crolla**). I am sure you know by now that I am a besotted Billecart fan. This small house is one of the finest producers of Champagne, full stop. Brut Réserve is one of the most reliable and over-delivering (flavour-wise) wines on the shelves today. It is creamy, smooth, uplifting and guaranteed to brighten your day. You simply cannot go wrong with this spectacular Champagne in your glass. Everyone needs a banker – a wine that will always delight and amaze the drinker – this wine does this and more.

£27.00 **Primo Joseph Sparkling Red, NV**, South Eastern Australia (**Australian Wine Club**). Who, what, where, when and how? Joe Grilli, a near-insane sparkling red wine, the outskirts of Adelaide, released recently and made from a fifteen-year-old Shiraz-base wine, with some Amarone-d Cabernet (dried grapes – heady and intense) and topped up with a seventies liqueured red wine. I've missed this in the past. How? The answer is, I have no idea, so don't ask any more questions! This wine has all the answers – it is mind-blowing.

£29.00 **The Wine Society's Cuvée Centenaire Blanc de Blanc, NV**, Champagne, France (**Wine Society**). The Wine Society, the oldest wine club in the world, is this year celebrating 100 years of collaboration with the prestigious Alfred Gratien Champagne house, which produces The Society's own label Champagnes. To mark their historic anniversary they have launched two exclusive, limited edition wines. Cuvée Centenaire is made from 100% Chardonnay (from the 2002 vintage) and it is fermented in French oak from Chablis. This is a stunningly crisp, fruity, fine wine. The second release is in magnums only (150cl) and only 2,000 were made – NV Cuvée Centenaire (£69.00) is 60% Chardonnay, 20% Pinot Noir and 20% Pinot Meunier from the excellent 1998 vintage. This bigger bottle has a much bigger, richer flavour – if you want something special for a celebration, hunt either of these smart wines down.

£30.99 **Laurent Perrier Ultra Brut, NV**, Champagne, France (**Berry Bros.**, **Boo**, **Fortnum & Mason**, **Goedhuis**, **Harrods**, **Harvey Nichols**, **Lea & Sandeman**, **Maj**, **Mitchells**, **Nicolas**, **Odd**, **Peckhams**, **Selfridges**, **Roberson**, **Roberts & Speight** and **Vintage House**). Ultra Brut (meaning bone dry) is a near masochistic style of Champagne, such is its searing dryness. I adore this cleansing style of fizz. It goes exceptionally well with food as the bracing dryness slices through flash canapés, sushi and spicy nibbles. It is also apparently the lowest calorie of any sparkler. Fill your glasses – I expect you'll end up losing weight with all that strenuous lifting of glass to lips!

scintillating beauty

£32.65 **Bollinger Special Cuvée, NV**, Champagne, France (**Berry Bros.**, **Fortnum & Mason**, **Odd**, **Sai**, **Selfridges** and **Wai**). You are either into Bolly or you're not. It is rich, full, firm, imposing, masterful, heady, mouth-filling, intense, aromatic, weighty, serious and takes no prisoners. And, if you're not into Bolly, you're missing something. Of course, I realise the taste of wine is personal and purely subjective, but surely Bolly can transcend that – it is omnipotent, after all!

£49.99 **Pol Roger Brut Chardonnay, 1998**, Champagne, France (**Bennett's**, **Berry Bros.**, **Fortnum & Mason**, **Haynes**, **Hanson & Clark**, **Luvians**, **Christopher Piper**, **Wine Society** and **Wright Wine**). This Blanc de Blancs (made from 100% Chardonnay) is a scintillating beauty. Not cheap, but ever so classy, this is a smooth, long, ripe glass of wine, with oodles of charm and buckets of breeding. It will leave you and your lucky fellow drinkers gasping for air and reeling with joy.

£65.00 **Billecart-Salmon Blanc de Blancs, 1998**, Champagne, France (**Harrods**, **Harvey Nichols** and **Uncorked**). Billecart's 1998 releases are sublime. My chosen BdB is the most forward of the trio and it is heart-achingly beautiful. The flavour is ethereal and it washes over the palate languidly, while you are left in a trance-like state of submission. The 1998 Cuvée Nicolas-François (£50, **Berry Bros.**, **Lay & Wheeler**, **James Nicholson**, **Odd**, **Selfridges** and **Uncorked**) is rich, youthful and imposing, forcing itself on to your palate and muscling its way into your dreams. This is a wine that will unravel incrementally over the next decade, but you can happily drink it from Christmas with confidence. The final wine in this line up of musketeers is the 1998 Cuvée Elisabeth Salmon Rosé (£75, **Berry Bros.**, **Fortnum & Mason** and **Uncorked**). It is nothing short of heroic, with unabashed, savage, wild-strawberry notes on the nose and a mighty lick of red fruit on the palate, too. This is a stunning wine and one that has nothing like the vinous density of the Bolly to follow but more sensitivity beneath its toned exterior. In short, this is the most complete family of 1998 releases on the market today.

£89.99 **Bollinger, La Grande Année Rosé, 1999**, Champagne, France (**Berry Bros.**, **Fortnum & Mason**, **Harrods**, **Harvey Nichols**, **Maj**, **Selfridges**, **Wai** and **Wimbledon**). I was totally floored when I first tasted this stellar wine. I find it hard to put into words just how perfect the nose, palate and finish of La Grande Année 1999 are. The cavalcade of flavours is frankly hilarious – I laughed for a day after experiencing this wine. The colour alone is a feast for your optical nerves. Deep, velvety, Regency glamour in a glass, it pleads with you to sprint down to the nearest costumier for a doublet and hose. You see fireworks and hear Rachmaninov playing on a Steinway. And you haven't even tasted it yet. Then things move fast – sensual nuances of wild, pagan, red fruit rush at you from all angles primping, prodding, stroking and soothing every flavour receptor in your being. Swallow and the world is a better place, but not as good as it is after another sip. This is as close to heaven on earth as you are going to get with a rosé Champagne. The problem is that you will like it too much. I am still in therapy. I adore this wine.

£89.99 **Pol Roger Cuvée Sir Winston Churchill, 1996**, Champagne, France (**Avery's, Bennett's, Berry Bros., Cambridge, Corney & Barrow, Hedley Wright, Jeroboams** and **Stone, Vine & Sun**). Winston would be proud. This 1996 is the finest for many years and it will live for two decades such is the intensity and finesse buried in the core of this unassuming, sleeping giant. It is a crime to open this wine now – I had to, it's my job – but it is woefully young. If you have the wherewithal, please stash some bottles away safely, because in five to ten years this will be a truly spectacular wine.

£115.00 **Krug, 1995**, Champagne, France (**Armit, Berry Bros., Connolly's, Corney & Barrow, Farr, Fortnum & Mason, Goedhuis, Harrods, Harvey Nichols, Hoults, Jeroboams, Lea & Sandeman, Nickolls & Perks, Raeburn, Roberson** and **Selfridges**). The 1990 Krug made the Top 250 two years ago. It is still one of the greats today, but I am convinced that the newly released 1995 is even more impressive ('What?' I hear you cry). It combines the sleek power, sensual wild honey and brazen, buxom fruit of the 1990 with a grip and vivacity that embodies the 1995 vintage and does wonders for the libido. Krug isn't cheap but I would forgo my late-night cheese on toast for a year to save up for a bottle of this beauty. It is every bit as good as you'd expect it to be.

£2.99 **Les Deux Colombard/Chardonnay, 2005**, Vin de Pays Côtes de Gascogne, France (**Boo**). The cheapest white this year (and the only one I would touch, I can assure you) is this cheery blend from Gascony. It is fruity and dry and finishes clean as a whistle.

£3.49 **Le Sanglier Old Vine Grenache Blanc, 2005**, Vin de Pays de l'Aude, France (**Boo**). Booths wine buyer Sally Holloway is a master at sniffing out bargain wines – here is the next one up the ladder and it is certainly worth the 50p more. With lemon and lime fruit and surprising depth, this is a proper little cracker and it looks smart, too.

£3.99 **Leopards Leap Lookout White, 2006**, Western Cape, South Africa (**Tes**). Made from the three Cs – Chenin Blanc, Chardonnay and Colombard, this zesty, brand new white from the Cape is a feisty, refreshing little number and it is also sealed with a screwcap, so it is guaranteed to be in perfect nick!

£3.99 **Muscadet, Jacques Arnoult, 2005**, Loire, France (**Maj**). This is a frighteningly good wine for its lowly price point. Muscadet has always had slightly dodgy street cred in the world of wine, but this is, in most cases, unfair. Muscadet does not set out to be a serious, or even very complex, style of white wine, instead it endeavours to please while perking up and invigorating the palate with light, dry, tickly, fresh, crisp fruit. Apples and crunchy pears and a whisper of white flowers are all you

LIGHT, DRY AND UNOAKED

need on the nose to guarantee a good glass of wine. Jacques Arnoult does all this for three and a half quid – *merci* Jacques.

£3.99 **Verdicchio dei Castelli di Jesi Classico, Moncaro, 2005**, Marche, Italy (**Wai**). Every year this wine comes up trumps. I can't believe it's only four quid – Moncaro is a stunner. This is emergency white, with more talent than virtually all of the ugly £4 wines that populate less discerning supermarket selections. Clean, aromatic and smooth apple and pear fruit tumbles across the palate like an ebullient toddler and the finish is a joy, too.

£4.99 **Alotzano Verdejo, 2005**, Gonzalez Byass, Vino de la Tierra de Castilla, Spain (**Boo**). There is a ton of vibrant lime juice going on in this crazy little wine. Like a wasp-stung donkey it kicks around in the glass with enthusiasm, scattering tropical fruit and cleansing acidity in all directions.

£4.99 **Quadro Sei Gavi, 2005**, Piedmont, Italy (**M&S**). Winemaker Claudio Manera is a shrewd cookie and he cunningly weaves some serious complexity into this budget Cortese. Normally a pretty dull grape variety, Cortese is responsible for the uber-fashionable white wine Gavi di Gavi. You would usually have to pay over a tenner to be assured of drinking a reasonable version of this chic wine, and even then you might end up with a flat, soulless offering, so when this tricky little number found its way into my glass I knew it would be a perfect white for entertaining your pals. Zesty

LIGHT, DRY AND UNOAKED

pineapple chunk fruit is balanced with keen, refreshing acidity and the overall impression is nothing short of the true essence of an Italian summer – bombing along on a Vespa with a male/female (delete as necessary) blonde riding pillion.

£5.49 **Quinta de Azevedo, Vinho Verde, 2005**, Barcelos, Portugal (**Boo**, **Maj**, **Wai** and **Wine Society**). Made from 70% Loureiro and 30% Pederña (can I dodge the explanation for these two varieties please?), this is a cracking good VV. Effervescent (unnervingly so) at first, this is a feisty number but after it settles in the glass it loses none of its verve as it goes about its job of electrocuting your taste buds one by one. Matched to seafood it sings loud and with perfect pitch. Don't drink too many bottles or you might explode from all the CO_2, but as a quick, refreshing apero or cunning crustacea partner, this is a terrific, joltingly chirpy five quid well spent.

£5.99 **Dourthe No. 1 Sauvignon Blanc, 2005**, Bordeaux, France (**Thr** and **Wai**). I have been following this wine for a few years now and it has finally hit the bull's eye. The 2005 vintage is brilliant; the flavour is mouth-watering and the value for money astounding. Made from Sauvignon (bonjour) but showing considerable depth and intensity, this is a superb party wine or lunchtime all-purpose white. It is lemony and succulent, with a perky, dry, tangy finish, and the bottle is sealed with a screwcap so you are guaranteed perfect condition. Congrats Dourthe.

£5.99 **Honeywood Sauvignon Blanc, 2005**,
Lodi, California (**Tes**). Strangely, this is not a typical
Sauvignon on the nose or palate. Leaving these
minor points aside, it is still a lovely white wine.
It is rich and fruity and yet dry and clean. There
isn't a herbal twang – more of a tropical, creaminess
which I really like.

£5.99 **Marks & Spencer Friuli Sauvignon
Blanc, 2005**, Friuli-Venezia Giulia, Italy (**M&S**).
Clean, herbal, tight and green, this is a perfect wine
for fishy, cheesy or creamy sauces (on fishy, cheesy
or creamy pasta dishes). The trademark Sauvignon
acidity cuts rapier-like through the richness of this
style of cuisine and refreshes the palate with verve
and vigour at the same time.

£5.99 **Peter Lehmann Chenin Blanc, 2005**,
Barossa Valley, South Australia (**Boo**, **La Riche**, **Wai**
and **T Wright**). This inexpensive beauty sprinted
into the list and set up camp. The bouncers tried to
eject it, knowing that PL is a specialist red wine
maker, but after encountering a tirade of well-
chosen Aussie expletives they left. Welcome PL
Chenin, you belong in this list because you have
balls! The more I taste this wine the more I get
hooked on the fresh pineapple and pink grapefruit
notes. The 2006 is a beauty, too, so slip into that
one when it arrives next year.

£5.99 **Stormhoek Sauvignon Blanc, 2006**,
Western Cape, South Africa (**Asd**, **deFINE**,
Harrogate, **Magnum**, **Sai**, **Thr** and **Wimbledon**).

LIGHT, DRY AND UNOAKED

This wine sports a 'drink by date' – Stormy were the first to come up with this inspirational concept. The team knows that this exceptional Sauvignon needs to be enjoyed in the first year of its life – which neatly mirrors the life span of this book. They use an 'ultimate freshness' guide on the bottle to ensure you drink it at its peak. Follow the instructions and bathe your taste buds in this wickedly refreshing, lime-juice-imbued wine. Stormy has always been a front runner – now they are the leader.

£5.99 **Stormhoek Pinot Grigio, 2006**, Western Cape, South Africa (**deFINE**, **Harrogate**, **Magnum**, **Thr**, **Wai** and **Wimbledon**). You wait all year for a £5.99 stonker and two come along at once. I was the first bloke to taste the new 2006s from Stormy Pants and I simply can't leave the PG out of the mix. It's wicked, its irreverent, it simply doesn't give a toss what you think – I expect really hard thugs are reduced to tears when they taste this wine, it has so much attitude. So are you up to it? Come and have a go … It's only Pinot Grigio, after all.

£5.99 **Tesco Finest Gavi, 2005**, Piedmont, Italy (**Tes**). On the face of it everything is wrong with this wine. Own label, Gavi, £5.99 – surely a treble recipe for disaster? Not so with this stunning white. Gavi has always been a trendy so'n'so, but here it transcends its chic (read over-inflated price point) status and delivers a seamless bolt of crisp, green-apple fruit and keen acidity, without even so much as a sideways wink. That's two Gavis already and we are still only in the foothills of this section!

£6.95 **Willow Bridge Dragonfly Sauvignon Blanc/Semillon, 2005**, Geographe, Western Australia (**Cheshire Smokehouse, Rodney Densem, Richard Granger, Old Forge Wine Cellar, Stevens Garnier, Thr** and **Wright Wine Co.**). This cheeky, cool-climate SBS is the sort of wine to take the spotlight off Marlborough's arrogant versions of this variety. Cunning, balanced and layered, Willow Bridge is as fresh as daisies and palate-titillatingly crisp, and just the ticket to wash away a grotty day in the office in seconds.

£6.99 **Glen Carlou Tortoise Hill White, 2005**, Western Cape, South Africa (**Odd**). Made by the mercurial, young winemaker David Finlayson, Tortoise is a Sauvignon, Chardonnay, Viognier blend and it really works well. With lemon, lime and apple notes on the mid palate and a whisper of apricots on the nose, this wine shows that blended whites can, in the right hands, equal more than the sum of its parts. Reports suggest the 2006 is a ripper, too.

£6.99 **Simonsig Chenin Blanc, 2005**, Stellenbosch, South Africa (**Thr** and **WRa**). Subject to a 'three for two' deal, this wine ends up at only £4.66 – not bad at all for a honeyed, greengage and lime-zest-stuffed white, with a perky gooseberry 'see-ya' on the finish.

£7.99 **Kaituna Hills Reserve Sauvignon Blanc, 2005**, Marlborough, New Zealand (**M&S**). It's funny how the tiniest things can influence the flavour of a wine. This Sauvignon

LIGHT, DRY AND UNOAKED

Blanc has only 3% of oak barrel fermented fruit in it, but that little addition of richness turns this wine from a 'nice enough white' into a 'drop dead stunner'. The complexity, depth of fruit and lift of citrus and green herb nuances on the nose is utterly delightful. This is Kiwi Sauvignon with an IQ. The much trumpeted 2006 follows and is set to be even more exciting.

£7.99 **Litorale Vermentino, 2004**, Cecchi, Maremma, Tuscany, Italy (**Wai**). Vermentino is a strange grape and it often disappoints, with edgy, acidity and tangy, underpowered fruit. But this version is amazing, with hypnotic, tropical fruit and a gorgeous, smooth, pulpy texture. It slides across the palate casting the fresh, lightly scented apricot nuances asunder. You can edge towards spicier dishes with this wine, as it has cooling acidity and enough weight of fruit to cope with stronger flavours.

£7.99 **La Prendina Pinot Grigio, 2005**, Lombardy, Italy (**M&S**). La Prendina is a clever little wine. With more body and texture than most PGs, this is an able aperitif white but, in truth, it has more to it than just pre-dinner-glugger status. This is a delicious seafood white and it can handle spicier dishes with ease because the finish is loaded with palate-quenchingly dry acidity and remarkable dynamism.

£7.99 **Pinot Grigio San Angelo, Banfi, 2005**, Tuscany, Italy (**Maj**). Look closely and you will see that this PG comes from Tuscany (not the far northeast of the country like the majority of Italian versions). It is warmer in Tuscany than it is in Friuli, for example, and this means the wine has more weight on the palate than you'd expect. The acidity is still typically crisp and refreshing, but the overall package is beguilingly yummy and more main course shaped than La Prendina above.

£7.99 **Wirra Wirra Scrubby Rise, 2005**, McLaren Vale, South Australia (**Old Forge Wine Cellar**, **Stevens Garnier** and **Whitebridge**). Thank goodness Wirra has now found its footing in the UK, because this company's wines should be on everyone's dining room table in the UK. This Sauv/Sem/Viog cocktail is destined to be hosed down 24/7 – yeehah! Scrubby is a lesson in blending skills: 1 + 1 + 1 = 6.

£7.99 **Wither Hills Sauvignon Blanc, 2006**, Marlborough, New Zealand (**Boo**, **Great Western Wine**, **Odd**, **Sommelier**, **Villeneuve** and **Wai**). It's made the list every single year – 2002–2007! All I need say, is that this wine gets better and better, and winemakers Brent, Ben and Nadine deserve a great vote of thanks for giving us the opportunity to drink GREAT Marlborough Sauvignon at a phenomenal price. It is too early to say where 2006 The Ned Waihopai Vineyard Sauvignon will be retailed this year, but this is Brent Marris's new project and it is made at the epic Wither Hills winery. Needless to say, it is sensational with even more linear drive and expression than even Wither Hills manages. Nothing is beyond this team. Smile wide – this is good news.

£8.50 **Quincy, Cuvée Villalin, Domaine Jacques Rouzé, 2005**, Loire, France (**Haynes, Hanson & Clark**). The most famous Sauvignon Blanc in the world is probably Sancerre. The best examples of Sancerre cost upwards of a tenner, but if you head to the villages neighbouring Sancerre, you can find terrific bargains for a few pounds less. Quincy (pronounced Can-see), is one of these little-known areas and the top producer here is Rouzé. Made from 100 per cent Sauvignon Blanc, this wine is drop dead gorgeous. The minerality, fresh green herb and nettle notes, and lime and gooseberry palate goes some way to explaining why this variety is now planted all over the world!

£8.99 **Springfield Special Cuvée Sauvignon Blanc, 2006**, Robertson, South Africa (**Maj**, **Sai** and **Wai**). Springfield's Special Cuvée is a triumph and it is one of the freshest and liveliest wines on the shelves today. 2006 is a crackerjack of a vintage in South Africa and the Sauvignons, in particular, are racy white-knuckle rides, guaranteed to thrill. Scream if you wanna go faster!

£9.25 **Grecante, Grechetto, Arnaldo Caprai, 2005**, Umbria, Italy (**Lea & Sandeman**). Lea & Sandeman is at the cutting edge of Italy's new and exciting wine scene. The selection of wines in their three London wine shops is very impressive indeed. One of their brand new whites that caught my eye and then mugged my palate was this stunning Grechetto. The depth of nutty, honeyed flavours, studded with quince, pear, greengage and lemon

LIGHT, DRY AND UNOAKED

zest is amazing. Even more so, because this wine doesn't use oak barrels at all – these flavours all come from the exceptionally serious grapes. It ticks every box, including the 'weird and wonderful' one, so if you like to blaze a trail with unusual but epic white wines, look no further.

£9.99 **Jackson Estate Sauvignon Blanc, 2005**, Marlborough, New Zealand (**Boo**, **Maj** and **Odd**). Jackson has always been one of the finest producers of Sauvignon in New Zealand and this 2005 and the 2006 are setting the mood for years to come. Winemaker Mike Paterson has rejuvenated this brand and John Stichbury (the founder and inspirational leader of this small but vital team) is beaming from ear to ear these days. He knows that Jackson is justly treasured by its loyal fan club and now that the 2004 Chardonnay and Pinot Noir are also up to racing speed this estate is a true force to be reckoned with.

£12.99 **The Berrio Sauvignon Blanc, 2006**, Flagstone Winery, Elim, South Africa (**Tes**). Winemaker Bruce Jack looked at me and said, 'Right Jukesy I have a job for you. Here are all the tank samples of Sauvignon Blanc for the 2006 harvest. You have ten minutes to put together the best blend you possibly can for The Berrio!' 'Aaarrgghh,' was all I could say. The 2003 and 2004 of this wine were landmarks in the history of SA Sauvignon but obviously this one will be even better! Sealed with a screwcap and hailing from surely the most exciting new region in SA, Elim, this should (cross fingers) be a blindingly serious Sauvignon. Watchathink?

£9.99 **The Gum Sauvignon Blanc, 2005**, Adelaide Hills, South Australia (**M&S**). The grapes for this tremendous wine come from one of the most idyllic properties in the Adelaide Hills – The Lane, owned by the irrepressible Edwards Family. Superstar winemaker Rob Mann converted them into wine with minimal intervention and the result is a direct reflection of the microclimate of this single vineyard site – it is sublime! The bone-dry, citrus fruit is exceptionally crisp and refreshing, and the finish lasts for minutes. This is the definitive refreshing white wine, as it goes with every al fresco dish and challenging starter imaginable. It also happens to be a proven crowd-pleaser – echoing the flavour of Loire staples Sancerre and Pouilly-Fumé but for a few pounds less!

£10.95 **Camel Valley Bacchus, 2005**, Cornwall, England (**Camel Valley**, selected **Waitrose** branches in the south west). This is the most impressive dry white wine of the year from our shores. It is every bit as rewarding and intriguing as any of the wines in this book, so if you are partial to English wine and want to taste the best or are willing to give this lime-juice-imbued wine a whirl, get on the blower now. The direct number for the winery is 01208 77959 and you can also access them online at www.camelvalley.com

£10.99 **Pinot Bianco, Franz Haas, 2004**, Alto Adige, Italy (**Maj**). This must be the most expensive Pinot Bianco I have ever written up in this book, but I can assure you it is worth every penny. Franz Haas is a magician and he summons up depth and texture in this variety that few can find. Ripe, creamy, smooth and complex, this is a superb and immensely classy wine that would be sensational with main course fish dishes. The pear, lemon balm, apple purée and white flower notes are simply superb.

£11.99 **Philip Shaw No.19 Sauvignon Blanc, 2005**, Koomooloo Vineyard, Orange, New South Wales, Australia (**Waitrose Inner Cellar**). He's back! The incorrigible Mr Philip Shaw (a kind of Kaiser Soze for the vinous generation) has brought us a range of epic wines from his beloved Orange region of New South Wales in Australia. They are all collectors' pieces and very few have found national distribution yet, but they will do – and fast. These wines are unmissable. Remember where you read this and electrocute your taste buds with No.19.

£12.99 **The Lane Gathering Sauvignon Blanc, 2005**, Adelaide Hills, South Australia (**Bacchanalia**). This wine has multiple personalities. It can be a giggly schoolgirl of an aperitif or a strict mistress marshalling a main course. Either way I love it. This is the purist, 'estate' wine from the same source as The Gun above, but it is the top of the line wine made in tiny quantities. It is usually sold through very top end restaurants for fairly nose bleed prices, but one merchant has popped up above the parapet and offered this wine to you. Don't delay. I know others will follow, but stock is limited. This is one of the world's finest Sauvignon Blancs. RUN and don't look back.

LIGHT, DRY AND UNOAKED

£13.95 **Keith Tulloch Semillon, 2005**, Hunter Valley, New South Wales, Australia (**The Cellar Door**, **Haslemere Cellar**, **Vin du Van** and **Wine Society**). Keith Tulloch is an inspirational technician. He handcrafts wine from the soil to the bottle and every stage is microscopically observed. This Semillon is spectacular – it is one of the most alluring versions of this grape in existence. It is also unoaked and has strangely low alcohol (10.5%) because this variety, in the right vineyards, gains its flavours earlier in the season than virtually any other white grape. The 2005 is also one of the best vintages I have ever seen and, believe it or not, this wine will last for a further eight years or more without missing a beat – piling on honey, lime and lanolin notes until it is golden, waxy and lush. In short, it starts off life as a perky aperitif, suited to oysters and light fusion dishes, and ends up with a full-on roast chicken or turbot on its lap.

£14.75 **Cullen Semillon/Sauvignon Blanc, 2004**, Margaret River, Western Australia (**Andrew Chapman**, **Bennett's**, **Flying Corkscrew** and **Oz Wines**). This is Willow Bridge (see above) with a doctorate. It ages like top white Graves (Bordeaux's finest dry white wines) and yet displays masses of class in its youth, too. Rare and a relative bargain given its dedicated following, this is a slice of pure excellence from one of the most beautiful wine regions in the world.

£14.95 **Gavi di Gavi, Vigneti Montessora, La Giustiniana, 2005**, Piedmont, Italy (**Flying

Corkscrew, Harrods, Hedley Wright and Noel Young Wines). This Gavi is the best I have ever tasted. Since its release I have drunk it no less than five times in various smart restaurants, because this is where wines of this calibre are usually found. The good news is a handful of merchants also have some stock, so don't delay and bathe in this invigorating, ripe, spring-blossom-scented white. It is as classy and alluring as a pair of Marnis or Manolos and a lot tastier, too!

£20.00 **Tyrrell's Vat 1 Semillon, 1999**, Hunter Valley, New South Wales, Australia (deFINE, Direct Wines, Christopher Piper, Great Grog, Hailsham Cellars, Nickolls & Perks, Roberson, Selfridges, The Vineyard, Wine Society and selected Wai). Vat 1 is a legendary wine and this 1999 is no exception. Lavish lemon meringue pie and wild honey cavort on the palate and the density of fruit is astounding. It started out life like the Tulloch wine above and six years on it is sassy, swinging its hips around like Marilyn Monroe! Jump on board.

● ●

£4.99 **Inycon Fiano, 2005**, Sicily, Italy (Boo). Fiano is a wicked little white grape that delivers terrific, quirky, fruity flavours. It is also a superb alternative to yet another Chardonnay or Sauvignon for the inquisitives out there. With honey, quince, greengage, peach and lemon verbena notes on the nose and palate, this is a wine that can handle fish or chicken main courses and at a fiver it is a real steal.

LIGHT, DRY AND UNOAKED/AROMATIC

£4.99 **Muscat Sec, Gérard Bertrand, 2005**, Vin de Pay's d'Oc, France (**Maj**). M. Bertrand seems to have populated our shelves with a vast number of wines in a very short space of time. The reason for this is clear - they all taste really good. This bright, grapey, dry, yet juicy Muscat typifies his approach to winemaking. It is exactly what you'd want from such a cheery grapey-tasting variety. Serve it as the perfect, cleansing aperitif and marvel at the value for money. Your granny will cartwheel around the room after a few glasses of this elixir – honest!

£5.49 **Torres Viña Esmeralda, 2005**, Penedès, Spain (**Odd**, **Tes**, **Thr**, **Wai** and **WRa**). The zesty, vivacious 2005 continues an unbroken run of excellence for this, my favourite, Spanish white wine. The value for money and sheer crowd-pleasing aroma and flavour of Esmeralda is staggering. I have sold/recommended this wine every year since I have been in the wine trade (I am in my twentieth). This is an unmatchable achievement – Miguel Torres is a superstar. Exotic on the nose and bracingly dry on the finish – a recipe for success!

£5.79 **Hardys Stamp of Australia Riesling/Gewurztraminer, 2005**, South Eastern Australia (**Tes**). This is a wonderfully bizarre style of white wine which won't please all palates, but will amaze those of you who like juicier, off-dry whites. The aroma gives you all the information you need to know – it is full on, with tropical fruit and exotic fruit salad notes. The palate is slippery and sleek, and the finish is round and smooth with a fair

AROMATIC

whack of grapey sweetness. If you chill it down ice cold it appears to 'dry out' a little, but if you drink it at fridge temperature the ripeness and sweetness is there for all to see. Love all, serve all – this may not be an original motto!

£5.99 **Sainsbury's Taste the Difference Albariño, 2005**, Galicia, Spain (**Sai**). I am not totally convinced with the 'Taste the Difference' range of wines at Sainsbury's, as some miss the mark completely, but this gorgeous white wine is a very worthy inclusion. Made by Lagar de Fornelos, a very reputable producer, this is a crisp, fresh, floral wine with a layered palate and aromatic, floral nose. Drink it with seafood and you'll be dead impressed.

£6.49 **Marks & Spencer Alsace Pinot Grigio, 2005**, Alsace, France (**M&S**). I think I am right in saying that this is the very first bottle of Alsatian wine to sport the grape variety name Pinot Grigio (instead of the historically preferred French term Pinot Gris). It says a lot for the cheeky, pioneering M&S team (Chris and Gerd in particular – hello boys!). The idea is that by labelling this wine thus it will appeal to a wider audience and it will also give you an idea as to what the flavour is in the bottle – uplifting, refreshing, zesty and bursting with vitality. It's all there, believe me.

£6.99 **Val do Sosego Albariño, 2005**, Galicia, Spain (**Odd**). I am an unapologetic fan of the beguiling Spanish grape variety Albariño. It wasn't long ago that there were only two or three of these

AROMATIC

wines available in any quantity in the UK. Now we are spoilt for choice and this is one of the finest of the year. The faint, haunting peach notes on the nose are complemented by crisp, green apple acidity and a sleek palate. You can pick through tapas-style dishes with this delicious white, but it really hits the high notes with crustacea and posh fish dishes.

£6.99 **Yalumba Y Series Viognier, 2005**, Eden Valley, South Australia (**Coo**, **Sai**, **Tes** and **Wai**). Winemaker Louisa Rose can do no wrong. This peach fuzz Viognier is in a league of its own. The 2005 Yalumba Eden Valley Viognier, for three quid more, is a dreamboat, too. She has nailed this variety quicker than any other winemaker in the southern hemisphere, and for seven pounds this is a wine that should stick two fat fingers up at the French and their legions of sweaty, soapy versions of this charming grape.

£7.00 **Sisquò Blanc, Château de Rey, 2005**, Côtes de Roussillon, France (**Haynes, Hanson & Clark**). This is a hauntingly pure wine made from Grenache Blanc and Macabeu (two relatively boring chaps normally). It is perfectly balanced, gently tropical and aromatic and totally bone dry. The finish is uplifting and you want to dive back in to see what you've missed, because this is an extremely complex wine for such a lowly price point. This is an oddity admittedly, and when Jim Eustace (buyer for HHC) poured me my first ever taste of Sisquò, his cheeky smirk gave away just how proud he was with this wine. He's right – it is incredible.

£7.49 **Concha y Toro, Winemaker's Lot 17 Gewürztraminer, 2005**, Casablanca Valley, Chile (**Odd**). From the Lo Ovalle Vineyard, this is a tremendous Gewurz, with great big lychee and rose petal bazookas firing heady scent up your hooter. The 2004 vintage will hand the baton to the 2005 in the late autumn (the '04 is stunning, too) and you will see what I mean – you can't miss it even if you were ten feet away. The handsome bottle, lascivious aroma and tumultuous fruit flavours leave you reeling, and you are left spent with an unexpected, bone-dry finish. It's one hell of a ride.

£7.49 **Rüdesheimer Burgweg Riesling Kabinett, 2005**, Leitz, Rheingau, Germany (**Tes**). This is simply one of the most attractive, juicy, off-dry, tropical-fruit-imbued wines I have tasted in years. It is also sealed with a screwcap. Chill it right down, close your eyes, take a sip and wash the day away with this utterly amazing Riesling. It is nothing short of magical. You'll go into orbit, too – see you there!

£7.99 **Brampton Viognier, 2005**, Stellenbosch, South Africa (**Wai**). I often get into trouble for calling this wine Brampton Viagra, but it performs admirably in that arena I am told, so I shall continue. Last year the 2004 made the Top 250 and this year the 2005 (a significant notch up in quality, but no increase in dosh) sits proudly in the line up. With an exotic apricot and peach blossom nose and a beautiful sleek palate, this is a wine that can't help in raising the temperature and pulse rate. Thank

AROMATIC

goodness for the dry, long finish (a plunge pool effect when you most need it). Sealed with a screwcap, this wine is guaranteed to perk you up – try it on with a game bird (sorry!).

£7.99 **Tim Adams Riesling, 2006**, Clare Valley, South Australia (**Tes**). Sadly Tim 'Bonecrusher' Adams didn't make it to the UK this year (good news for my hand that has only just recovered from his last wince-inducing handshake!), but he kindly posted over early samples of his brand new '06s and they are all delish. I always marvel at this wine, as it has layers and layers of cool lime and honeysuckle fruit. It is still only £7.99 a bottle and yet even at this relatively affordable price tag it challenges all comers across the globe in the dry Riesling department. Good work mate.

£7.99 **Vinha da Urze, 2005**, Douro/Castello Rodrigo, Portugal (**M&S**). Made from Verdelho, Rabigato, Sira and Arinto, this is a beautifully intriguing wine from the far left field. Greengage, fig fruit and serious acidity mark it out as an oddity, but this wine redefines the term 'weird and wonderful'. I was captivated with Urze when I first tasted it and I went back for more and more, finding new flavour nuances every time. This is the wonderful world of wine in a glass.

£8.99 **St Hallett Riesling, 2005**, Eden Valley, South Australia (**Bibendum**). You'd think these guys would concentrate on Shiraz, what with Faith, Old Block and Blackwell in their armoury, but they

AROMATIC

can't stop making epic Riesling, too. Pure, light-sabre limejuice – you may need two hands to wield this bottle.

£8.99 **Terrunyo Viognier, Block 19, 2004**, Casablanca Valley, Chile (**Odd**). Chile has started to produce some pretty smart Viogniers recently and Terrunyo's version is the best I have seen. With a lovely nose of peach and ginger, and a fleshy, smooth palate, this is a very sexy wine. Match it to chicken or fish main course dishes and you will see Block 19 at its best. Viognier is a heady grape and most first-class examples cost a bomb. At nine pounds this is one of the best-value/grandest-tasting versions around. The follow-on 2005 is a beaut, too.

£9.09 **Ona Riesling/Chardonnay/Viognier, 2005**, Rapel Valley Chile (**Odd**). The 2003 made this book last year and the 2004 has just sold out, so how good is my chosen 2005? Bloody brilliant. The best to date. And while you are at it, grab its brother, too – the huge, beastlike, charred-barrel-scented, plum-stuffed 2004 Ona Syrah (£9.09, **Odd**). These are immensely professional wines and they have a particular Chile-ness to them that is hard to explain, but it is a unique sense of place that I adore. The white is a brilliantly balanced blend of three important grapes where the lime zest, peach blossom and wild honey notes are in perfect synergy. You're Ona your own now.

£9.95 **Pikes Riesling, 2005**, Clare Valley, South Australia (**Great Grog, Lea & Sandeman, Vin du**

Van, **The Vineyard** and **Noel Young**). This is one of the star Rieslings of the terrific 2005 vintage. Neil Pike is a trouper and this wine cascades over the palate like an ice cold mountain stream. I cannot recommend this wine enough. It is amazing now, but will age for a decade and will end up being one of the best investments for your taste buds that you have ever made. Yum.

£9.99 **Ernst Loosen Erdner Treppchen Riesling Kabinett, 2005**, Mosel, Germany (**M&S**). Awesome wine! I went straight up to 18.5/20 in my notes and then re-scribbled a 19 over the top of it! Superb honed fruit coupled with density and length and topped off with gripping acidity, this is the master of the Mosel at his very finest. Erni Loosen never lets you down – this wine is my number one aperitif wine of the moment and if I could I would have a butler bring me an ice cold glass every day at 6pm to signal the end of the working day. We can all dream.

£9.99 **Feudi di San Gregorio Fiano di Avellino, 2005**, Campania, Italy (**Wai**). Intensely scented with tropical flower and fruit nuances and laden with waxy honey notes on the palate, this Fiano (another wicked white grape from Southern Italy) is a lovely wine for top class dinner party fish main courses. Funnily enough, I always tend to drink this wine with pasta dishes, so a fish and pasta combo would be spot on. Watch out for the tremendous whoosh of acidity which zooms into view as the exotic fruit notes fade. It is shocking!

bum-clenchingly dry

£9.99 **Knappstein Ackland Vineyard Riesling, 2005**, Clare Valley, South Australia (**Bibendum**). Coming from 35-year-old vines in Watervale, this is winemaker Paul Smith's finest Riesling to date. Teeth-bleachingly pure and bum-clenchingly dry, this is a wicked wine. You can't go wrong with Clare 2005s, but with so many to choose from you may as well buy the best and this one is a classic.

£9.99 **Off the Leash No Oak White, 'Finn', 2005**, The Lane Wine Co., Adelaide Hills, South Australia (**Odd**). Is it possible to see into the future? I think so, and this wine proves it. Finn is based around a core of seamless, smooth, apple-blossom-imbued unoaked Chardonnay (a Chablis-esque chassis if you will). But the genius element here is the cunning addition of spiky, green, tangy Semillon, lush, textural pear-scented Pinot Gris and a whisper of exotic peach-skin-scented Viognier. This is another wine from the tremendous Edwards family team at The Lane. If this grabs you by the short and curlies then fill your boots with its brother – 2005 Off the Leash Max (£9.99, **Odd**) – a Shiraz/Viognier that will send you on safari without your suit!

£9.99 **Tim Adams Pinot Gris, 2006**, Clare Valley, South Australia (**Australian Wine Club**). TA makes a small amount of ridiculously delicious Pinot Gris. This is a stunning wine with perfect balance between fleshy pear and apple juiciness and crisp, crunchy acidity. Hurry though – and make an orderly queue!

AROMATIC

£9.99 **Yering Station MVR, 2005**, Yarra Valley, Victoria, Australia (**Maj** and **Wai**). MVR has seemingly been given another retune and the result is a lighter, racier, more manoeuvrable wine but with more power and class. Marsanne, Roussanne and Viognier has never been so fit and agile. In fact, I can't think of a competitor for this wine on the planet!

£11.99 **Grüner Veltliner, Bergdistel Tegernseehof, 2004**, Wachau, Austria (**Odd**). Grüner is a superb grape variety and Austria makes the very best in the world. This unpronounceable wine has a panoply of flavours which rolls on seamlessly for minutes. From the gripping grapefruit and lime zest nose to the smooth, languid, pear and Granny Smith palate, this is a sensational wine. The classic spiciness that the very best Grüners always sport is there in spades. If you haven't yet tasted this white grape variety then sprint to Oddbins and grab this wine – it will scare you!

£12.99 **Mount Langi Ghiran Pinot Gris, 2004**, Grampians, Victoria, Australia (**Great Northern Wine**, **Oz Wines**, **SWIG**, **Villeneuve** and **Wimbledon Wine**). Sleek, sultry PG, with curvy hips and a devastating décolletage, this is wondrous wine with enough acidity in its killer heels to keep it all in check.

£13.95 **Grosset Watervale Riesling, 2005**, Clare Valley, South Australia (**Bennett's**, **Philglas & Swiggot**, **Roberson** and **Noel Young**). Jeff Grosset

AROMATIC

fashions serious Rieslings for his knowing audience. The beautiful 2005 vintage has allowed the Watervale cuvée to show very well in its youth. Buy it – this is GREAT wine. There is a lot of joy in owning his wines, let alone drinking them. They look and feel good – like serious art.

£14.99 **mesh Riesling, 2005**, Eden Valley, South Australia (**Handford**, selected **Odd**, **Philglas & Swiggot** and **Roberson**). '05 mesh is back to top form. A stern, no-nonsense nose is followed swiftly by a genial palate and desperately long finish. It's drinking now or in a decade. 2005 really is the 10/10 vintage we all thought it was.

£16.95 **Manna Cru, Franz Haas, 2004**, Trento-Alto Adige, Italy (**Bennett's**, **Fortnum & Mason**, **Hedley Wright**, **Philglas & Swiggot**, **Valvona & Crolla**, **Villeneuve** and **Noel Young**). This is one of the finest white blends in the world. Made from Riesling, Sauvignon, Traminer and 20% of oak barrel fermented Chardonnay, this is a masterful wine. Heavenly on the nose and luxurious, luminous and long on the palate, this is a wine worth tracking down. I have followed Manna Cru for over a decade and it never disappoints.

£19.99 **Condrieu Les Vins de Vienne, 2004**, Northern Rhône, France (**Tesco Premium Range**). This is one of the best Condrieus I have seen in the last twelve months and it is the cheapest. This village is where Viognier started its campaign to win over our hearts. Now all Viogniers in the world

AROMATIC

are compared to this wine and a few others like it. In fairness I know twenty pounds is a lot of dosh, but a mediocre bottle of Champs can set you back ten quid more than this celestial wine, so I reckon it is a total and utter bargain. The sensational peach and apricot notes that flow from the nose to the palate and onwards, for minutes on the finish, are simply astounding.

● ●

£4.99 **Yalumba Chardonnay, 2005**, South Australia (**M&S**). This is my favourite cheapy Chardonnay of the year. As I am sure you already know, Yalumba is a very slick, family-owned operation in Oz and the wines they make are of the very highest order. M&S have, once again, convinced a BIG name to fashion a wine for their adoring wine drinkers. This is classic, mildly oaked Aussie Chardonnay, with terrific integrity and awesome balance. I thought it tasted two or three quid more when I first had a go!

£5.99 **Argento Chardonnay, 2006**, Mendoza, Argentina (**Coo**, **Maj**, **Sai**, **Tes** and **Wai**). Welcome back Argento Chardy. After a few years in the wilderness, and a pretty good 2005 (which may still be out there in dribs and drabs), the revival of this brand is complete with this stunning 2006 release. Not 'oaky' as such, but intense, floral and certainly honeyed, this is a very good bottle of wine and it looks classy, too. If you want to try another brilliant wine in the family look to the 2006 Pinot Gris (£5.99, **Maj** and **Mor**). It is richer and more succulent than the Stormhoek (page 24) and is a delicious return to top form.

£8.99 **McManis Family Vineyards Chardonnay, 2004**, California (Tes). The complete opposite of the restrained Neil Ellis Chardonnay that follows, this loudhailer of a wine is a joy to behold because there is no mystery about what is going on in the glass. It lets you know with its wild garlic, lemon blossom, sweet oak and crème brûlée nose, and super-succulent, fleshy, honey and almonds palate. This would be the perfect wine for a chicken pie or blanquette de veau, such is its utterly amazing howdeedoodee approach to life. By the way, its brother a 2004 Cabernet (£8.99, Tes) does exactly the same thing except it wears a Stetson and it 'boot scoots' its red fruit all over your body.

£8.99 **Neil Ellis Chardonnay, 2004**, Stellenbosch, South Africa (Tes). Neil is a very highly respected winemaker in South Africa and he goes about his work quietly, impressing everyone who tastes his wines. For £9 you can taste all that is great about South African Chardonnay in this wine. The sunshine and fruit integrity, the cool nights and perky acidity, the technical know-how and perfectly judged oak, and the finesse and class that is intrinsic in their greatest wines. This is a stunner.

£8.99 **Penfolds Thomas Hyland Chardonnay, 2005**, South Australia (www.tesco.com). This is the best Thomas Hyland to date – it is made with extreme precision and very few wines in the world

OAKED

are as balanced in their youth as this stunning Chardonnay. The reason for this class is that Penfolds makes a number of stellar Chardonnays and their quality rubs off – one of them is the 2004 Penfolds Reserve Bin 04a Chardonnay (£19.99, selected **Wai**) which is big boned and beautiful. Bin 04a is a sassy Chardonnay, with unashamed succulent oak and brazen, moreish peach and mandarin blossom fruit. I would rustle up a big lamb roast with spring veg and couscous and dive off the highest board into a brimming flagon of this nectar! Just having this wine in the winery means that Thomas Hyland at half the price learns from its older, flashier sibling.

£8.99 **Pouilly-Vinzelles, Domaine Thibert, 2005**, Burgundy, France (**Wai**). Christophe Thibert is a fastidious winemaker and his smart Pouilly-Fuissés are among the best Burgundy has to offer. Waitrose sells his usual P-F for £14.99, but my selected wine, from the lesser known area of Vinzelles, is well under a tenner and I actually prefer it! Balance, elegance and control are the hallmarks of this delightful Chardonnay and the length of flavour on the finish is amazing. Made using exactly the very best materials and expensive French oak barrels, you'd have imagined it would cost a bomb, but no. The word Vinzelles seems to be holding it back and so this is reflected in the price. I adore this wine – it is near perfect in my opinion – so make sure you find a bottle. There is so much overpriced white Burgundy around these days, but occasionally a wondrous bargain comes along – and this is it.

OAKED

£9.99 **Chapel Hill Reserve Chardonnay, 2005**, Adelaide Hills, South Australia (**Australian Wine Club**). Wow, what a change of tack for this wine! Gone is the oaky chubster – hello lithe hotty! Chapel Hill must have a catwalk in the winery. This is the best CHRC I have ever seen and it is destined to shock New York, Paris, Milan and London with its sleek curves and tight turns. The 2006 Chapel Hill Unwooded Chardonnay (£6.99, **Tes**) is the nude version of this wine – imagine how good that would be! I can assure you I have given it a thorough test drive and everything is in perfect condition.

£9.99 **Château Tour Léognan, 2004**, Pessac Léognan, Bordeaux, France (**Wai**). This is the 'second wine' of Château Carbonnieux and it is sealed with a screwcap for the very first time – congratulations guys, we thought you'd never make the leap! I adore this wine, not least because it is very well-balanced and the oak barrel flavours are perfectly knit within the framework. This is a robust white wine, but it is in no way heavy or ponderous. I wish more winemakers who use oak to enhance the class and appeal of their wines would do so with the sensitivity of Tour Léognan. If you like the weight and style of Premier Cru Chablis, but find the prices a little punitive, then switch to this classy white Bordeaux – you'll be impressed.

£11.99 **Raats Chenin Blanc, 2005**, Stellenbosch, South Africa (**Cheshire Smokehouse**, **de FINE**, **Handford**, **Harrogate**, **Charles Hennings** and **Wimbledon**). Bruwer Raats has perfected his

OAKED

celestial Chenin Blanc and it now delivers everything he always knew he could conjure up in the glass. This is a profound wine with layers of fruit and not sheer weight making up its charm. If you want to experience the unoaked version of this wine, 2005 Raats Chenin Blanc The Original, then the wine merchants above sell it for £7.99 and it is as refreshing as a cool breeze on a summer's day. Bruwer has also outdone himself with his sterling 2004 Cabernet Franc (£16.99, same again) – it is a magnificent example of what this underrated grape can do when you have complete understanding of you vineyards.

£12.95 **Lugana Brolettino, Ca' dei Frati, 2004**, Lugana, Italy (**Bennett's**, **Flying Corkscrew**, **Luvians**, **SWIG**, **Valvona & Crolla** and **Noel Young**). The finest Lugana on the shelves today is this super-cuvée, Brolettino, from Ca' dei Frati. This is an oak-fermented wine (although you'd never know), made from 35-year-old vines and boasting one of the most complete and balanced flavour packages of apple, pear, honey and wild flowers I have seen in an Italian white wine. This is a desperately classy wine for a very good price.

£12.99 **De Bortoli Chardonnay, 2004**, Yarra Valley, Victoria, Australia (**Odd** and **Tes**). This is a smorgasbord Chardonnay, with a little of everything you could possibly want in the glass. The trick is that no matter how much this wine is loaded with fruit, it is still impeccably balanced. It is made by Steve Webber, one of Australia's most dynamic

OAKED

winemakers and the class in this Yarra Valley wine is sensational. With honeyed succulence, nutty oak nuances and sensational balance, this is a serious glass of wine. If you dabble with white Burgundies such as Meursault and Chassagne-Montrachet, then you'll find this stunner every bit as enticing at a tenner less.

£13.99 **Cape Mentelle Chardonnay, 2004**, Margaret River, Western Australia (**Amps, Fortnum & Mason, Harvey Nichols** and **Selfridges**). Mentelle Chardonnay is often forgotten about in favour of the famous Cabernet Sauvignon it produces, but that would be a grave error, because the fruit quality and skill behind this wine is breathtaking. We are still only in the lower reaches of white Burgundy's price points and yet this Aussie Chardonnay is nearing the peak of the nation's wines.

£16.25 **St-Aubin, 1er Cru Murgers des Dents de Chien, Domaine Gérard Thomas, 2004**, Burgundy, France (**Jeroboams** and **Wai**). This is delightful white Burgundy, with serious depth of fruit and potential to age. It will evolve incrementally over the next four or five years, revealing honey, hazelnut and citrus notes. This is one of the most underrated villages in Burgundy and the value afforded here is amazing. Neighbouring Chassagne-Montrachet and Puligny-Montrachet have the street cred, but St-Aubin wins my vote every year in the sub-twenty bracket.

OAKED

£19.95 **Grosset Chardonnay, 2004**, Piccadilly, Adelaide Hills, South Australia (**Bennett's**, **Andrew Chapman**, **Moriarty** and **Noel Young**). With perfect balance between the swishy, white flower and honey fruit and the suave oak, this is one of Grosset's sexiest Chardonnays ever. Rare, but essential, this is yet another wine from this iconic producer that life is too short to miss out on.

£24.25 **Pierro Chardonnay, 2004**, Margaret River, Western Australia (**Jeroboams**). You will have to be patient for this wine to unravel, but when it does it may just pip the other Margaret River wines (like the cosmic Leeuwin Estate and imposing Voyager) at the post. Uncommunicative at present, but ever so intellectual – this wine is worth the wait. You wouldn't rush into top white Burgundy, so don't hurry this Zen-like precision winemaking.

£29.99 **Penfold's Yattarna Chardonnay, 2003**, Australia (**Berry Bros.**, **Harrods**, **Maj** and **Odd**). Yattarna continues its exponential path in pursuit of perfection. We are nearing that goal and in the 2003 there is a mineral core which grabs the palate and never lets go. Awesome and celebratory!

● ●

£5.49 **Domaine Saint-Antoine Rosé, 2005**, Costières de Nîmes, France (**Odd**). Antoine is a chunky rosé with a fine line of blackberry juice and liquorice running down its spine. Well-balanced and inexpensive this is a juicy, barbecue-style meat

OAKED

favourite, as it has enough structure to handle charred creations and it is a wine that everyone is sure to love.

£5.75 **Les Grès Rosé, XL, 2005**, Coteaux du Languedoc, France (**Jeroboams**). Les Grès is a rich wine (nearly red in colour) and is the perfect picnic wine as you can drink it with virtually any dish imaginable. With layers of spice and juicy red and black berries on the nose and palate, this is a cracking rosé and it is great value for money, too. It packs a punch – it's a forceful chap with a knuckle duster in its pocket.

£5.99 **Casillero del Diablo Shiraz Rosé, 2005**, Concha y Toro, Chile (**Maj**, **Odd** and **Sai**). The ever reliable Concha y Toro wine company has made yet another stunner this year – a funky, new rosé! Bright, cheery, juicy and perky on the palate, this is a wine that looks as good as it tastes – the colour is wicked, glowing in the glass and begging you to set it free! This is a deeper, foody-style rosé that adores all dishes. So, you'll only need one wine even if you are serving a smorgasbord. I tasted the first sip of the 2006 and it is a joyous wine, too.

£5.99 **Cousiño-Macul Cabernet Sauvignon Rosé, 2005**, Maipo, Chile (**Castang**, **deFINE**, **Portland**, **Roberts & Speight**, **Selfridges** and **Taurus Wines**). This is the most vibrant, livid, lipstick-pink rosé of the year. The nose is spectacular, with a fanfare of juicy strawberry and raspberry fruit. The palate weight is a little heavier and spicier than expected, which makes this wine perfect for everything from aperitif glugging to lighter, meaty main courses. It's fruit is dense, but the acidity and verve on the finish is mouth-watering. At six pounds there is an awful lot of flavour and character here – think of it as a very light red more than a rosé and you'll get the picture.

£5.99 **Jacob's Creek Shiraz Rosé, 2005**, South Eastern Australia (Asd, Mor, Sai, Tes, Thr and Wai). JC has the most complete entry level portfolio of wines – they are justifiably very famous, but you should know that technically, too, they are very sound. But something has been missing … Ah, the best-value rosé of the year – here it is! Professional to the end, and a great advert for Australia, with JC in to bat for you, you know you're on to a good wicket!

£5.99 **Stormhoek Rosé, 2006**, Western Cape, South Africa (Asd, deFINE, Harrogate, Magnum, Thr and Wimbledon). Stormy Pants Rosé just keeps getting better. If the White Stripes were a wine, this would be it – only a different colour! Packed to the rafters with ridiculously classy red berry fruit, this is a swaggering pickpocket of a wine because, before you know it, it'll have emptied your wallet of its contents in double time and you'll be skipping home to share the spoils with your nearest and weirdest!

£6.24 **Domaine Bégude Pinot Noir Rosé, 2005**, Vin de Pays d'Oc, France (Maj). Feather-light Pinot rosé from high up in the hills of Limoux, this is a delightful wine with a whisper of raspberry and cranberry fruit on the nose and a long, cool finish. Sancerre rosé eat your heart out – you can't even begin to do this at the price! 2004 Bégude Chardonnay (£8.99, Wai) is another cracker from James and Catherine Kinglake's idyllic property as they continue their quest to prove that the 'no going back' dream really can work.

£6.99 **Louis Jadot Beaujolais Rosé, 2005**, Burgundy, France (**Wai**). Made from the Beaujolais grape Gamay, this is a lovely, light, red-cherry-scented wine with superb packaging (it really does look amazing) and a distinctly balletic air. Only graceful ladies (and particularly camp men) need apply.

£7.95 **Château de Roquefort 'Corail' Rosé, 2005**, Côtes de Provence, France (**Lea & Sandeman**). My annual competition for most heart-achingly beautiful rosé of the year has been won by a wine called 'Corail' (in English - coral) – this perfectly describes the colour of the wine. It looks amazing and also tastes unnervingly serious, too. More like a wild-strawberry-scented white wine than a rich rosé, this is the perfect wine for a lobster salad. I adore the length of flavour and the haunting aroma – this really is a sensational wine.

£7.95 **Pinot Grigio 'Ramato', Visintini, 2005**, Friuli-Venezia Giulia, Italy (**Lea & Sandeman**). Last year the 2004 pink-skin-stained (this is what ramato means) Pinot Grigio narrowly missed a slot in this book because it had the temerity to sell out before the publication date! What cheek. Luckily this 2005 is even better – hard to believe, I am sure you will agree if you are one of the lucky people who managed to taste last year's wine. Patrick Sandeman assures me that he has a much larger allocation this year, so make that call and load up with one of the most beautiful, ethereal, wild-cherry-scented, refreshing wines of the year. Despite its pinkish colour it very much drinks like a white wine and it is the ideal buffet/grazing number – jaw-dropping beauty and precision in a glass.

£7.99 **Château de Sours Rosé, 2005**, Bordeaux, France (**Corney & Barrow**, **Goedhuis**, **Maj**, **Tanners**, **Playford Ros**). Majestic knocks this wine out at the £7.99, but the indies are a quid or so more. Either way, Château de Sours has made another great wine in 2005. Free run Merlot is the driving force here and there is plenty of weight and strawberry style on offer (thanks to some Cabernet making the cut, too). Even a steak is not beyond this wine! The knock down version of Château de Sours is called 2005 Domaine de Sours Rosé (£5.99, **Sai**) and it is good, too, but not great, so don't get them mixed up.

£8.99 **Marks & Spencer Bourgogne Rosé, 2005**, Epineuil, France (**M&S**). This is another beautiful Pinot Noir rosé, whose grapes come from 20 kilometres north east of Chablis (so about as far north as Burgundy gets). This is a fleshier wine than the colour suggests, but it still retains a superb, tight, mineral line on the finish, which shows off the red fruit with style.

£9.50 **Linda Domas Shot Bull Shiraz Rosé, 2006**, Southern Fleurieu, South Australia (**Adnams** and **Bedales**). The 'best' rosé in Australia? It is certainly up there with Turkey Flat and Charlie Melton's Rose of Virginia. I urge you to find a bottle and let me know your thoughts – rosé has never been so big, rich, dry and juicy. Linda is one of the hardest working people in the industry and her wines have so much passion and energy they are a true treat.

•••••••••••••••••••••••

£2.99 **Les Deux Grenache/Syrah, 2005**, Vin de Pays de Vaucluse, France (**Boo**). Continuing their domination of the inexpensive sections of this book, Booths gives us another winning wine. Made from the same grape combo as a Côtes-du-Rhône this is a happy-go-lucky rouge with pure, clean red fruit and a neat little finish. Party wine – Booths deliver nationwide – got it?

£3.49 **M&S Ardèche Gamay, 2005**, France (**M&S**). This is made from the Beaujolais grape Gamay, but it comes from the South of France, so has a little more warmth and juiciness behind that unassuming façade. Price wise this is a steal, because the Ardèche is not prime real estate. This is a fairy-light, juicy red for those who prefer white, but like to dabble occasionally!

FRUIT DRIVEN

£3.99 **Côtes-du-Rhône, Les Airelles, 2005**,
Enclave des Papes, Southern Rhône, France (**Odd**).
This is an unlikely star, because four pound C-d-R
usually tastes like vegetable peelings soaked in
muddy water. So, imagine my delight when this
perky, spicy little chap rocked up. Hello mate!
Come on in! This is a midwinter, midweek, budget
red that won't let you down.

£3.99 **Santa Julia Fuzion, Shiraz/Malbec,
2005**, Mendoza, Argentina (**Wai**). The inexpensive
Santa Julia Fuzion duo, which includes a cheeky
Chenin Blanc /Chardonnay, look clean, smart, funky
and refreshing. Designed to be early-drinking and
crowd-pleasing in equal measure, you would be
hard pushed to find a more professionally made,
party-style offering from the South American
section of the store.

£4.49 **Montepulciano d'Abruzzo, 2004**, Umani
Ronchi, Marche, Italy (**Wai**). This pocket rocket
is a cracker. If you are looking for a bargain wine
to serve with a monster pasta or pizza session, then
this is it. Blackberry and plum notes, coupled with
crisp acidity and a twist of fresh herbs, make this
a ton of wine for the money. I drink gallons of this
stuff each year and have already sniffed and slurped
the 2005, too – it's a winner!

£4.95 **Castillo de Montblanc Tempranillo,
2004**, Conca de Barberà, Spain (**Jeroboams**). This
inexpensive Spanish red is a complete and utter star.
Made from Tempranillo, the grape responsible for

FRUIT DRIVEN

Rioja, it is a juicy, smooth, blackberry-stuffed red, with a cunning twist of warm, sweet spices and a smattering of fresh herbal aromas. This is a very complex wine for its sub-fiver price tag and it shows that Spain is a great place to look for inexpensive reds. As I taste my way around the planet, I am increasingly disappointed with sub-fiver wines, and I implore my readers to trade up whenever and wherever possible. Montblanc is a wine that is extremely well made and it's great value, too – I wish this happened more often, but I know you are a discerning audience and I will not recommend sub-fiver wines that are not up to your and my standards. The 2005 is winging its way to us soon and it continues in exactly the same mould.

£4.99 **L'Oc de la Bouysse, 2005**, Domaine de la Bouysse, Languedoc, France (Maj). When I first tasted this wine back in the summer, it was very juicy but a little abrupt on the finish. By the autumn this will have softened out into a really balanced, fruit-driven red wine, with a fair amount of complexity and charm. This is the sort of red that you should open when cooking shepherd's pie or hot pot, as it has that comforting feeling that makes you want to crash out on the sofa and catch up on missed episodes of *Lost*.

£4.99 **Marks & Spencer Casablanca Valley Pinot Noir, 2005**, Chile (M&S). This is my favourite inexpensive New World pinot on the shelves at the moment. It is very aromatic with vanilla, plum, raspberry and cherry fruit leaping

FRUIT DRIVEN

from the glass. Knock it down to a cool temperature and these flavours really come into their own – perking up the palate with a summer pudding theme shining through. I love this wine with cold chicken or meaty terrines and pâtés or even fish stews and seafood pies – fish and red wine do work if you pick the right wine!

£4.99 **SO Organic Valpolicella, 2005**, Veneto, Italy (**Sai**). This funny little chunky red wine is a cheery so and so, and it is just the ticket for a tomato/meaty, pasta-based dish. Fresh, crunchy tannins enliven the finish and make the mouth water. The palate is stuffed with dark berry flavours and the nose is perky and attractive. You can't do much better for a five-pound, Italian organic red wine – job done!

£4.99 **Saumur Rouge Les Nivières, 2004**, Loire, France (**Wai**). If you chill this wine down a few degrees in the fridge you will find a blackberry-juice theme, with whispers of green, herbal notes and an aromatic lift which is perhaps more akin to a Loire white than red. The shape of Les Nivières' palate is also much lighter than you'd expect from the deep garnet colour of the wine. It has crisp acidity, too, which makes it perfect for cutting through sauces and marinades. You could even drink it with 'meatier' fish, which is what the locals from Saumur do, as these vines are only a stone's throw from the mighty Loire River.

£5.99 **Chinon Cuvée de Pâcques, 2005**, Domaine de la Roche Honneur, Loire, France (**Boo**).

Just along the river from the Saumur above lives this little beauty. 2005 is a great vintage and the Cabernet Franc grapes in this wine are singing from the rooftops with blackberry jelly notes and clean, crunchy tannins. Fruity and aromatic, this is a bargain Chinon and one that is ready to drink now.

£5.99 **Côtes-du-Rhône, Domaine de l'Amandine, 2004**, Southern Rhône, France (**Odd**). This is the French version of Peter Lehmann's Grenache (below) and it is very good, too. Darker perhaps in colour and more or less the same weight, this is an earthier number with more tannin and grip, and you have to respond accordingly in the kitchen. Game is good but bangers are better – go on, you know you can't resist a gourmet toad-in-the-hole.

£5.99 **Peter Lehmann Grenache, 2004**, Barossa Valley, South Australia (**Boo**, **Mor**, **Odd** and **Tes**). This is a cheeky red with a jaunty air and a lot more depth than expected beneath the surface. On the nose the blueberry and damson fruit is tempered with herbal notes and on the palate the finish is broad and long. This is a wine with two distinct characters. Do you chill it down and heighten the crisp fruit and tangy acidity, allowing it to slice through chilli salsas, fiery dips and barbecue marinades? Or do you drink it at normal red temperature and combine it with rare roast beef or veal? Either way this wine relishes a challenge. And I am delighted to report that the 2005 is fresher and redder than ever, too.

FRUIT DRIVEN

£5.99 **Porta Pinot Noir Reserve, 2005**, Bio-Bio Valley, Chile (**Tes**). This is an amazing Pinot at a teeny price point! Open, ripe, accurate and spicy, this is a model of the variety at half the price it should be. OK, it's a little raw, but that's nothing a good plate of food wouldn't mask. All thongs (yes, I mean thongs) considered, this is a wild plum and damson treat.

£5.99 **St Hallett Gamekeepers Reserve, 2005**, Barossa Valley, South Australia (**Coo, Odd, Sai** and **Wai**). On paper this 56% Shiraz/36% Grenache/5% Touriga/3% Mourvèdre could be a discordant mess but, in fact, it is pure gold. I would even go so far as to say it is Australia's finest, inexpensive, youthful red blend. You MUST taste this wine – it is a fundamental cornerstone of your wine diet. Winemaker Matt Gant is nothing short of a necromancer, such is his magical touch with this wine.

£6.25 **Château Roubaud, Tradition, 2004**, Costières de Nîmes, France (**Yapp**). 2004 was a good vintage in the southern Rhône and this stylish mini-Châteauneuf-du-Pape taste-alike is a real find. Made from exactly the same grapes as its more famous near neighbour, with the same methods, but for half the price, Roubaud is a juicy, all-rounder, suited to wintry dishes and well-stocked cheese boards.

£6.70 **Château Puyanché, 2003**, Côtes de Castillon, Bordeaux, France (**Haynes, Hanson & Clark**). This is a rare find – a red Bordeaux under

FRUIT DRIVEN

£7 that really hits the spot! For every zillion bottles of cheap claret that I see on my tasting table, I am likely to only find two or three that I like, so enjoy this rare slice of Cabernet quality while you can. 2003 was a stunning, warm vintage in Bordeaux and this wine is mobbed with fruit. I am in awe of the value and flavour impact that Puyanché delivers.

£6.99 **Beaujolais-Villages, Combe aux Jacques, Louis Jadot, 2005**, Burgundy, France (**Asd**, **Tes** and **Wai**). Classic, fresh, new season Beaujolais is one of the finest styles of red wine to serve with virtually any dish (see the Food and Wine chapter). Jadot is a legend in this department and Combe aux Jacques is a model wine. I have tasted so many 2005 Beaujolais and I keep coming back to this superb wine.

£6.99 **Secano Estate Pinot Noir, 2005**, Leyda, Chile (**M&S**). There are some very sexy 'cherry crumble with vanilla ice cream' notes on this wine. It is slippery on the palate and ever so fruity on the finish – you barely need to engage the brain, as this wine does it all for you. Too easy.

£6.99 **Windy Peak Pinot Noir, 2005**, De Bortoli, Victoria, Australia (**Sai**). This may be the best value Pinot Noir in Australia. I certainly haven't found anything to compete with it and I have already tasted literally thousands of Aussie wines this year. The pure, strawberry, plum and rose petal nose is delightful and the medium-bodied, silky palate is hypnotic. One trick to play with this wine is to taste

FRUIT DRIVEN

it at different temperatures. Served cold it is perfect with salmon and fish dishes, but at a more normal red wine temperature it can handle chicken, meat and cheese.

£7.99 **Serpaiolo, Rosso Toscana, Serpaia, 2004**, Maremma, Tuscany, Italy (**Adnams**). Made in Tuscany from Merlot, Cabernet, Petit Verdot and Mourvèdre (all French grapes) by the fabulous Endrizzi family from Trentino (see the Prosecco in 'Sparkling') in the north of Italy, this could, on paper, be a disaster! But Serpaiolo is a stunner. Medium-weight, juicy, ripe, red- and black-fruit flavoured, and with a twist of fresh herbs and spices, this is a dream wine for all purpose food-and-wine matching. The bottle looks very cool, too.

£7.99 **Swan Bay Pinot Noir, 2005**, Scotchmans Hill, Geelong, Victoria, Australia (**Odd**). 2005 Swan Bay improves on last year's excellent 2004. This is the 'second wine' of the famous Scotchmans Hill Pinot Noir, and it is a very worthy stablemate. Screwcapped, bright, pure, aromatic and heaving with berry fruit, you will not believe just how gorgeous this wine is. I would say it is my favourite sub-tenner Pinot release so far this year, but Windy Peak runs it to the wire. Bring the temperature down a few degrees from room temp and you will be hypnotised with the wild strawberry, plum and cherry notes.

£8.85 **Chiroubles, Domaine de la Grosse Pierre, 2005**, Alain Passot, Beaujolais, France

(**Haynes, Hanson & Clark**). With a notch more intensity and a slightly weightier feel (albeit still fresh and light) than the Jadot B-V above, this Beaujolais Cru – from one of the recognised ten best villages, in this instance Chiroubles – is sublime. Passot is one of the most talented Beaujolais producers and there is a whisper of black fruit embedded in this heady red fruit cocktail. What amazes me is that, for one of the most renown wine regions in the world, the top offerings can cost as little as £9. Please take advantage of this wine – it will not let you down this week or the next, or any other for the next one hundred!

£8.99 **De Bortoli Gulf Station Pinot Noir, 2004**, Victoria, Australia (**Odd**). Make sure you serve this wine 'cool' not cold or warm (heaven forbid), and you will be grabbed by the ethereal wild strawberry nuances wafting up your nostrils and wooing your senses. This downright delicious wine is another one made by Pinot guru Steve Webber and he uses every trick in the book to make sure that you come back for more. Hand-picked grapes, French oak barrels and the utmost care and attention, make this a masterful wine for an eminently affordable price tag. Australia is finally cracking the code of the most difficult red grape on the planet and De Bortoli is leading the way. The 2005 is also a sensational follow on to this wine. It is his best Gulf Station Pinot to date – so keep you eyes peeled.

£8.99 **Nepenthe Charleston Pinot Noir, 2004**, Adelaide Hills, South Australia (**Great**

FRUIT DRIVEN

Western Wines, Oz Wines and Victor Hugo). The sultry, dark chocolate and plum fruit are content in this juicy, sweet and sour Pinot. Give it some air, let it relax and you'll meet a temptress who won't take no for an answer. Bring it on!

● ●

£3.49 **Le Sanglier de la Montagne Old Vine Carignan, 2005**, Vin de Pays de L'Aude, France (**Boo**). With more than enough dark berry fruit and a decent kick of earthiness and depth, this is a stunning wine for autumnal, meaty dishes. These old vines have done the trick – all of those years applying themselves are paying off at last. Good on yer, Grandpère.

£4.49 **Le Carredon Merlot, 2005**, Vin de Pays d'Oc, France (**Maj**). Brilliant, ripe, pure, plummy fruit and a serious mid-palate whoosh of velvetiness make this a wonderful budget Merlot. This grape rarely performs at this price point, but 2005 is a great vintage and this wine has lined all of its ducks in a perfect row. Duck and Le Carredon! Mmmmmm, now there's and idea.

£4.99 **Cruz de Piedra Garnacha, 2004**, Aragon, Spain (**Odd**). We all need a winter warmer that swings in under the fiver barrier and this tremendous little Garnacha, which tastes like juicy Rioja but for a fraction of the price, is the wine for emergency purposes this winter. You will love this wine.

£4.99 **Norton Barbera, 2005**, Mendoza, Argentina (**Wai**). This is one of the best value Barberas on the planet, and that includes all of those from the famous Piedmont region in the northeast of Italy! Norton has always been a great red wine producer, but this is a stunning little wizard of a red. Pizza, pasta and all things Italian wouldn't mind being tackled by this lusty little red. The fruit flavours are darker and feistier than expected, with a lick of crisp tannin to allow you to cut through a juicy steak with confidence.

£4.99 **Viña Fuerte Garnacha, 2004**, Calatayud, Spain (**Wai**). Fuerte is a Top 250 regular, and it always comes up trumps. Plummy, bright, herbal and juicy, this is a Rioja taste-alike for a few quid less. You can open a few bottles of this for a party and relax, as it goes with practically any main course meat, game or chicken dish. If you feel frisky, have a swipe at the 2005 Fuerte Rosé (£4.79, Wai) – it's a wondrous little filly.

£5.99 **Beyerskloof Pinotage, 2005**, Western Cape, South Africa (**Sai**). This is the best vintage to date of Beyers Truter's famous, inexpensive Pinotage, and they continue to fly the flag for this variety with their plum, spice, blueberry and foresty notes. Lamb shanks and this wine – bring it on. Don't dawdle, I am starving.

£5.99 **Tesco Finest Valpolicella Ripasso, 2005**, Veneto, Italy (**Tes**). Made by the Casa Girelli team this is an excellent Valpol with real black

MEDIUM WEIGHT

cherry fruit and a nice tangy aftertaste. Get cooking – this wine might be fairly cheap to buy, but it will want to be taken seriously in the glass and any old re-heat dinner will simply not do.

£5.99 **Tinto da Anfora Bacalhôa, 2003**, Alentejo, Portugal (**Bat & Bottle**, **Cambridge**, **Corkscrew**, **S H Jones**, **Le Riche**, **Noble Rot**, **Stanton** and **Wai**). This is the best value Portuguese red I have tasted in ages. I remember tasting around 200 wines one day in my office and this was the only one that stood out! It is made from five or more indigenous Portuguese red grapes and aged for around a year in oak barrels, but beyond that all I can say is that for six pounds you will not find a more enticing red wine, nor a more exciting advert for Portugal on the shelves today. Rich, full and dark, and packed with spice and fruit, this is a stunning wintry red.

£6.25 **Adobe Merlot, 2004**, Central Valley, Chile (**Maj**). This organically grown Merlot fruit is really singing in the glass in this delicious wine. Vanilla, plums and raspberries cavort around the glass and you need not worry what you're eating when you demolish this wine, as long as it is beef in one form or another.

£6.25 **Anjou Rouge, Domaine des Forges, 2005**, Loire, France (**Haynes, Hanson & Clark**). This is one of the most surprising and impressive wines of the year. It has an amazing extra dimension of mulberry fruit wedged into the middle of the

MEDIUM WEIGHT

action and there are even mild pencil-lead notes and crunchy acids making it a dead ringer for very smart (and bloody expensive) Right Bank Bordeaux; not a lowly but frighteningly self-assured Cabernet Franc from the Loire. Save some cash and blow your mates away at the same time with this bottle.

£6.49 **McWilliams Hanwood Cabernet Sauvignon, 2004**, South Eastern Australia (**Mor**, **Som**, **Tes** and **Thr**). This does exactly what it says on the tin, and it does it incredibly well for such a competitively priced wine. Bravo McWilliams – I know how hard it is to do this.

£6.95 **Montepulciano d'Abruzzo, Vigne Nuove, Valle Reale, 2004**, Abruzzo, Italy (**ten-acre**). Made from the younger vines on this amazing estate, this is a spectacular red wine, bursting with vibrant red and purple fruit. I kept staring disbelievingly at the price of this wine when I not only tasted it but drank the entire bottle I loved it so much!

£6.99 **Trincadeira, JP Ramos, 2004**, Alentejo, Portugal (**Wai**). Portuguese red wines are really making waves over here as this funky, juicy, blueberry, liquorice and cinnamon-stuffed wine shows. This is a change of tack for those of you who fancy something a little different for the weekend.

£6.99 **Yering Frog Shiraz/Viognier, 2005**, Yarra Valley, Victoria, Australia (**Maj**). Everyone seems to be making SVs these days. And they should all have a look at this wine to see how it's done (and it's the cheapest!). I have tasted this innumerable times and the package is so complete that even Linford Christie would faint at the sight of it.

£7.55 **Cosme Palacio y Hermanos Rioja, 2004**, Rioja, Spain (**Wai**). Not too oaky, not too heavy, not too tannic or too heady, this slinky, mellow, seamless Rioja is in perfect balance. And this is easily the best vintage of Cosme I have ever tasted. The clincher is that it continues to be sensational value for money. You should treat yourself to this wonderfully proportioned wine. It is my favourite Rioja of the year.

£7.95 **Château La Hase, 2004**, Bordeaux, France (**Lea & Sandeman**). After last year's pumped up 2003, it is nice to return to normal with the elegant, classically dimensioned 2004. La Hase always manages to engender the purity and succulence of the Cabernet grape at its best. The blackcurrant energy and Old World charm in this wine is beautifully balanced. If you like red Bordeaux – hurry and buy this wine. 2005 looks like being a good year, too, but you'll have to wait another year until you'll see any of them!

£7.99 **Château Ségonzac, 2004**, Premières Côtes de Blaye, Bordeaux, France (**Wai**). The 2002 and 2003 have made this list in the past and this delightful 2004 is here to keep them company this year. Sealed with a screwcap and bursting with black fruit and sweet leather nuances, this is a delicious

MEDIUM WEIGHT

red wine that would benefit from an hour in a decanter to unwind and mellow out before you tuck in.

£7.99 **Lacrima di Morro d'Alba, Rùbico, 2005**, Marotti Campi, Marche, Italy (**Odd**). This is definitely the strangest wine I have ever written up in TWL. Believe it or not, the grape used here is actually called Lacrima di Morro d'Alba (the tears of the Moors of Alba) and it is one of the most aromatic red grapes on the planet. With extraterrestrial liquorice, rose petal, Turkish Delight, red cherry, prune and violet notes (I could go on for hours) this wine is sensational with lamb main courses or meaty sauces – Moroccan food works really well, too. Made in minuscule quantities, this is a wine for the fully fledged wine geek – I, of course, love it (I'm not a geek, though, honest!).

£7.99 **Lucky Country Shiraz/Cabernet, 2004**, Langhorne Creek, South Australia (**Odd**). Lucky Country indeed! This cheeky blend is a fireball of flavour and it benefits from being made at the smart Two Hands facility in the Barossa Valley. This is a classic Aussie blend and I know you will fall for its charms.

£8.49 **KC Shiraz, Klein Constantia, 2004**, Stellenbosch, South Africa (**Maj**). Made by the historic estate Klein Constantia, this is one of the most relaxed wines I saw on my visit to Cape Town earlier this year. Winemaker Adam Mason is a laid-back dude and this shows in the wine. Smooth,

MEDIUM WEIGHT

supple and laden with juicy fruit, this is a bargain price for such competent winemaking.

£8.49 **Vergelegen Mill Race Cabernet/ Merlot, 2003**, Stellenbosch, South Africa (**Maj**). This is the best Mill Race I have ever tasted. If I was poured a glass of this wine blind, I would be at least a tenner over on my guesstimate. Lovers of red Bordeaux sit up and take note – this is very serious wine indeed and it will age for a further three or four years, too. A plate of roast lamb with Dauphinoise potatoes and cabbage is calling – I must obey.

£8.99 **Bourgogne Rouge Cuvée Gérard Potel, 2004**, Potel, Burgundy, France (**Boo**). Nicolas Potel celebrates his famous father's memory with this exceptional wine. Made from old vine Pinot Noir and tasting much grander than a mere generic red Burgundy, this is a truly brilliant wine. The 2004 is still a little youthful, but this is one wine that you must find. Buy a case – it will get better and better over the next two to five years.

£8.99 **Château Tour Prignan, 2003**, Médoc, France (**Odd**). Well-chosen 2003s are very exciting. Having said that, they are also usually pretty dear. This is a lovely, juicy, blackcurrant-driven wine that does the lunchtime claret thing with style. With 2004 being a more backward vintage in Bordeaux, it is time to load up with these wines.

£8.99 **Cumulus Climbing Merlot, 2004**, Orange, New South Wales, Australia (**Maj**). Philip Shaw's

MEDIUM WEIGHT

baby Merlot is a joy. Dark and dense, but with aromatic high notes and seamless red/black flavours, this is a very good wine. Watch out for offers on this chap in the autumn!

£8.99 **Fitou Les Quatre, 2003**, Mont Tauch, France (**Wai**). Made from fifty-year-old Carignan, Grenache and Syrah vines, this is one of the finest Fitous I can remember. It is liquid crushed velvet bound around summer pudding fruit and smart, seasoned oak.

£8.99 **Katnook Founders Block Cabernet Sauvignon, 2003**, Coonawarra, South Australia (**Bibendum** and **Odd**). Even better than last year's 2002, Founders is a revelation. Affordable Coonawarra Cab, with a sense of place and a guarantee to satisfy – how often does that happen? I will answer for you – never!

£8.99 **Walker's Pass Private Bin Zinfandel, 2003**, California (**Adnams**, **Cellar Door Wines**, **deFINE**, **Handford**, **Harrogate Fine Wine**, **Magnum**, **Roberson**, **Thr** and **Wine Society**). What is it about this wine that caught my interest? It is drinking beautifully, it is from stunning stock (I cannot divulge this top secret information) and it is only £9. This is a criminally low price for the class in the glass. Flavour-wise, this is a briary, black-fruit-imbued, spicy, velvety monster. It is smooth, sexy, ripe and lusty and you will love it. Please don't ask me the secret though – I won't tell. Or will I?

MEDIUM WEIGHT

£9.49 **Fox Gordon 'By George' Cabernet/ Tempranillo, 2004**, Barossa Valley, South Australia (**Cooden, Haslemere Cellar** and **Odd**). Fox Gordon Eight Uncles has taken a well deserved year off from the 250 and by George, here's 'By George' to keep you entertained. The value afforded here is overwhelming. This is a superb blend of Spanish grape Tempranillo and blockbuster Cabernet. I can't get enough of this wine. Tash Mooney (the winemaker) has, once again, shown just what a talent she is.

£9.49 **Rioja, Viñas de Gain, 2002**, Artadi, Spain (**Boo**). I have said this before, but surely Sally Holloway, esteemed buyer at Booths, has got the price wrong again! This tastes like twenty-five quid's worth of Rioja. Shush though. Don't tell a soul – we can have it all to ourselves. I don't care whether you live near Booths in the north of England or not, get on the dog and bone now! They deliver – sort it out.

£9.95 **Glaetzer Wallace, Shiraz/Grenache, 2004**, Barossa Valley, South Australia (**Great Western Wine**). Ben and Colin Glaetzer have made my favourite ever Wallace in 2004. The sweet American oak seasons the stunning blackberry and cherry fruit, and the result is a refined, yet impressive wine. The Rhône struggles to compete with wine of this quality and brightness of fruit – this is a wicked wine.

£9.99 **Tim Adams Fergus, 2004**, Clare Valley, South Australia (**Maj**). A great, great, great wine.

MEDIUM WEIGHT

Grenache is the main variety embedded in this wine and it is celestial. The complexity is terrifying and the screwcap keeps it all in place. I drank a bottle over three days and it just got better and better. Awesome. Tim's 2004 Shiraz is also £9.99 in Tesco and this will show you the exact taste difference between these two world famous varieties – sounds like it's time for a wine tasting to me!

£9.99 **Wirra Wirra Church Block, 2003**, McLaren Vale, South Australia (**Amps**, **Nidderdale**, **Old Forge**, **Sai**, **Stevens Garnier**, **Whitebridge Wines** and **Wine Society**). Wirra Wirra is one of the most professional outfits in Australia. Church Block is a heroic red wine, boasting yards more flavour and breeding than many wines twice its price. Made from a fascinating blend of Cabernet Sauvignon, Shiraz and Merlot, this is a seamless red wine, with spice, earth and fruit characters covering every base from crunchy red to intense black. There is a superbly suave oak element to this beauty that lengthens the flavour and makes it all seem so effortless and all-encompassing. Decant this wine an hour before drinking it and you will have a front row seat at one of the best-value operas in a glass there is.

£10.99 **Chianti Classico, Castello di Brolio, 2003**, Tuscany, Italy (**Sai**). The Barone Francesco Ricasoli's estate was founded in 1141. He is a lovely chap, who travels the world opening bottles of his wine and spreading the word about his superb Chiantis. Made from the Sangiovese grape and

MEDIUM WEIGHT

matured in French oak for ten months, this is a superbly suave Chianti, with glossy damson and blueberry fruit, and a wonderful twist of leather and tangy spices on the nose and palate. This is a seriously good wine and it's another one that benefits from an hour in a decanter and a mountainous plate of hearty, wintry Italian food.

£11.55 **Moss Wood The Amy's Blend Cabernet Sauvignon, 2003**, Margaret River, Western Australia (**Jeroboams**). Sealed with a screwcap and more forward than the normal estate wines, Amy's is the equivalent of Les Forts de Latour (the second wine of Bordeaux Premier Cru Château Latour) from a juicy, early-drinking vintage! I love this wine – it is so honest, engaging and rewarding.

£11.99 **Château Sérilhan, 2003**, St.-Estèphe, Bordeaux, France (**Boo**). This is not a Château I am familiar with, but I will certainly be following its progress from now on, because this 2003 is a wondrous creation. It was a very hot year in 2003 and communes like St.-Estèphe really played a blinder. This is a deep, dark, brooding red Bordeaux with muscle and breeding. You can drink it now, but it is not going to fade for a decade!

£13.99 **Majella Merlot, 2004**, Coonawarra, South Australia (**Cooden** and **Noel Young**). I love Majella Cabernet and the 2003 (£13.99, **Cooden**, **OFW** and **Noel Young**) was in the running for this book as well, but I went for the Merlot because they are few and far between at this quality and value for money.

MEDIUM WEIGHT

Stuffed with fruit cake, red currants and fat black plum fruit, this is a sexy, brooding wine with a delicious bedside manner.

£14.99 **Wither Hills Pinot Noir, 2005**, Marlborough, South Island, New Zealand (**Ballantynes**, **Decorum**, **Michael Jobling**, **Odd**, **Old Forge**, **Sommelier Wine Co.**, **Villeneuve**, **Wai**, **Wicked Wines** and **Wine Society**). This is better than ever before – how is that possible? You can't keep doing it year in year out, unless you are totally and utterly committed to making stellar wine. Brent Marris and the team at WH are single-minded in the pursuit for perfection. Surely they cannot better this brilliant 2005 – it is positively glittering it is so encrusted with excellence. This is very smart wine – you must taste it.

£15.35 **Two Paddocks, Last Chance Pinot Noir, 2004**, Central Otago, New Zealand (**Haynes, Hanson & Clark**). Owned by Sam Neill, this property is one of the finest producers of Pinot in New Zealand. It is also important to stress that the price of this wine has not gone up over the last three years either, unlike many of the vastly overpriced Pinots from Central Otago. Screwcap-sealed, like virtually every top wine in NZ, this is a delightful wine.

£16.95 **Kooyong Pinot Noir, 2003**, Mornington Peninsula, Victoria, Australia (**Lea & Sandeman**). The rich, hedonistic, gallant red fruit strides forth and takes complete command of your olfactory

MEDIUM WEIGHT

system. It will give your senses back when it has finished. I adore serious Pinot Noir. It is the Holy Grail of the wine world, as this grape is desperately fussy outside of its spiritual home in Burgundy. Having said this, Kooyong, made by the phenomenally talented Sandro Mosele, is one of the New World's finest proponents of this variety. Sleek, sultry, harmonious, erudite and ever so long on the palate, this wild-strawberry-scented wine is nothing short of heavenly. If you want to push the boat out even more, then Sandro makes three other single vineyard wines from his beloved Pinot – 2003 Ferrous, Haven and Meres Pinot Noir (all £22.75, L&S). This may sound ridiculous, but I love them all. You should try all three just to see how different a wine can be from one vineyard to the other, even though they are only yards apart.

£16.99 **Château Belgrave, 2002**, Haut-Médoc, Bordeaux, France (selected **Coo** and **Handford**). This is one of the best value red Bordeaux I have tasted in ages. Made from the classic recipe of Cabernet Sauvignon, Cabernet Franc and Merlot, this is the definitive Sunday lunch wine and it is drinking beautifully now. Remember to decant it to give it a little air, and the velvety blackcurrant and cedar notes will flow uninterrupted from the glass.

£18.00 **De Bortoli Reserve Pinot Noir, 2004**, Yarra Valley, Victoria, Australia (**Odd**). With a cool, calm exterior, it is easy to assume that all is well. But one sip will show that controlled chaos is ensuing under the surface of this maelstrom of a wine. I, for one, want to join the melée. Do you? You had better be up for it – this wine is seriously good.

£18.95 **Seghesio Barbera, 2004**, North Coast, California (**Bennett's** and **Noel Young**). I was one of the first people in the UK to taste this new vintage of Seghesio Barbera with none other than Camille Seghesio herself. They are one of California's most exciting producers and, in a world-Barbera, context this wine is up there with the true greats. Sealed with a screwcap and bursting with dense damson and blackberry fruit, this is a wine that demands respect and it gets it. Brooding, wildly intense and totally complete, this is a serious red wine with immense class and terrific ageing potential.

● ●

£5.99 **Argento Malbec, 2006**, Mendoza, Argentina (**Coo**, **Maj**, **Sai** and **Tes**). Our least expensive blockbuster this year was featured in the very first TWL back in 2002. The 2005 vintage is on the shelves and it is delicious, but I had the very first peek at the 2006 and it is sublime. Black in colour, but very succulent and pulpy on the palate, this is a cascading squashed blueberry and blackcurrant style of wine with a lusty chassis and an eager demeanour. There is spice and power there, too, and it looks very smart in its new livery.

£5.99 **Casillero del Diablo Cabernet Sauvignon, 2005**, Maipo Valley, Chile (**Asd**, **Boo**, **Mor**, **Odd**, **Sai**, **Som**, **Tes**, **Thr**, **Wai** and **WRa**).

MEDIUM WEIGHT/BLOCKBUSTER

swarthy assassin

As every year passes CdD Cabernet cements its position as the best-value Cabernet on the planet and it distances itself from its competitors. The 2005 is incredible. It is inspirational. Nearly ten million bottles of this wine are made every year – this is nothing short of extraordinary. Marcelo Papa is a very humble winemaker, but I know he understands how much pleasure he brings his acolytes around the planet and this must be part of the reason that every year he forces himself to better the vintage before. He is a genius, and a kind one at that. Footnote – the 2005 Chardonnay and Syrah are both widely available and top notch, too!

£5.99 **Tesco Finest Old Vines Garnacha, 2005**, Campo de Borja, Spain (**Tes**). This is a dark, swarthy assassin on the nose and palate. Keep your wits about you, as you won't know where he's going to strike next. Give it some air before it catches you out, and this Rioja-shaped wine will calm down a touch and start to behave. Food-wise this is a dead cert for anything gamey or meaty.

£6.49 **Château Camplazens Syrah, 2005**, Vin de Pays d'Oc, France (**Maj**). I went into orbit when I first tasted this wine. I gave it 18.5/20 in my notes and rated it one of the best wines of the 165 that I tasted at Majestic that day! It is dense, dark, brooding, chocolaty and stuffed with blackberry fruit. This is a truly brilliant winter red and, although I would normally urge you to trade up as often as possible, with this quality of wine in your glass, you could happily stay sub-seven until it runs out!

£6.49 **Concha y Toro, Winemakers Lot 137 Malbec, 2005**, Chile (**Odd**). This is an utterly heroic red wine. The least expensive of Marcelo Papa's 'Lot Series' reds, this Malbec is a miraculous number at £6.49, combining every shade of red and black fruit, and a delightful core of sweet oak running the length of the minutes-long palate. Steak, crunchy greens and potato salad is the order of the day – you'd better make sure you have a few extra bottles in the cellar because your guests won't be able to put this wine down.

£6.99 **Château Cazal Viel, Cuvée des Fées, 2004**, St-Chinian, Languedoc, France (**Wai**). This is a monstrously impressive Syrah/Viognier blend that shows that the Aussies are not the only people getting this blend right at the sub-tenner level. The bizarre thing is that there is no oak whatsoever used in this wine. It is malevolent brooding, inky black, almost menacing – and I love every single solitary drop in the bottle. If you are remotely serious about big, black, scary wines, do not miss Cuvée des Fées.

£6.99 **Linda Domas Swensen Shiraz, 2005**, McLaren Vale, South Australia (**Odd**). Linda's baby Shiraz is a stunner. For seven pounds you can drink first-class wine from one of the greatest wine regions in the world – not bad, hey? If anyone else made it, you'd walk on by, but when this lady waves her wand around the winery, extraordinary things happen – I don't know how she does it because she works in cramped conditions with old kit, but her touch and control are second to none. Treat yourself to any wine with her name on it – you will be mesmerised.

£6.99 **Porcupine Ridge Syrah, 2005**, Coastal Region, South Africa (**Wai**). Screwcapped 2005 Porky Pie Syrah is the best version of this wine ever. It is bristling with pepper, spice, squashed plums (ouch), swollen blackberries and fat cranberries. Made by Marc Kent at the Boekenhoutskloof winery in Franschhoek this wine is the little brother of the £25 estate Syrah and the familial relationship is clear to see in the glass. At seven quid this is a true bargain – Côtes-du-Rhône is 'NFI'.

£6.99 **Saint-Chinian Roches Noires, 2003**, Languedoc, France (**Tes**). This is a succulent ripe, blackberry-coulis-stuffed red wine, with some serious complexity beneath the rumbustious exterior. Slip beyond the frontage unnoticed and wallow in the layers of deep, dark plum and berry fruit. This is a superb wintry red and the value for money here is cracking.

£6.99 **Yalumba Y Series Shiraz/Viognier, 2004**, South Eastern Australia (**Wai**). I know Yalumba very well and this new wine is utterly fantastic. I gave it 19/20 in my personal wine tasting notes and marvelled at the precision and depth of fruit on the palate. This is not a heavy wine, but an intense mouthful of flavour. I adore well judged S/V blends, but so many miss the mark and end up tasting too soapy – Viognier's perfume can be too much (gaggy and cloying) even for mighty, swarthy Shiraz. But this wine is absolutely spot on, and it's great value, too. The 2005 follows this awesome debut wine and further improves on the recipe.

£7.99 **Cortegiara Valpolicella Ripasso, 2003**, Veneto, Italy (**Tes**). Goodness me, this is a superb Italian red wine. For eight pounds you can be assured of a roller-coaster ride. Crammed with sweet-and-sour cherry fruit, and piled high with intensity and impact, this is a sensational creature and one that could grace the very finest tables and most competent of cooking. Once in a while these superb Valpolicellas come along. You wouldn't know it from the label but, believe me, this is a wickedly impressive wine.

£7.99 **Hardys Oomoo Shiraz, 2004**, South Eastern Australia (**Mor** and **Thr**). If Rob Mann (now with Cape Mentelle in Margaret River) was to be remembered for a single red wine during his tenure at Tintara (Hardy's historic winery in McLaren Vale), I expect he'd like it to be an Eileen Hardy Shiraz or a Tintara Grenache. But I think that '04 Oomoo Shiraz is his legacy – it's phenomenal. 2004 is a brilliant year in Australia and Rob captured £15 worth of excellence in this £8 bottle. The complexity in this briary, bold wine is breathtaking.

£7.99 **St Hallett Faith Shiraz, 2004**, Barossa Valley, South Australia (**Bibendum**, **Sai** and **Tes**). Matt Gant has made his best ever Faith Shiraz in 2004. This snake-hipped, clean-shaven musketeer

BLOCKBUSTER

has not only re-discovered his Faith (cue George Michael), but he's also decided to share it with us. We are not worthy.

£8.49 **Concha y Toro Winemaker's Lot Syrah, 2005**, Llanuras de Camarico Vineyards, Limari, Chile (**Maj**). Hang on to your hats because this wine is a Lamborghini at warp factor five careering down the highway! It has so much momentum that you are sucked into its vortex. The Syrah fruit is mesmerising and the build quality is second to none. Marcelo Papa is not only a great winemaker, but he also 'designs' these wines to be jaw-droppingly gorgeous, too!

£9.99 **Marananga Dam, Grenache/Shiraz/ Mourvèdre, 2004**, Barossa Valley, South Australia (**M&S**). My goodness this wine is a real treat. It is a game of two halves, with brilliant, ripe, sweet, red berry fruit on the nose and initial attack on the palate. But it builds and builds on the mid-palate and finishes with deceptively rich and long black fruit flavours. Made by Dave Powell and his stellar team in the Barossa, this is a world-class wine at a very smart price. The M&S buyers are an experienced lot and they manage to convince some of the world's best winemakers to make wine especially for them. Dave Powell is the mind behind Torbreck (look up this cult estate on the internet!) and this is a tremendous GSM (the same blend as Châteauneuf-du-Pape, in fact). It comes from 80-year-old, un-irrigated vines in the heart of the Barossa Valley. After eighteen months in French oak barrels you are left with a sublime, intensely perfumed, mightily juicy red wine. This is half the price of Dave's normal beauties. Nice.

£9.99 **McLean's Farm Reserve, Shiraz/ Cabernet, 2003**, Barossa Valley, South Australia (**Tes**). Sir Lunchalot, Bob McLean, tackles the Shiraz/Cabernet challenge with aplomb. He doesn't know any other way mind you. Great impact and bravado (that's just Bob), the wine is fantastic, too. Make sure you've pan-fried your yak with just the right amount of fresh sage to lift the nose and expose the tender underbelly of this delicious wine.

£9.99 **Hegarty Chamans, Cuvée 2, 2004**, Minervois, Languedoc, France (**Adnams** and **Odd**). Made from 70% Grenache, 20% Syrah and 10% Carignan, with bright red fruit, lashings of sweet spices and beautiful balance, this is a true treat if you are into the darker side of the arts. With more gaminess than a Laird's Barbour and more polish than Cary Grant on form, this wine is a classic dichotomy – part genial host, part daydreaming psycho. Do you want to play with your guests palates a while before delivering the coup de grace? If so, then treat them to this Cuvée 2 during the main course and then open a two-hours-previously-decanted bottle of Cuvée 1 (£12.99, **Odd**) and release a mesmerising Minotaur of a wine. Good Luck – make sure you have a well-rehearsed exit strategy, because a ball of wool won't help you now.

BLOCKBUSTER

£9.99 **Kangarilla Road Zinfandel, 2004**,
McLaren Vale, South Australia (**Maj**). Zinfandel is
very closely related to the swarthy southern Italian
red grape Primitivo. You may be used to me
recommending Californian versions of this grape,
because it is California's most famous red variety,
but no! Zin is also planted in a few other countries
and Kangarilla's is a cracker. Blueberry, loganberry,
sweet spices and plums all reverberate around on
the palate, and the texture is as velvety as can be.
Unlike the USA blockbusters, this is a distinctly
medium-weight affair and it's perfectly suited to
well-hung meat.

£9.99 **Linda Domas Top Hat Grenache, 2005**,
McLaren Vale, South Australia (**Novum**). This is the
wine I have been waiting all year for. Herbal, tricky,
pipe smoke on the nose, squashed blueberries and
mulberries on the palate, and a zany, tangy finish
make this an utterly hypnotic red wine. Linda's
wizardry is near legendary – this wine is pushing all
of the buttons, but where the magic spell comes
from originally is beyond me. I have two decades of
experience in this industry but every year she
demonstrates to me just how much there is to learn
about this fascinating art. Tired of 'top hat, no
rabbit'? Try this wine – it is 'top hat, full warren'.

£9.99 **Yering Station Shiraz/Viognier, 2004**,
Yarra Valley, Victoria, Australia (**Maj** and **Sai**). A
slightly heavier red wine than you might expect from
Pinot Noir specialists Yering Station. This Shiraz/Viog
is the silky smooth charmer that you want to sip on

BLOCKBUSTER

the sofa with a lump of real Cheddar and a few crackers in front of a movie after your mammoth feast. With a perfect black fruit nose and a velvety palate, Yering Station has pulled out all of the stops for this eminently classy wine. Well done Tom!

£10.03 **Q Tempranillo, 2003**, Familia Zuccardi, Mendoza, Argentina (**Tes**). The Rioja grape variety has never been so happy on its hols than in this frighteningly dark, densely appointed wine. This is a velvety, inky mouthful of red that requires a modicum of chewing to turn it into liquid form. After that, all you need is a lasso and a forest full of wild boar. Fire up the Land Rover, get the boys around and let's have us a hog roast!

£10.03 **Ravenswood Amador Zinfandel, 2001**, California (selected **Som**). In the A-Z of wine there is only one 'Z' – Zinfandel (I simply ignore the preposterous variety Zibbibo). Ravenswood is a legendary producer of Zin and Amador is one of the best wines that they make. Huge, inky, brooding and spicy, this is a monstrous wine, with a devil-may-care attitude. Charge your glasses and then sink into the sofa (or someone's arms, you lucky sod) with a grin on your face. This is one of the most languid, laid-back wines on the planet. You will melt, I can assure you, when you fall under the spell of this wine. If you find the passion level too much for everyday wine work, then slot a bottle of 2003 Ravenswood Vintners Blend Zinfandel, California (£7ish, **Maj**, **Som**, **Tes** and **Wai**). I have gone on record saying that this is one of the ten most reliable and affordable red wines in the world. It is loaded with dark plum, blueberry, vanilla, chocolate, blackberry and sweet cinnamon spice notes. Buy this wine. It is an icon.

£10.99 **Clos de los Siete, 2005**, Tunuyan, Argentina (**Maj**, **Odd** and **Wai Canary Wharf** branch). Once again, I was lucky enough to taste the first sample bottle of the 2005 CdlS in the country. And, as I've said before, I think this is Argentina's greatest value red wine by a mile. Needless to say, it is better and more relaxed in its shell than last year's marauding but incredible 2004. You must taste this wine – its impact on Argentina's red-winemaking psyche should not be underestimated.

£10.99 **Penley Estate Condor Shiraz/Cabernet, 2004**, Coonawarra, South Australia (**Cooden** and **Moreno**). It is impossible to see the join between these two varieties in this impressive wine, such is the masterful melding that has gone into its construction. Mellifluous, erudite and rewarding, Kym Tolley, owner and winemaker of Penley, is a fastidious sort (and a dead ringer for Michael Douglas in his prime), and his care and undeniable talent shines through in Condor.

£11.99 **Bardou, Saint-Chinian, 2003**, Laurent Miquel, Languedoc, France (**Sai** and **Tes**). This is a marvelously gamey red designed for candlelit venison main courses and after-dinner, cigar-chewing conversations. It is deceptively large, despite having a medium-weight body, as the flavour builds on the palate like a monsoon about to break. And when it comes down, it drenches your taste buds with damson, plum, black cherry, boot polish, bonfire ember and back seat of the Jag leather moments.

£11.99 **d'Arenberg Laughing Magpie, 2004**, McLaren Vale, South Australia (**Bibendum** and **Odd**). The loopy team at d'Arenberg cracked the Shiraz/Viognier game years ago and this glossy, polished wine is a stormtrooper already, despite its youth. Saddle up for some swamp-yomping hilarity.

£11.99 **Eldredge Blue Chip Shiraz, 2004**, Clare Valley, South Australia (**Australian Wine Club**). Definitive Clare Shiraz is a fascinating class of wine and Blue Chip is one of the best (it is blue chip after all). The fruit is direct and remorseless, but not in any way heavy or ponderous. Waves of blue and black fruit crash on your palate and leave you satiated. There seems to be no tannin whatsoever, because the velvetiness is all-encompassing, but it is there, hiding under the skirt layers and peeping out when you least expect it.

£11.99 **Heritage Shiraz, 2004**, Barossa Valley, South Australia (**D Byrne**). Steve Hoff may have even eclipsed his '02 (a past Top 250 alumni) with this sensational 2004 Shiraz. It has every element of classic Barossa Shiraz but the volume is turned down a notch, so the effect is profound, contemplative and not a little shocking. Imagine a dark, spooky, rainy night and Steve suddenly

BLOCKBUSTER

rapping on the window pane, looking hungrily at you inside, huddling, shaking behind the sofa. Fun, hey?

£12.99 **Tesco Finest Barolo, 2001**, Piedmont, Italy (**Tes**). Made by Matteo (the bear) Ascheri, this Barolo is, not surprisingly, a bit of a beast. Huge and tarry with black cherry and blackberry fruit crammed into the glass and topped off with spice and liquorice, it needs half an hour minimum in a decanter to unwind and relax, and then you must serve it with a full-on carnivorous dish or top-class cheese. This is as imposing as Italian wine gets and it is wicked value, too.

£12.99 **Turkey Flat Grenache, 2004**, Barossa Valley, South Australia (**Halifax**, **Harrods**, **Nidderdale** and **Selfridges**). Old Vine Grenache is one of Australia's strong suits, but it usually plays second fiddle to Shiraz. Not this time, because this one's a Stratocaster! Drink it with everything but flat turkeys.

£14.99 **Leconfield Cabernet Sauvignon, 2003**, Coonawarra, South Australia (**Boo**, **Harrods** and **Wimbledon**). Sealed with a screwcap, winemaker Paul Gordon has not allowed a cork to interfere with his most exciting work in years. There is a sprig of mint, a bar of Green and Black's finest and a bolt of velvet in every glass – unbridled joy. The 2004 (which I saw very early doors in the strictest confidence) is a stormer, too. This is the sort of wine to resurrect Coonawarra's slightly dented pride.

raucously appointed

£15.29 **Penfolds Bin 389 Cabernet/Shiraz, 2003**, South Australia (**Maj**, **Mor**, **Sai**, **Selfridges** and **Tes**). I have followed this wine for years and it never disappoints. Almost every bottle of 389 is drunk too young, but this lush vintage is an atypical cracker and you can get on with it whenever you're ready. Now, in other words. You will encounter one of the most lavish flavours of the year – black in colour and raucously appointed, this is a Broadway production of amazing complexity coupled with fine footwork. You may think this an old label and that it doesn't move with the times. Far from it – 389 is setting the pace for everyone else to follow. If you want to taste a baby Penfolds wine that rocks, then for a mere £6.99 2004 Koonunga Hill is a stonker (**Asd**, **Mor**, **Sai**, **Tes** and **Wai**).

£17.99 **Château Le Boscq, 2003**, Cru Bourgeois Supérieur, Saint-Estèphe, Bordeaux, France (**Handford**). With all of the recent fuss surrounding the superb 2005 vintage in Bordeaux, it is easy to forget that these bottles won't be delivered into the UK for two years, so you have to find something suitably flash to drink in the meantime. 2003 was another remarkable vintage – this time for its heat and the resulting intense, brooding wines. Saint-Estèphe performed very well in '03 and Le Boscq, a perennial overachiever, made stunning wine. Dark, rich, full and glossy, this is top-flight claret at an eminently affordable price tag. Decant it and give it an hour or so to gather its thoughts before diving into layer upon layer of blackcurrant and cedarwood notes.

BLOCKBUSTER

£19.99 **Battle of Bosworth White Boar Shiraz, 2004**, McLaren Vale, South Australia (**Stratford's**). The estate 2005 BoB Shiraz Viognier is a stunner (£9.99, **Odd**), but if you want to open the throttle and accelerate away from the screaming masses, find a bottle of White Boar, an Amarone-style Shiraz, made from part-dried grapes – it is Herculean. You will need a helmet and gloves to attempt this wine, and after a glass you'll need a chaise longue to collapse on to.

£19.99 **Shelmerdine Single Vineyard Shiraz, 2004**, Heathcote, Victoria, Australia (**OFW** and **Sommelier**). With shockingly pure fruit and an aura that is frankly unnerving, this is a very interesting wine indeed. The flavour builds like a whirlwind on the palate and it crashes into you with a fantastically destructive force. Incredibly, you are left feeling bizarrely calm. If you wondered why people like me bang on about wine in full, florid form, taste this red – it's all there! You try to write something straightforward about the flavour!

£24.50 **Wirra Wirra Dead Ringer Cabernet, 2002**, McLaren Vale/Coonawarra, South Australia (**Richardson** and **Whitebridge Wines**). Hallelujah, this wine's sonorous tone envelops the planet. Monumental – perfect in every way. 2002 was an awesome vintage and Wirra nailed this wine. Just about drinking, Dead Ringer (named after a threatened law suit from Angélus in Bordeaux – the previous name of this wine – geddit?) has twenty years ahead of it.

BLOCKBUSTER

£24.99 **Penfolds St Henri Shiraz, 2002**, Barossa Valley, South Australia (**Maj**). This is the finest St Henri I have ever tasted. I gave it 19.5/20 in my notes and want to weep tears of joy when I remember the flavour onslaught that this wine brought me. At a quarter of the price of Australia's most famous red wine (and this wine's brother), Grange, this is, in my opinion, a monumental offering. There is nothing I would rather do than sip this wine right now. It is everything you could possibly wish for in a red wine. It really is that good. It will also live for another thirty years, too, such is the balance and perfection that dwells within this plainly labelled bottle.

£27.95 **Mitolo Serpico Cabernet Sauvignon, 2004**, McLaren Vale, South Australia (**Andrew Chapman**, **Cooden**, **Farr Vintners**, **Fine & Rare Wines**, **Harvey Nichols**, **Oz Wines**, **Philglas & Swiggot** and **Sommelier**). Lock up your daughters, here comes a fleet of Vikings, primed to slaughter anything in their way. Serpico is the definitive destroyer – it makes you forget every other wine you've ever tasted, not least because you'll feel so ravaged you'll suffer temporary memory loss. When you start to come around, you'll also feel curiously aroused – all good!

£29.95 **Clonakilla Shiraz/Viognier, 2004**, Canberra District, Australia (**Philglas & Swiggot** and **Noel Young**). Tim Kirk makes immensely serious wines. This 2004 is a model wine for the world to marvel at (yes this includes Côte-Rôtie

BLOCKBUSTER

producers in the Northern Rhône), because at £30 it simply can't be done anywhere else. The depth and texture of fruit are heavenly. If I could, I would buy cases and cases of this wine for my own cellar!

● ●

£5.59   half bottle, **Moscato d'Asti, Nivole, 2005**, Michele Chiarlo, Piedmont, Italy (**Boo** and **Odd**). At a fiver a half bottle, this is a fairly expensive wine and, unfortunately, you'll have to buy quite a few of these halves because one glass each is simply not enough. I have opened this for loads of people over the last few months on my book tours and at lectures and everyone, and I mean everyone, loves it. It is mildly sweet and juicily grapey, and the sparkle lifts the palate beautifully. It is perfect with strawberries and fruity puds. Chill it down, ice cold, and then watch your guests grin like idiots when the first whoosh of tingly, frothy grape juice hits their taste buds.

£5.99   half bottle, **Brown Brothers Orange Muscat & Flora, 2005**, Victoria, Australia (**Asd**, **Boo**, **Coo**, **Maj**, **Mor**, **Som** and **Wai**). This is justifiably one of the most famous sweet wines in the world. A few companies have tried to copy it but no one has ever come close to the bizarre mandarin segment and runny honey notes that this wine has in spades. If you like chocolate puds, then drink this wine with it. If you've never tasted it, you will be shocked at just how delicious and unusual Orange Muscat is.

BLOCKBUSTER

£5.99 half bottles, **Hermit's Hill Botrytis Semillon, 2002**, Riverina, New South Wales, Australia (**M&S**). Fresh fruit tart, summer pudding, strawberries and other summery deserts are among the lighter styles of the sweet food arena and you need a fresh, mildly tropical sweet wine to complement these dishes. Hermit's Hill is a honeyed, smooth, juicy, sweet white wine with a touch of caramel and tangerine running through the palate. It is a stunner and you could get six good glasses from this half bottle – one pound a glass ain't bad.

£6.99 half bottle, **Bimbadgen Myall Road Botrytised Semillon, 2005**, Griffith, New South Wales, Australia (**Maj**). This is a pretty little thing with oodles of fruit salad flavours and lashings of fresh honey. The clean acidity perks up the palate perfectly on the finish. Drink it with spotted Dick – or any of your other mates.

£6.99 50cl bottle, **Casa de la Ermita Viognier Dulce, NV**, Jumilla, Spain (**Bibendum**). This is a curio, but one worthy of a slot in this hallowed roll call of greats. It is a sweet Viognier, with tropical fruit on the nose and lush peaches all over the palate but I particularly like the finish, which dries up and perks up your palate. It would be perfect with a fresh and fruity tart, if you're lucky enough to know one.

£8.49 **Moscato d'Asti, Saracco, 2005**, Piedmont, Italy (**Maj**). This is one of the most exciting Moscatos I have ever tasted. Off-dry, frothy, juicy and grapey,

Saracco has managed to capture so much life and energy in this sparkler it is amazing. I liken this style of wine to a jet of ice-cold, soda-siphon grape juice on your palate. Serve it with light puddings or even on its own, as the fine bubbles and cheery air make it a guaranteed crowd-pleaser. Smiles all round. Kit off guaranteed in T minus twenty seconds!

£12.95 half bottle, **Keith Tulloch Botrytised Semillon, 2004**, Hunter Valley, New South Wales, Australia (**D Byrne**, **Haslemere Cellar** and **Vin du Van**). A complete contrast to the Bimbadgen above, this is a deep, intense, exotic wine, with extraordinary fruit concentration and immense class. It is only right to compare this to Sauternes (Bordeaux's great sweet white wines) and I think you will be blown away by the complexity that this wine possesses. There is no competition in value for money, either! Well played Keith.

£14.49 half bottle, **Mount Horrocks Cordon Cut Riesling, 2005**, Clare Valley, South Australia (**Bennett's**, **Philglas & Swiggot** and **Noel Young**). Australia's most famous sweet Riesling is a joy, with layer upon layer of lemon balm, lime zest and greengage fruit. Drink now or keep it for a decade!

£14.49 half bottle, **Torcolato, Maculan, 2003**, Veneto, Italy (**Odd**). Maculan's top sweetie Torcolato is the big brother to a favourite of mine, Dindarello (£7.89, half bottle, **Odd**). Torcolato is much richer and sweeter than its sibling and instead of just being limited to fresh fruit puds and lighter tarts, this wine can handle more exotic desserts. The orange, quince and honey flavours are hypnotic, and the sensual texture is amazing. In fact, this is so good you could have it instead of a pud, but you'd probably need a half bottle each, it is so delicious.

£15.99 50cl bottle, **Royal Tokaji 5 Puttonyos Aszú, Blue Label, 2000**, Hungary (**Cambridge**, **Jeroboams**, **SH Jones**, **Maj** and **Tanners**). This is one of the most captivating sweet wines of the year. The colour, nose and palate are nothing less than theatrical in their intensity, delivery and effect. The orange blossom, hazelnut and caramel notes are sensational and the slight sherried/tropical undertones support the main cast with reverence and accuracy. This is a wondrous wine and one that will alert your taste buds to the only reason (to date) why Hungary should form part of your vinous diet.

£24.99 **Billecart-Salmon, Demi-Sec, NV**, Champagne, France (**Harrods**, **Odd** and **Uncorked**). Demi-Sec (or Rich) Champagne embraces a much fruitier style of wine than the normal Bruts. This is Demi-Sec at its best! I absolutely adore this wine. It is refreshing and cleansing on the finish, but much more succulent and juicy on the palate. Anyone who loves Champagne will fall for this wine. But it will also bowl over those of you who have found traditional Brut (dry) styles too acidic.

£25.00 50cl bottle, **Klein Constantia, Vin de Constance, 2000**, Constantia, South Africa

(**Laithwaites**, **SWIG**, **Wai** and **Wine Society**). This historic wine has at last made me sit up and pay attention. I could never really understand why this expensive sweetie got so much attention, but in more recent vintages the purity and depth of the luscious fruit flavours seems to have been heightened and beautified. I now feel happy to give the 2000 vintage my seal of approval. Made from naturally raisined berries of Muscat de Frontignan, this is the apogee of dried apricots and zesty, thick-cut English marmalade in a glass. What is really bizarre is that it is all held together with lashings of stern acidity. Its ideal partner is an entire home-made cake trolley in a wonderfully appointed, fading English seaside resort. You could drink tea, eat cake and get marvellously and expensively pissed and watch the rainy world go by – heaven.

● ● ● ● ● ● ● ● ● ● ● ● ● ● ● ● ● ● ● ●

£6.99 **La Gitana, Manzanilla, NV**, Bodegas Hidalgo, Sanlúcar de Barrameda, Spain (**Boo**, **Cambridge**, **Maj**, **Sai**, **Villeneuve** and **Wai**). This is a call to arms! For a mere seven quid everyone in the UK can drink one of the most famous styles of wine the world has ever seen. There is nothing more uplifting than an ice-cold glass of dry Manzanilla sherry. Now don't turn your nose up at this idea – you will be shocked by how refreshing, joyous and cleansing this flavour is. Grab some salami, chorizo, olives, cashews, caperberries, in fact any nibbly bits and pieces and pick away knowing that your glass of Manzanilla (pronounced man-than-ee-ya) will take everything in its stride, dousing the vinegar, cutting through the fat and not missing a beat. You can get ten good glasses from a bottle, which makes this one of the best value wines on the planet.

£6.99 50cl bottle, **Sainsbury's Taste the Difference 12 year Old Oloroso Sherry, NV**, Spain (**Sai**). Made by Lustau, one of the top producers in Spain, this is a stunning sherry, with nutty richness and a toffeed, raisiny core. There is a lot of tangy sweetness here on the palate and you will find this an addictive sipper, as it is so delicious. Great with a big tin of choccies and nuts (Brazils and macadamias are essential).

£9.99 **De Bortoli Show Reserve Muscat, NV**, South Eastern Australia (**Maj** and **Odd**). Maybe one year we will have more fortified wines in the UK to choose from but, until then, you can't find a better wine to exchange for a tenner than this one. Liquidised, boozy Christmas cake in a glass. This is the sort of wine that the Aussie rugby team trains with in their bellies!

£11.00 **Fonseca Terra Prima Port, NV**, Portugal (**Amps** and **Raeburn**). This is an organically grown Port which shows stunning intensity and purity of black fruit and loads of dark chocolate on the finish, too. It is my favourite value Christmas Port of the year. Smooth, plump, succulent and round, the only disappointing thing is that the UK wine trade hasn't woken up to just how good this wine is. Philip Amp and Scooby-Doo (Zubair Mohamed at Raeburn) take a bow! This is what wine buying is all about – finding a great wine and getting it in even if it is a brand new release no one has previously heard of. I wish more people in the UK trade worked this hard.

£11.50 **Fonseca Unfiltered LBV Port, 2000**, Portugal (**Bennetts**, **Friarwood** and **Maj**). While we are dwelling on the Port and Fonseca thing, let me also recommend this brute. You have to decant it because it needs to breathe and there is a mild sediment, but once unleashed, this Shrek turns into a Prince Charming (don't worry kiddies, he's the same guy underneath!). Hang on to your seats because unlike the calm, erudite Terra Prima above, this is a berserker under the surface – get ready for some fun when you play spin the bottle (after it's empty, of course)!

£12.69 **Blandy's Harvest Malmsey, 1998**, Madeira, Portugal (**Sai**). This is a stunning Madeira that is an after-dinner treat for any wine lover. You only need a small glass and this wine lasts for ages when opened, so it is very good value indeed. Packed with toffeed, nutty sweetness and with a finish that lasts for half an hour, you will be in no doubt as to why Madiera is one of the world's most unique and famous wines.

£14.00 half bottle, **Turkey Flat Pedro Ximénez, NV**, Barossa Valley, South Australia (UK agent is **Mentzendorff** tel. 020 77840 3600). I know there are no retail stockists yet because the bottles arrive in the country after my copy deadline for the book, but I can't leave this wine out, so I have given you the UK agent's details above and you can ring them for information. PX is a grape that, when fortified, turns into the most ridiculous of boozy elixirs. Very dark brown in colour and tasting like liquorice toffee, espresso beans, brandy snaps and prunes in a blender, this is the ultimate in sweet wines. Drink it with coffee or dribble it over vanilla ice cream (or someone you lust).

£16.99 **Taylor's 10 Year Old Tawny Port, NV**, Portugal (**Boo**, **Fortnum & Mason**, **Sai**, **Selfridges**, **Tes** and **Thr**). With more weight and balance than its rivals, this is my choice of the Tawny ports this year. Everyone loves a Tawny port, particularly if you chill the bottle down a little. It is so glorious it goes with Christmas pud as well.

£17.00 50cl bottle, **Delaforce Colheita Port, 1988**, Portugal (**Off the Vine** and **Noel Young**). I love this Port because it is fully mature and really decadent. The nose of caramel, plum, hazelnut and fig, coupled with the rich raisiny palate, really shows off just how delicious Port can be when it has some age under its belt. The spirit has burned off and the wine element underneath is exposed. This is a totally mellow, after-dinner sipping wine.

£25.00 **Taylor's Quinta de Vargellas Port, 1996**, Portugal (**Fortnum & Mason**, **Harrods**, **Odd**, **Selfridges**, **Tes** and **Wai**). The BIG GUN this year comes from Quinta de Vargellas, the pick of Taylor's vineyards. Massive, inky, dark and swarthy, the 1996 is a full-bodied port that takes no prisoners. Vintage style in every way, this is £25 well spent!

A–Z OF FOOD
AND WINE
COMBINATIONS

INTRODUCTION

The most challenging chapter to compile in this book is undoubtedly The Top 250. It takes months and months of tasting to put together. And yet, when I ask readers which chapter they'd put first there is always a split decision. It seems the A–Z of Food and Wine is used as much, if not more, over the course of the year as readers regularly scour these seventy or so pages while deciding what to drink with their cooking. This delights me because, as you all know, there is nothing better than a glass of well-chosen wine with a plate of well-judged food.

People panic about choosing wine for dinner parties – the last thing you want to do is 'get it wrong', and 'getting it right' is so satisfying for both you and your guests. This chapter removes that worry, so hopefully you can now rest easy and let me help you out. Food-and-wine matching isn't rocket science, though; rather it's a case of telling the truth about what works and what doesn't in the flavour-combination arena. By thinking things through and paying attention to your tastes, you will find that you can swiftly learn the basic rules. You probably have most of them cracked already. After all, you match food ingredients all the time without even thinking. When making a sandwich it is generally accepted that ham goes well with mustard and beef with horseradish, but not necessarily the other way around. I know the flavour of most of the wines out there because I spend every day tasting them, so flick through these pages and avoid the ham and horseradish!

I realise that everything is a matter of taste – this is a subjective topic if ever there was one. So, if you are new to this book, it is important you realise that I don't tell you exactly what to drink with your dinner (I could only get it precisely right for my own palate). Instead, I tell you what not to drink and gently guide you to a flavour or group of wines that would work well. The final decision is up to you.

When I am not writing wine articles or books, I work as a wine consultant to restaurants around the world. My job involves writing wine lists and teaching waiting staff about wine and how it matches their restaurant's dishes. This invaluable experience, over twenty years, has helped me compile this chapter. There is nothing more exciting than setting up a wine list for a new restaurant. Talking to the chef and manager, tasting the dishes, anticipating the clientele, seeing the size of the cellar or storage area, and formulating a budget, all help me towards my decisions. The same thought processes happen when you are cooking dinner for friends – albeit on a smaller scale.

Your first step is to think of a menu. Next, find the dish in the A–Z and read through my recommendations. Now you have a choice. Either dive into this year's Top 250 and find the exact bottle you need – just hunt by style and price and you'll be there in a trice. This is quick and easy and you'll be drinking one of the best wines in the world in a moment. Alternatively, peruse the Gazetteer section and make a shopping list of several producers in the category of wines you need, flick through the Merchants pages and phone around to buy the perfect bottle. Or, if you are feeling brave, just head out of your front door, book in hand, and wing it. This is the way to gain confidence and, if you play your cards right, you could well find a real surprise on the shelves. Whatever you decide, I wish you the best of luck in balancing your wine and food in a well-thought-out and superbly enjoyable way.

One small tip – make sure you grab a few bottles of a multi-purpose, multi-talented style of wine while you're at it. Some names pop up in this chapter more often than others – Sauvignon Blanc, the crowd-pleasing, refreshing, dry, citrussy, white grape, is always a winner and definitely a safe haven if you need to hedge your bets. As are the juicy, smooth, black-fruit-driven, New World GSM (Grenache, Shiraz, Mourvèdre) blends. Try to keep a few bottles of these styles of wine at home in readiness for unexpected guests or impromptu cooking. It is also worth pointing out that Beaujolais, once one of the most derided styles of red wine in France, is incredibly versatile in the kitchen. It is savoured by knowledgeable gourmands the world over, but suffers from a down-market image thanks to 'Nouveau'. Stick to the proper estates in the Gazetteer and you will be delighted. It appears over twenty-five times in this chapter alone – there's proof for you!

APÉRITIF WINE STYLES

Pre-dinner nibbles like dry *roasted almonds*, *bruschetta*, *cashews*, *canapés*, *crostini*, *crudités*, *olives* and *gougères* (those addictive, cloud-shaped, cheese puffs served by the basket-full in Burgundy) are designed to give your palate a jump-start and get your juices flowing before a banquet. It is important at this stage of the proceedings not to overload your taste buds with big, weighty, powerful wines. Save those bottles for later and home in on refreshing, taste-bud-tweaking styles that set the scene, rather than hog the limelight: Champagne is, not surprisingly, the perfect wine if you're feeling flush but, if not, sparkling wines from the Loire (Saumur), the south of France (Limoux) or Crémant de Bourgogne (Burgundy) would do the job nicely. Italy offers up superb, dry, palate-enlivening fizz in the form of Prosecco from Veneto, or some more serious sparklers from Franciacorta, Trentino or Alto Adige. I never really drink the Spanish fizz Cava unless I'm dining out in Barcelona because there are only a few worthy versions to be found in the UK. The best and most authentic Champagne-taste-alikes come from the New World. These are all unusually good value, too (around half the price of Champs) – New Zealand, Australia (particularly Tasmania) and California are the places to go to find awesome quality. Fino- and manzanilla-style sherries are wonderful palate cleansers, too, particularly with salty dishes, despite being thought of as perpetually 'out of fashion'. Buck the trend and buy a bottle, they cost bugger all! Check out the Top 250 fortified section. The least expensive option (and often safest, particularly if you are eating out) is a zesty, uplifting, palate-sprucing, dry white wine. Even a moderately expensive number is often half the price of a bottle of Champs and there are thousands of these around. Look for screwcap-sealed wines for failsafe, pristine, unadulterated flavours. There are also loads of first-class examples in this book. Stay with unoaked styles and keep the price under control, and then step up the pace with the next bottle when the food hits the table. If the choice on offer is poor, then grab a neutral, dry, inexpensive white wine (Loire Sauv) and pep it up with a dash of Crème de Cassis (blackcurrant liqueur) to make a Kir. Use the same liqueur to turn a dry, sparkling wine or inexpensive Champagne into a glitzy Kir Royale, and suddenly everyone will want to be your friend.

STARTERS AND MAIN COURSES
Anchovies Strongly flavoured whether they are fresh or cured, these little, hairy fish require dry, unoaked, tangy, acid-rich whites or juicy, bone-dry rosés for maximum impact. Head to Italy, Spain or France and keep the budget low – a fiver is all you need. There are a few worthy rosés from the New World (check out The Top 250), but watch the alcohol level, as they can stray a little high up the scale (stay under 14% vol for safety). Dry sherry is also spot on, but consider what is in the rest of the dish, as it can pack a punch.

Antipasti The classic Italian mixed platter of *artichokes*, *prosciutto*, *bruschetta*, *olives*, *marinated peppers* and *aubergines* enjoys being serenaded by chilled, light Italian reds like Valpolicella and Bardolino, or clean, vibrant, refreshing whites like Pinot Grigio, Pinot Bianco, Frascati, Falanghina, Fiano, Cattarato, Vernaccia, Greco, Est! Est!! Est!!!, Orvieto, Verdicchio or Gavi.

Artichokes Dry, unoaked, refreshing whites are best here, especially if you are going to drown the artichoke leaves in *vinaigrette* (see 'Vinaigrette'). Alsatian Sylvaner (boring but worthy), Pinot Blanc, lighter, dry Riesling, Loire Sauvignon Blanc or Aligoté from Burgundy are perfect partners from France, as are the Italian whites listed above for 'Antipasti'. If you want to head to the New World, then keep it angular and edgy with South African, Chilean or New Zealand Sauvignon Blanc, or Argentinian Torrontés – don't spend up.

Asparagus Because of its inbuilt asparagusy characteristics (see my tasting note on page 174), Sauvignon Blanc is the perfect match here. New World styles of Sauvignon from Chile (Casablanca), Australia (Adelaide Hills) or New Zealand (Marlborough) have tons of flavour and would be better suited to asparagus dishes that have *hollandaise*, *balsamic vinegar* or *olive oil* and *Parmesan*. Old World styles, like those from the Loire (Sancerre, Menetou-Salon and Pouilly-Fumé) are great if the dish is plainer. Northern Italian whites like Pinot Bianco or Pinot Grigio, as well as South African Sauvignon Blanc (somewhere between New Zealand and Loire geographically and in style, too) would also do the job.

Aubergines If served grilled with *pesto* or *olive oil*, *garlic* and *basil*, as always you must identify the most dominant flavours in the overall dish. In both of these recipes they are the same – garlic and basil – so tackle them with a dry Sauvignon Blanc or keen, white Italians like Verdicchio, Inzolia, Vernaccia or Falanghina. Plain aubergine dishes are fairly thin on the ground as these glossy, sleek, bulbous, black beauties are often used within vegetarian recipes (for example, *ratatouille* or *caponata*). If cheese or meat (*moussaka*) is involved, these flavours take over, so light, youthful, crunchy reds are required. Southern Italian or Sicilian Primitivo, Nero d'Avola or Aglianico, southern French Grenache-based blends (most Côtes-du-Rhônes), Chilean Carmenère, Spanish Garnacha or Aussie Durif (g'day) are all good matches (and great value, too). Just make sure they are not too ponderous or alcohol heavy. If the dish is hotter (spicier) or the aubergines are *stuffed*, you will need a more feisty, characterful red. But don't be tempted by anything too heady (avoid tannic red grapes like Cabernet, Pinotage, Nebbiolo, Zinfandel and Malbec). *Imam bayildi*, the classic aubergine, onion, olive oil and tomato dish, is a winner with juicy, slightly chilled Chilean Merlot, youthful, bright purple Valpolicella, spicy Sardinian Cannonau or black-fruit-imbued Italians – Barbera d'Alba, Carmignano, Montepulciano d'Abruzzo or Morellino di Scansano.

Australian The masters/inventors of Asian fusion Down Under manage to juggle the freshest of land and sea ingredients, and weave into them the best of Asia's spices and presentation. This beguiling and thoroughly delicious style of cuisine is a real hit worldwide, as the cooking is virtually fat free and it's packed with zesty, palate-enlivening flavours. It is no surprise that in trendy Sydney, Brisbane, Adelaide, Perth and Melbourne restaurants they reward their palates with finely tuned Clare and Eden Valley Rieslings, fresh, grapey Verdelhos, zippy, perky Adelaide Hills and Western Australian Sauvignon Blancs, assorted Pinot Gris, Semillon/Sauvignon blends and keen, fresh, unoaked Chardonnays. Not all Aussie reds are huge and porty, with the vogue for more aromatic wines coming from McLaren Vale, Great Western or Frankland (Shiraz), Tasmania, Mornington Peninsula, Geelong or Yarra (Pinot Noir and Shiraz), Hunter Valley (Shiraz) and cooler Margaret River or Orange (Cabernet/Merlot) really hitting form. It is no wonder they are so fit and healthy down there with such glorious local produce, awesome wines and inspired chefs!

Avocado If the avocado is *undressed*, you need light, unoaked whites, in particular Loire Sauvignon Blanc, Muscadet or fresh, cheap, clean Italians. If *dressed* with *vinaigrette* or with *Marie Rose sauce*, richer Sauvignon Blanc (NZ and the Cape), Pinot Gris (smart Italians, Aussies and New Zealanders) or Australian Verdelho and Riesling are spot on, as are young, white Rhônes and Alsatian Pinot Blanc. *Guacamole*, depending on its chilli heat, needs cool, citrusy, dry whites to douse the palate and cut through the gloopy green matter.

Bacon This usually pops up as an ingredient in a dish and not often as the main theme – unless you've had a heavy night on the sherbets and need the pinnacle of all miracle cures – a *bacon sarnie*! If you feel like a glass of wine to accompany this classic bread and pork delight or to sip alongside your *full English breakfast*, then chilled red Côtes-du-Rhône, Languedoc Rouge or smart, Cru Beaujolais would be a joy. If you are brave (or foolish, or both) try it with a sparkling Shiraz from Down Under. If you are using fried or grilled *pancetta* or *lardons* in a salad, remember that the salty flavour and/or smoked taste could prompt a move away from a salady, light white wine to a juicy, fresh red or rosé.

Barbecues The unplanned, out-of-control, ever-so-slightly flammable nature of the British barbecue, combined with pink, uncooked meat, spicy, lurid marinades and intense, mahogany-coloured, smoky sauces ensures an informal, cave-men-hugging, flavour-packed occasion. Aim for good value New World gluggers (white or red), as long as they are assertive, juicy and fruit-driven. Lightly oaked Chardonnay, Chenin Blanc or Semillon for whites, or inexpensive Zinfandel, Merlot, Carmenère, Cabernet Sauvignon or Shiraz for reds all work. Don't be afraid of chilling both the whites and reds for maximum effect. Chile, Argentina, Australia, South Africa and New Zealand are the most likely candidates for your guest list – stay under a tenner to avoid credit card statement shockers.

Beans With *baked beans* you simply need to find fruity, berry-driven reds because the tomato sauce flavour is so dominant and it takes over the palate. Any youthful reds with refreshing acidity, such as those from the Loire, Spain, Portugal, South Africa, South America or Italy, will work well. Remember to keep the price down – it's not worth spending much for a *beans-on-toast* wine, unless you are a little loopy or feeling unnaturally flush! Not surprisingly, anything goes with *green beans*, as they are the least flavourful of veggies. You'd have to mince along with a light, dry white to let a green bean truly express itself! *Tuscan bean salad* needs slightly chilled, light-bodied reds or fresh, zingy whites to cut through the earthy, brown flavours. If you throw some beans into a stew, *cassoulet* or any of a wide variety of Spanish dishes, then Grenache/Carignan blends from the south of France (Fitou, Corbières, Faugères or Minervois) or Garnacha-based wines from Spain (Navarra, Terra Alta, Priorato, Campo de Borja, Calatayud or Tarragona) will easily deal with the beanie ballast – yum.

Black bean sauce requires a few moments' meditation and trepidation. The curious, oil-slick texture and sheer intensity of dark sweetness must be countered by huge, juicy, mouth-filling, velvety smooth reds – Zinfandel is the only red grape with the right gung ho attitude and armoury to cope.
Refried beans, either in *tacos* or other *Mexican* dishes, have a fair degree of earthy sludginess that needs either rich whites like a bright New World Chardonnay (Chile, South Africa and Australia give the best value) or fresh, fruity reds. I would try Bonarda, Sangiovese or Tempranillo from Argentina as a starting point, then head over to Chile for some Carmenère or Merlot if you have no joy. My favourite bean is the noble *cannellini*, the base for all great bean-frenzy soups. What should you uncork? Unlucky – you'll have to wait with tureen, spoon and glass at the ready for the 'Soups' entry.

Beef As there are so many different beef dishes, it is lucky the rules are not too tricky. Reds, predictably, are the order of the day. But it is the size and shape of them (the wines not the cows) that determines just how accurate the match will be. *Roast beef* (or *en croûte/beef Wellington*) served up for Sunday lunch deserves the utmost respect. When you gather around the dining room table do, by all means, push the boat out. It is at times like these when old-fashioned, gentleman's red Bordeaux really comes into its own. Don't ask me why, but classy wines such as red Bordeaux, Bandol, erudite northern Rhônes – Hermitage, Crozes-Hermitage, Cornas, St-Joseph or Côte-Rôtie – or even Italy's answer to an Aston Martin Rapide, the Super-Tuscans (see the stellar list in the Gazetteer) are simply magnificent with this king of beef dishes. As you'd expect, not one of these wines is remotely affordable. They are all special-occasion wines, so if you are looking to shave a few pounds off your spend, I would recommend heading to the top Cabernets from Australia's Margaret River (Western Australia), Coonawarra (South Australia) or Napa Valley in California. You've guessed it, these are fairly dear, but at least these reds will give you the richness and complexity that you are craving. If you are on a strict budget, then don't change regions, just buy cleverly – not all wines from Bordeaux are exorbitantly priced. Try first-class sub-regions like Lalande de Pomerol, Haut-Médoc, Côtes de Castillon and Fronsac, and go for a good vintage (see my Vintage Table on page 240). Hearty Southern Rhône or Languedoc reds would also do very well. Most Aussie (try Clare Valley and McLaren Vale in particular), South African, Chilean and Argentinian Cabernets or Cab/Shiraz blends around the tenner mark offer charm, complexity and competence, especially if you stick to my recommendations. It is at this price point that the New World leads the pack. But even if you drop down to around a fiver you can still have fun, just remember to stick to hotter-climate wines, as red Bordeaux and red Rhônes at this price are bloody awful. If you are a keen carnivore and a fan of *rare* beef, you can safely drink younger, more tannic red wines, as the tighter tannins balance perfectly with juicy, rare meat, slicing through the flesh and making your mouth water. If, however, you like your beef *well done*, then choose an older wine with smoother, more harmonious tannins. *Stews*, *casseroles* and *meat pies* need richer, more structured reds, particularly if meaty, stock-rich gravy is involved. Cabernet Sauvignon, Syrah (Shiraz), Pinotage, Piemontese (northern Italian) reds, Zinfandel and Malbec are but a few of the superb, hunky, robust grapes to go for. Look for wines from South Africa, Australia, California and Argentina. Southern Rhônes like Gigondas, Lirac, Cairanne, Rasteau or Vacqueyras will also be superb, as will Provençal or Languedoc reds made from a similar blend of swarthy red grapes. Portuguese wines are worth considering with rich beef dishes – the red wines from Dão and the Douro Valley are still woefully under-priced and, if you peruse my Gazetteer recommendations (see page 171), mightily impressive. Cahors in southwest France also deserves a mention, as it is a beautiful blunderbuss of a beef partner. *Bollito misto*, the Italian stew made from beef and just about everything else you could find in your larder, demands the presence of local wines – Teroldego and Marzemino from Trentino in northern Italy, would be a quirky and yet inspirational place to kick off, as would smart Valpolicella, Nebbiolo, Barbera and Dolcetto. *Boeuf bourguignon*, as the name suggests, usually pressgangs the help of red Burgundy. But please don't cook with anything expensive – save your money for the drinking wine and cook with a generic bottle (Beaujolais or Bourgogne Rouge). *Steak and kidney pie* loves manly, rustic reds with grippy, palate-crunching acidity and sturdy tannins. These wines slice through the gravy and often-chewy kidneys – Madiran and Cahors from France, Malbec from Argentina, and New World war-horses, like South African Pinotage and Syrah and Aussie Cabernet/Shiraz blends also enjoy this challenge. *Cottage pie* rarely requires anything more challenging than an inexpensive, fun lovin' red. You could even try your hand at Eastern Europe (although don't expect me to join you), or southern Italy or Sicily (a much safer bet), and go crazy and buy two bottles. A heroic *Beef stroganoff* demands rusticity in its dancing partner, so gather together some southern Rhônes (Sablet, Valréas, Cairanne or Vacqueyras); even a straight Côtes-du-Rhône from the right domaine can be a joy (see the Gazetteer page 171). *Hungarian goulash* would be wonderfully authentic if a Hungarian red wine joined it. Good Luck! If you want to play a straighter bat, then head to Rioja, Navarra, La Mancha or Toro (Spain) or Chilean

Cabernet Sauvignon – success guaranteed. Straight *steak* has a more direct and controlled meaty flavour than a rich stew, so finer wines can be dragged kicking and screaming out of the cellar (or local merchant). Bathe your buds in Chianti, Brunello di Montalcino, Ribera del Duero, Californian Merlot, Zin or Cab, top-end Cru Beaujolais (still only a tenner!), Crozes-Hermitage, St-Joseph (both Rhônes), and South African, Argentinian, cool-climate Australian and New Zealand Cabernet Sauvignon or Shiraz. Watch out that you don't OD on *Béarnaise sauce* – though great with a mouthful of steak, it can clog up the taste buds (and the waist band). With *steak au poivre*, the pungent, pulverised peppercorns make their presence known in each and every mouthful, so look for meaty (and pepper-flavoured) wines like northern Rhône reds (Syrah) or their cousins from further afield – Shiraz from Australia would be first choice, followed by Chile or South Africa. *Burgers* – heaven in or out of a bun – crave fruity reds like Italian Dolcetto or Barbera, Spanish Garnacha, young Rioja Crianza, juicy Californian Zinfandel, South African Pinotage, Chilean or South African Merlot, and Australian Petit Verdot (hard to find, but well worth it) or Cabernet/Shiraz blends. Once again, go for younger wines if you like your burger rare, and older, mellower wines if you dwell at the well-done end of the spectrum. *Chilli con carne* is a difficult dish to match with wine … search for fruitier styles like Aussie Merlot, or Negroamaro and Nero d'Avola from southern Italy and Sicily – I quite like chilling them a touch, too. *Steak tartare* is a strange one but does work terrifically well with very light reds and rosés – Tavel (southern Rhône) and other Grenache-based rosés (try Spain or Australia) are perfect, as are Shiraz rosés and snooty Pinot Noirs like Sancerre red or rosé. If you fancy splashing out, then rosé Champagne is the ultimate combo (although people are bound to think you're a tosser, but who cares?). Whatever you do, make sure you go easy on the capers if they are served alongside – as far as your palate is concerned, they are mini, green hand grenades. *Cold, rare roast beef salad* and other cold beef dishes enjoy the company of fresh, lighter reds with low tannins – Beaujolais, Valpolicella, red Loires (either Cabernet Franc or Gamay) or Argentinian Tempranillo or Bonarda would all work well. Pinot Noir is also a treat with this style of dish – Burgundy (France, but you knew that), Martinborough, Marlborough or Central Otago (all NZ), Tasmania, Yarra Valley and Mornington Peninsula (all Oz). The only occasion when you are allowed to break the red-wine-with-beef rule (of course there has to be one) is with *carpaccio* (raw/rare) or *bresaola* (air-dried). These wafer-thin-sliced beef dishes can handle whites and rosés. Any dry, apéritif-style Italian white, French dry rosé, Spanish Rosado or light Montepulciano-style red would be *fantastico*.

Cajun see 'Mexican'.

Capers Sauvignon Blanc, from almost anywhere, Vinho Verde from Portugal or very dry Italian whites like Soave (Veneto) or Greco, Fiano or Falanghina (Campania) are very good matches, as they can cut through the peculiar, otherworldly, vinegary tanginess you experience when you crunch and burst open the scarab-like exoskeleton of an unsuspecting caper. (For more suggestions see 'Apéritif'.)

Caviar I know it is a sin, but I adore good caviar. Sevruga or Oscietra (not Beluga – ridiculously decadent and a little too 'fishy' for my taste) are my faves and Champagne is definitely the call of the day. Avoid rosé styles, though (they always tend to taste metallic with caviar, in my experience), and there is no need to pop the cork of a prestige cuvée unless you're desperately trying to impress the ladies. If you want to keep the budget down, and there is nothing wrong with that, then Sancerre, Pouilly-Fumé (Loire) or tighter, leaner South African and New Zealand Sauvignons are all stunning combos. These styles also work if caviar is used in a sauce, but do look to the main ingredient as well as the caviar for guidance.

Charcuterie A selection of charcuterie (*assiette de charcuterie* to be precise, including *saucisson, salami, ham* etc.) contains loads of diverse flavours along a similar textural theme. I love smart rosés (I am not afraid to admit it and nor should you be) and top-quality, slightly chilled Beaujolais or Gamay from the Loire. Light- to medium-weight Italian reds, like Freisa (Piedmont), Valpolicella (Veneto), Morellino di Scansano (Tuscany), Montepulciano d'Abruzzo (Marche) or Aglianico (from the south) would also be good matches (take a few degrees off these, too, in the fridge). If you favour whites, then stick to firm, rich white grape varieties like Riesling or Pinot Gris, which usually manage to harness at least as much flavour intensity as the reds anyway. Do watch out for pickles, gherkins, cornichons (wicked, but delicious, little French numbers) or caperberries, as excess vinegar will guarantee that you'll not be able to taste the next mouthful of wine! My advice is to shake your gherkin (close the curtains first) and knock off as much vinegar as possible before hamstering them away. (For *chorizo* and *spicy salami*, see 'Pork'.)

Cheese (cooked) There is a groaning cheese-board section at the end of this hedonistic chapter, so flick on for uncooked cheese-chomping joy. *Cauliflower cheese, leek Mornays, cheesy pasta dishes* etc. and straight *cheese sauces*, depending on the strength of cheese used, need medium- to full-bodied whites such as New World Chardonnay, Chenin Blanc and Semillon. For reds, you must join the quest for fresh acidity coupled with pure berry fruit. This hunt should lead you to the delicious wines from the Loire (Saumur-Champigny, Chinon or Bourgueil) or Chilean, Australian or South African Merlot, Italian Cabernet Franc, Lagrein, Dolcetto or Freisa, or youthful Rioja, Navarra, Somontano or Campo de Borja reds from Spain. *Fondue* needs bone-dry whites (or pints of frothy lager!) to cut through the waxy, stringy, molten cheese. If you are a perfectionist then you'll be trekking off, wearing waterproofs and silly hat, in search of the inoffensive, and frankly frighteningly dull, wines from Savoie – Chignin-Bergeron, Abymes, Crépy or Apremont. However, if you are keen to reward your palate with pleasant-tasting, accurate wines, then well-balanced, fully ripe (as opposed to upsettingly lean and enamel-challengingly acidic) styles like Alsatian Pinot Blanc, Riesling and Sylvaner, and fresh Loire Sauvignon Blanc or Chenin Blanc would be ideal. You could even try dry Portuguese whites and various northeastern Italian single varietals like Pinot Grigio, Ribolla Gialla or Pinot Blanc. *Raclette* loves to be partnered with light red Burgundies or, better still, juicy Beaujolais-Villages. With *cheese soufflé* (one of the true highlights in the cooked cheese repertoire) you can really go out on a limb. Argentinian Torrontés or any aromatic dry whites like Muscat (Alsace), Riesling (from Alsace or Tazzy or Clare Valley/Eden Valley/Frankland in Australia), or even lighter Gewürztraminer (Chile or the Alto Adige in Italy are worth a punt) would all be delicious. If the soufflé has any other hidden ingredients inside it remember to consider them before plumping for a bottle – with *smoked haddock soufflé* you'd be wise to follow the fish so opt for punchy, lemony whites, like Hunter Valley Semillon (Australia) or Austrian

Riesling. *Melted mozzarella,* with its unusual milky flavour and play-doh texture, is well suited to Italian Pinot Bianco, Pinot Grigio, good Vernaccia, Arneis, Gavi and Verdicchio. Yes, these are all Italians! *Grilled goats' cheese* is equally at home with Sancerre (remember the best goats' cheese hails from Chavignol, Sancerre's finest village) and Pouilly-Fumé (across the other side of the Loire river) and all other Sauvignon Blancs from around the world (South Africa would be my first choice if your Loire fridge is empty). Lighter reds also work, particularly if you are tucking into a salad that has some ham joining in the fun. Goats' cheese is pretty forgiving when it comes down to it, but avoid oaky whites and tannic or leaden reds.

Chicken Chicken is very accommodating – it loves both whites and reds. But be careful because it is a touch fussy when it comes to the precise grape varieties you want to pair it with. Chardonnay is chicken's favourite white grape by far, with Riesling coming in a close second. Pinot Noir is the bird's favourite red (it's every bird's favourite red – be honest!), with Gamay, perhaps surprisingly, claiming the runner-up spot. This means that a well-educated, classy chicken loves every village in my beloved Burgundy region, and who can blame it? Lighter dishes such as *cold chicken* are fairly versatile, so look to my al-fresco-style wines in the 'Picnics' section. *Cold chicken and ham pie* works well with lighter, fragrant reds and deeper-coloured, sturdy rosés from the southern Rhône, Languedoc, Beaujolais, Portugal and Australia. If you are feeling adventurous, then try chilling down a bottle of Beaujolais-Villages to white temperature – it's a super, if unusual, match. *Poached chicken* can handle the same sort of wines but with a little more flesh on the bone – both Old and New World Pinot Noir work exceptionally well here. White wine companions include lighter New World Chardonnay or French Country Viognier and Marsanne/Roussanne blends. Possibly my favourite dish of all time, *roast chicken*, follows this theme once again, but takes it a stage further. Finer (i.e. more expensive) red and white Burgundy, elegant, cooler climate New Zealand or Australian or Californian Chardonnay, Pinot Noir and top flight Beaujolais (again) are all wonderful matches. *Coq au vin* works well with red Burgundy, but you can scale the wine down to a Chalonnaise version, a Hautes-Côtes or Bourgogne rouge (from one of my reputable Domaines, of course). *Chicken casserole* or *pot pie* ups the ante even further and it enjoys a broader wine brief. Medium-weight Rhône reds and New World Grenache-based wines, as well as mildly oaky Chardonnays, are all in with a shout. *Chicken and mushroom pie*, *fricassee* and other *chicken dishes with creamy sauces* call out to Chardonnay and beyond – dry Riesling from Germany, Alsace (France), Clare Valley, Eden Valley, Frankland or Tasmania (Australia), Alsatian Tokay-Pinot Gris and funky Rhône whites. New World Pinot Noir (from California, New Zealand, Tazzie or Victoria in Oz) is the only red variety to feel truly at home here.

OK, so far things have been fairly straightforward, but I am now going to poke a stick in the spokes of our free-wheeling, feathered friend, because *chicken Kiev* changes the rules completely. Full, rich and even part-oak-aged Sauvignon Blanc or Sauvignon/Semillon blends are needed to take on the buttery garlic onslaught – white Graves (Bordeaux) and California does this well with their Fumé Blancs, as does Margaret River in Western Australia and the stunning Hunter Valley Semillons, but watch this space as these styles are starting to be made all over the world, too. On to the next hurdle, *coronation chicken*, depending on who is making it (I like a lot of spice in my sauce), can also have a bit of a kick, so dry Riesling from New Zealand or

Clare Valley/Eden Valley in Australia would be worth unscrewing. Lastly, *barbecued chicken wings* can be nuclear-hot (my brother Simon is a veritable Jabba the Hut when slotting these) and, in my experience, beer is usually the safest bet. However, if, for some reason, you want to open a bottle of wine (are you mad?), then a clean, inexpensive, ice-cold New World Chardonnay will work.

Chilli *Enchiladas*, *chimichangas* (nuclear waste in a wrap), *fajitas*, *chilli con carne*, *dragon's breath pizzas* and any other fart-lightingly hot Mexican dishes 'embrace the dark side' with a hefty dose of chillies. Thirst-quenching, chillable Italian red grape varieties like Freisa, Primitivo, Nero d'Avola, Frappato or Negroamaro, or juicy New World Bonarda, Durif, Cab Sauv and Merlot are needed to cool you down and rebuild your damaged taste buds. If you prefer a bottle of white, then New World Chardonnay or Semillon, thoroughly chilled, will have enough texture and body to handle the heat. I love Clare Valley Riesling or Adelaide Hills Sauvignon Blanc with chilli-laden seafood or chicken dishes, but keep the price sub-tenner.

Chinese The perennial problem when matching wine to Chinese food is that, the second you and your pals see the menu, everyone wants something different. So, in the end, you settle on sharing and find yourself tasting every dish on the table, thus mixing flavours wildly in your bowl. Sweet-and-sour dishes slam into spicy ones, stir-fried dishes envelop crispy chilli ones, while poor old plain-boiled food struggles for a break in the non-stop, kick-boxing palate action. John Woo would be proud of the mayhem but your taste buds are crying for a break. All this means Chinese-friendly wines must be multi-skilled, pure, fruit-driven offerings with lashings of all-important, crisp acidity. Tannic, youthful reds and oaky, full-bodied whites are completely out of bounds. White grape varieties to consider (in unoaked form) are Sauvignon Blanc, Riesling, Semillon, Pinot Gris, Greco (southern Italy), Verdelho (totally underrated from Australia) and bone-dry Gewürztraminer. Reds are a little more difficult, as there are only a few truly juicy varieties, but New World Merlot, Argentinian Bonarda and cheaper Californian Zinfandels are all good bets. It is no surprise that Antipodean wines work well with this style of cooking as Asia is on their doorstep. *Hao chi, Ganbei.*

Chutney see 'Pâté' and 'Pork'.

Duck *Roast* or *pan-fried* duck is often served with fruit or fruity sauces, so you need to be prepared to balance this with a fruity wine. Reds are *de rigueur* here – New World Pinot Noir (loads to choose from), good quality Beaujolais, Italian Barbera or Negroamaro, Australian Chambourcin (OK, that is a rare and slightly ridiculous suggestion, but what the hell!), lighter Californian Zinfandel and any other super-juicy, berry-drenched wines would do the business. *À l'orange* swings the colour firmly to white, but full-flavoured, juicy wines are still the vogue. Alsace or top Aussie Riesling, Alsatian Tokay-Pinot Gris, or Southern French and Rhône Viognier all have enough richness and texture to crack this dish, as do top-end northern Italian white blends – see Trentino, Alto Adige and Friuli in the Gazetteer for the best estates. With *cherries*, 'village-level' red Burgundy (utilising the beautifully cherry-scented red grape Pinot Noir), top notch Barbera from Piedmont, smart, new wave, fruit-driven, Reserva-level Rioja and medium-weight but classy Zins from California are all excellent. The more robust dish of *confit de canard* demands meatier reds with backbone, grippy acidity and tannin to cut through the sauce and fat that makes this dish sing, like those from Bandol in Provence, the Languedoc-Roussillon or the southwest of France – Madiran or Cahors for example. For an unlikely but first-class combo, give *crispy aromatic duck* a whirl with chilled Chambourcin or Durif from Australia, or juicy, fruit-driven Californian Zinfandel (you need only spend £6 or £7) – these are all a dead cert.

Eggs For *quiches, soufflés* or *light, savoury tarts* consider the main flavours (ham, cheese, salmon, herbs etc.) and their impact on the dish. Also, think about what you are eating with it – these dishes are always served with something else. Once you have nailed these flavours, unoaked or lightly oaked Chardonnay is a fair starting point – Chablis is the classic, but northeastern Italian Chardonnays would also be spot on. New World unoaked Chardonnays are now creeping on to the market too. *Omelettes, frittata* and *savoury pancakes* follow the same rules. However, for *oeufs en meurette* (the legendary Burgundian dish of poached eggs in red wine with lardons – *à genoux*) a red wine is definitely called for – mid-priced Beaujolais or a fresh, young, acidic red Burgundy would be accurate. For *fried* and *poached* eggs, look at the other ingredients involved. If combined with a salad utilising stronger-flavoured ingredients, try Beaujolais but, if you'd rather go white, Alsatian or German dry Riesling or a top Pinot Blanc would be just fine. For *quails'* eggs, see 'Apéritif wine styles'. Finally, eggs *Benedict* has an awful lot going on, from the muffin base and bacon or ham, to the ridiculously wicked hollandaise sauce, so a youthful Côtes-du-Rhône is needed *now*, preferably a magnum.

Figs The only entry to feature in both this section and the pud category. If you are anything like me then these are the most irresistible of fruits. Served with serious ham (in Italy) or in a salad, they manage to hold their own irresistibly carnal flavours despite coming up against ingredients as combative as Gorgonzola and balsamic vinegar. Clearly those are the dominant flavours but if you really want to know what a fig likes to be drunk with, there is only one answer – slippery Riesling made with passion, knowing and all-enveloping sensitivity. Figs are, after all, the most erotic of ingredients and they must be rewarded with the most exotic and sensual of grape varieties – phew, I made it to the end without overheating.

Fish The flavour intensity of fish depends not only on the sort of fish you are cooking but also, crucially, on how it is cooked. The general rule is: the milder the flavour, the lighter the white wine; the richer the flavour, the heavier the white wine. I know this is obvious, but it is worth stating. Fish cooked in red wine is one of the few exceptions to this white-dominated section, as a light, fresh red would simply meld better with the sauce. From Bianco de Custoza and Soave (Italy), Austrian Grüner Veltliner, Menetou-Salon and Sauvignon de Touraine (Loire), white Burgundy (Mâcon, Rully, Pouilly-Fuissé, Meursault and so on), fine Californian Chardonnay, zesty Jurançon Sec, heady Australian or New Zealand Pinot Gris, plump Marsanne or whip-cracking Hunter Valley Semillon, to any aromatic Riesling or Viognier – the opportunities are literally endless. Just remember that poaching and steaming are gentler, non-taste-altering ways of cooking fish, while grilling, searing, frying and roasting all impart distinctive charred or caramelised nuances to the flesh. Also consider what you are cooking the fish with; check through your recipe for strongly flavoured ingredients, such as lemon, capers, balsamic vinegar, flavoured olive oil and pungent herbs.

Often, the finer the piece of fish, the more money you should chuck at the wine. *Dover sole*, *lemon sole*, *turbot* and *sea bass*, at the top of my Premier fish league, are all pretty pricey and, if you are that committed to a dish, you should endeavour to complete the picture by splashing out on a worthy bottle of white Burgundy. Failing that, for under a tenner you could pick up a top South African Chardonnay, Australian Semillon, Eden Valley or Clare Valley Riesling, Adelaide Hills Chardonnay, Riesling from Alsace, posh Lugana or Gavi from Italy, dry white Graves (Bordeaux), white Rhône or trendy Spanish Albariño or Godello to go with these fish. *Halibut*, *John* (Hunky) *Dory*, *sea bream*, *skate* and *brill* all enjoy these styles of wine, too, while *swordfish*, *monkfish* and *hake* can take on slightly weightier whites (or even a fresh, light red, such as Beaujolais). *Salmon* (poached or grilled) likes Chardonnay, whether it is from the Old or New World, but give oaky styles a wide berth. *Trout* loves Riesling and the all-time classic Chablis. But, for an especially wicked combo, try to track down the unusually scented, dry French wine, Jurançon Sec. *Fish cakes*, especially proper ones with a high salmon content, go wonderfully with dry Riesling, richer Sauvignon Blancs or fresh, young Semillons, particularly if you are keen on a generous spoonful of tartare sauce (those grapes can handle it – they've been in training for years). *Red mullet* has more than enough character to cope with rosé wines, making a beautiful pink partnership between plate and glass. *Kedgeree* is trickier (and if it's breakfast, slow down – wait for 10 o'clock at least!), as the combo of smoked haddock, cayenne, parsley and egg might make you lean towards red. But don't! Rapier-like acidity is needed to slice through this dish and I'm sure you know which white grape does this best – Sauvignon Blanc. Sauvignon is also the grape to enjoy with *fish 'n' chips* (*cod*, *haddock* or *plaice*) because it can handle the batter and, to a certain degree, the vinegar (but go easy), and it shines with *fish pie* – poshest partnership being the Loire all-stars Pouilly-Fumé or Sancerre. If you fancy a trip to the New World, then Marlborough in New Zealand has to be the starting point for fans of this zesty grape, with South Africa's finest from Elgin or Elim being next and Australia's Margaret River giving the best Sem/Sauv blends outside Bordeaux. *Fish soups* and *stews* need more weight in the glass and one of the finest matches is white Rhône, made from Marsanne and Roussanne, or Viognier. Aussie Marsanne (rare) or Pinot Gris (loads) would also be a great option. *Sardines* require masses of perky acidity to cut through their oily flesh and, once again, Sauvignon Blanc is the winner. Having said this, don't forget poor old Muscadet or Italian Pinot Grigio, Arneis, Verdicchio or Gavi. Spanish Albariño, French Aligoté and even light reds, like Gamay. *Canned tuna* just needs unoaked, dry white wine – yawn. However, *albacore*, the finer, paler version, is more delicately flavoured so take care not to swamp it. The Italian trio, Lugana, Bianco di Custoza and Soave Classico, would do this job inexpensively and with the required chic. *Fresh tuna*, seared and served rare, desperately craves juicy, fresh, baby-light reds and chilled rosés (you could sneak a Sauvignon in, if you wish). *Brandade de morue* (salt cod), with its garlic and oil components, can stand up to whites with a little more soul. Albariño, from Galicia in Spain, is a perfect choice. However, Penedès whites and even light rosés are all within its grasp. Don't forget good old Vinho Verde either – it is a cracker with tricky fish dishes. *Herrings, kippers* and *rollmops* have a more robust texture and aroma thanks to the curing process. Once again, dry whites and rosés work well, but steer clear of oaked whites, as the pungent barrel nuances will overshadow the subtleties of the dish. *Smoked eel* is often served with crème fraîche, and cream is always a little problematic for wine. Look to Austrian Riesling or Grüner Veltliner, top end Italian Pinot Grigio, bone-dry, world-class Riesling, and almost any dry white wine from Alsace. These will all relish the challenge. *Smoked salmon* is perfect with Gewürztraminer, whether it is from Alsace, Oz or Chile. Just make sure you buy a 'bone-dry', not 'off-dry' version. The scent and tropical nature of Gewürz may work amazingly well, and so does Viognier and even Canadian Pinot Blanc. Don't forget Champagne or top-end Tasmanian or Californian sparkling wine, particularly if serving blinis topped with smoked salmon and caviar. *Smoked trout* or *smoked mackerel pâté* is a challenge – fishy, smoky and creamy flavours all in one dish. Victorian Riesling, Hunter Valley Semillon, Adelaide Hills Sauvignon Blanc or Pinot Gris (all Aussies), southern French Viognier, lighter Alsatian Riesling and Pinot Blanc are all perfect matches. Lastly, *curries* or *Asian* fish dishes often sport spices, such as turmeric, ginger and chilli, so turn to two of our favourite saviour white grapes for the solution – New World Sauvignon Blanc and Australia's world-class, mind-blowing array of Rieslings – and these are all stunning value. Yum.

Frogs' legs Aim for smooth, mildly oaked Chardonnay from Burgundy (Chablis, St-Romain, St-Aubin or Mâcon), Australia, South Africa or New Zealand. Consider what you've cooked these cheeky little blighters in and then tweak your wine choice accordingly – if *garlic butter* is involved, stick to Sauvignon Blanc. Come on, hop to it! (Sorry – I couldn't resist!)

Game All flighted game, including *pheasant, quail, guinea fowl, woodcock, teal, grouse, snipe, wild duck* and *partridge*, adore the majestic red grape Pinot Noir. This means red

Burgundy is my first choice, with California, New Zealand, Tasmania, Victoria and Oregon somewhere in the pack behind the leader. The longer the bird is hung, the more mature the wine required (this can mean ten- or even twenty-year-old bottles). I have enjoyed red Bordeaux, Super-Tuscan, northern Rhône, Spanish wine from Ribera del Duero or Priorato, and many other top reds with this heady style of cuisine. But it is important to aim for complex wines with layers of fruit and a bit of age, and this inevitably means spending up. *Jugged hare* often uses port and/or redcurrant jelly in the recipe, so a pretty feisty red wine is needed. New-style Piemontese reds made from Nebbiolo or Nebbiolo/Barbera blends would have the stuffing to cope, as would more structured Australian Shiraz (Clare, McLaren Vale, Heathcote, Hunter or Barossa Valley), Zinfandel from California or South African Shiraz and Pinotage. One slightly cheaper and worthy source of full-bodied red is the Douro Valley in Portugal – not only would you have a meaty wine, but it would also be in perfect synergy if you've used port in the recipe. *Rabbit*, as well as being a less athletic version of hare, is also less pungent and has lighter-coloured flesh so, although big reds are essential, they don't need to be quite as powerful as those suggested above. The classic combo of *rabbit with mustard and bacon* packs a pungent flavour punch, so aim for swarthy bottles of red with feisty tannins and a youthful, purple hue – Chianti, Carmignano, Vino Nobile di Montepulciano (all from Tuscany), Bandol (from Provence), Lirac, Rasteau, Vacqueyras, Cairanne and Gigondas (from the southern Rhône), Argentinian Malbec, South African Cabernet and Shiraz, and smarter Chilean Cabernet blends would be spot on. *Wild boar* favours rich, brooding reds and, depending on the dish, you could choose any of the aforementioned wines but, this time, include some of the finest of all Italian wines – Brunello di

Montalcino, Barbaresco and Barolo. The only problem is you might need to win the lottery to buy a bottle. *Venison* loves reds and any bottle mentioned in this section would do, including top Australian Cabernet Sauvignon and some of the better New Zealand Hawke's Bay reds. Finally, *game pie* – served cold it behaves like cold chicken and ham pie (see 'Chicken') but served hot needs any wine suggested for steak and kidney pie (see 'Beef').

Garlic *Roast garlic* tends to emasculate fine wines so, if you are partial to lobbing a few bulbs in the oven, keep the wine spend down and follow the main dish's theme. *Garlic prawns*, *mushrooms* and *snails* all need aromatic, bone-dry, rapier-sharp Sauvignon Blanc. If you fancy being ahead of the pack and ever-so patriotic, then try dry, herbal English white wines. Watch out for *aïoli* (*garlic mayonnaise*) because you'll get a shock if your wine isn't up to it. Once again, Sauvignon Blanc can provide you with a shoulder to blub on, but you will have to find a bottle with a lot of character and vivacity – Marlborough in New Zealand is probably the answer. (For *chicken Kiev* see 'Chicken'.)

Goose The best wines for roast goose lie somewhere between those suited to game and those for chicken. In short, this means lighter red Burgundies and smooth, cherry-scented New World Pinot Noir in the red camp, and big, rich, sassy Chardonnays and Rieslings in the white. If you can afford it step up to Alsatian Grand Cru Riesling: you'll be in heaven.

Greek see 'Mezze'.

Haggis Traditionally accompanied by a wee dram of whisky but, if it could speak for itself (and some apparently do), a haggis would love to get down with a rich, textured, aromatic white wine. Depending on your palate, you could choose a broad, luscious New World Chardonnay or a scented white Côtes-du-Rhône. If you really want to go over the top, try any Grand Cru Tokay-Pinot Gris from Alsace, or a Condrieu from the northern Rhône. If you want to save a few quid then look to the Eden Valley in South Australia for a funky, juicy Viognier. Many Scots swear reds are better, but on this occasion they're wrong!

Ham Smart Cru Beaujolais, Chilean Merlot or Carmenère, youthful Spanish Tempranillos, Italian Nero d'Avola, Montepulciano or Negroamaro, and youthful, inexpensive South African Merlot all have the essential juiciness to complement a glorious ham. The golden rule is to avoid any tannic or heavily acidic reds – stick to more mellow styles. There is a splinter group for whom heady whites also work – busty Viognier and lusty Chardonnay would do the task well. *Parma ham and melon, prosciutto, jamón Serrano* and *pata negra* all like dry German Riesling (Mosel, Rheingau or Pfalz), many of the aromatic whites from Trentino, Alto Adige and Friuli (northern Italy), and Verdejo or lightly oaked Viura from Rueda (Spain). *Honey-roast ham* needs mouth-filling, textural, bone-dry whites like dry Muscat, Viognier, Verdelho and Riesling. Search for these in Alsace, Australia, the Rhône Valley and from the vast array of terrific French Country wines (and grab some ripe figs to eat alongside it – so exotic and erotic!). *Ham hock* with lentils or boiled Jersey potatoes and beetroot (or garden peas) is a treat with posh, dry rosé, and there are a fair few out there, so head to the southern Rhône or to richer examples of Sancerre rosé or Grenache rosés from McLaren Vale in Oz or Garnachas from Spain. *Smoked ham* has a fairly strong aroma and lingering flavour, so Tokay-Pinot Gris and young

Vendange-Tardive-level Rieslings from Alsace would be exact, as would older Aussie Rieslings. If you favour red wine then choose a Merlot, a Cabernet Franc (from Australia or the Loire) or a Beaujolais, and chill it a degree or two to perk up its acidity. *Gammon steak* (sling the farcical addition of pineapple or peaches) makes a neat partnership with oily, unoaked whites. All Alsatian wines and most dry German Rieslings would be delicious, as would the world-class Rieslings from Australia's Clare Valley, Eden Valley, Tasmania and Frankland. New Zealand Pinot Gris would also be fantastic. Semillon rarely gets the call up for a specific dish, but Aussie versions from the Hunter Valley with a few years under their belts and dry white Bordeaux (both with a smattering of oak) are simply stunning with ham, too.

Indian My Indian food-and-wine-matching career is complete. It is now nothing short of a fully fledged passion. When I designed and wrote the wine list for the re-launch of top London Indian restaurant Chutney Mary, it was clear to me that unoaked, fruit-driven whites were to be the driving force in my selection. Smooth, juicy rosés were also essential, as were overtly fruit-driven reds, avoiding any that were noticeably tannic. The surprise came when I made the final selection and found that Italy, Australia, South Africa and New Zealand had claimed the lion's share of the list. There were a few wines from other countries but virtually no classics like red Bordeaux, Burgundy or Rhône. Shock horror! This just proves that, depending on the style of cuisine, a wine list can be balanced, eclectic and hopefully thoroughly exciting, without relying on France. The grape varieties or styles of wine that go particularly well with Indian food are: whites – Pinot Grigio, Verdicchio, Sauvignon Blanc, Pinot Bianco, Fiano, Torrontés, Riesling, Viognier, Verdelho, light Gewürztraminers and Albariño; reds –

Valpolicella, Gamay (Beaujolais), Grenache (and Spanish Garnacha), Negroamaro, Pinot Noir, Nero d'Avola, Zinfandel, Barbera, Lagrein and Merlot. Other styles that work well include rich rosé, Prosecco, Asti (with puddings), rosé Champagne, Aussie sparklers and good-quality ruby port. Chutney Mary won Indian Restaurant of the Year at the Carlton Food Awards and then Amaya, a new sister restaurant, came along at the tail end of 2004 – wham bang! Best New Restaurant of the Year and also overall Restaurant of the Year in 2005 – you can see why I am having a good time!

Japanese *Sushi* is a strange, but undeniably delicious, dish to match wine to. Surely green tea or sake would be more appropriate? Well, I beg to differ. Sparkling wines and Champagne are a treat with the best sushi, especially bone-dry cuvées – 'Ultra Brut', Zero Dosage or 'non dosage'. Not surprisingly, the ever-ready Sauvignon Blanc grape is waiting in the wings to save you and the bill. You could always look to zesty, unoaked Italian whites for joy – Vernaccia, Arneis and Gavi are all ideal. Perky Pinot Gris and the brilliant dry Rieslings from Australia and New Zealand would also be great. *Teriyaki* dishes are a nightmare, though, as the sweetness and fruitiness in the glossy soy and sake glaze is incredibly flavour dominant on the palate. Zinfandel or rich, glossy Pinot Noir from California, super-ripe Chambourcin, lighter, modern Shiraz or Merlot from South Australia, and Nero d'Avola or Negroamaro from Sicily would just about manage this scary challenge – chill for effect. You will always be offered a blob of nuclear green matter with your sushi called wasabi. I'm afraid wasabi is a stealthy, committed, highly trained and silent, Ninja wine assassin – thank God it's green and it moves slowly so at least you have time to react.

Junk food What on earth should you drink with a hamburger, cheeseburger, chicken nuggets, bargain bucket of fried off-cuts, blanched brontosaurus, sweaty stegosaurus or any of the other palate-knackering, mass-produced, burp-mongering, fast-food delicacies? A high-sugar, monstrously carbonated, brain-banging soft drink, of course, for that all-encompassing, explosive gut, nauseous, cold-sweat feeling that you look forward to enjoying ten minutes after plunging this demonic matter down your cakehole. If you are seriously considering opening a bottle of wine (*Broadmoor's calling*), try Chilean Carmenère, entry-level Aussie Shiraz/Cab, or South African Chenin/Chardonnay (just keep the price down, you don't want to regret opening it in the morning). If you are well organised you'll always keep an 'emergency' white in the fridge and red in the cupboard for times like these. That way you can't open a serious bottle by mistake. Either way, while you are guzzling, Dante is hastily reworking his epic and inventing yet another circle of hell for your internal organs to be poached in while you slumber.

Kidneys Lambs' kidneys tend to absorb a fair amount of the flavour from the ingredients in which they are cooked, so follow those as your guide. Mustard is often used, so keep the reds firm, chunky and with a lick of crunchy, palate-refreshing acidity – Chianti, Morellino, Lagrein, Barbera, Montepulciano, Rosso Conero (all Italian), Rioja, Toro, Calatayud, Navarra (all Spanish), Languedoc-Roussillon and the Rhône Valley (both French) would all be worth a whirl. (For *steak and kidney pie* see 'Beef'.)

Lamb Red Bordeaux is, strictly speaking, THE classic combination with *roast lamb* or *lamb chops*. However, reds from nearby Bergerac or Madiran and, further a field, Burgundy, South Africa's smarter Pinotage and Shiraz,

California's Merlot, Australia's Shiraz and Cabernet blends, Spain's Rioja, and Argentina and Chile's Cabernets and Merlots are all in with a very solid shout. Keep the wine firmly in the middleweight division and you will do well. You can, of course, go bonkers on the price or stick within a tight budget, as lamb is less choosy than beef or game. The way it is cooked, though, should definitely influence your final choice. If cooked *pink*, the range of suitable wines is enormous (any of the above). If *well done*, then a fruitier style of red should be served, so head to the New World's treasure chest, as lamb tends to dry out and it needs moisture-resuscitation. Watch out for gravy and mint sauce, as an abundance of either could test the wine. *Lamb pot roast* and *casserole* tend to be a little richer in flavour than a chop or roast lamb because of the gravy. Again, don't spend too much on the wine, as authentic Languedoc or southern Rhône reds will do fine. *Shepherd's pie* is incredibly easy to match. In fact, just open whatever you feel like – if it's red and wet, it will be spot on – switch your brain off for an hour. Plain *lamb shank* is another relatively easy dish to match to red wine, with inexpensive European examples from Portugal, Spain, Italy and France all offering enough acidity and structure to cut through the juicy, mouth-watering meat. *Moussaka*, with cheese, onion, oregano and aubergines, is altogether different. Lighter, fruit-driven reds such as New World Pinot Noir, inexpensive workhorses from Toro, Alto Duero or Campo de Borja in Spain, or cheaper South American reds will work well. *Stews* like *navarin* (with vegetables), *Irish stew*, *cassoulet* or *hot pot* all have broader shoulders when it comes to reds. Beefier southern French examples from Fitou, Corbières, St-Chinian, Madiran, Faugères, Minervois or Collioure would be perfect. From further afield, Malbec from Argentina or Carmenère from Chile, as well as medium-weight, scented

Aussie Shiraz (McLaren Vale, Pemberton or Yarra Valley) would also suit these dishes. *Cold roast lamb* follows the same rules as cold slices of beef and, to a certain extent, ham, in that fruity, light reds and juicy medium- to full-bodied whites work pretty well. Beaujolais, served cool but not cold, is a great partner, while Chardonnay in any of the following guises would augment the dish – try medium-priced ('village') white Burgundy, Chardonnay from Margaret River, Adelaide Hills or Yarra Valley (Australia) or Nelson or Marlborough (New Zealand), or lighter South African and Chilean styles. Also, don't forget proper manly rosés – they are such an underrated drink, especially with cold cuts and there are loads out there these days. Lastly, *kebabs*, one of lamb's most exciting and gastronomically enlightening incarnations whether you've lovingly marinated and skewered the meat yourself or just adoringly watched it being shaved off that abhorrent, elephantine mass of grey flesh in your kebab shop. I suspect you'd struggle to balance a kebab and a goblet of wine while stumbling down the street after a late-night gig but, on the off chance that you make it home before tucking into the nuclear-hot dish, a glass of big-brand, sub-fiver New World Chardonnay or Semillon/ Chardonnay would be a welcome break between mouthfuls.

Liver *Calves' liver with sage* (an ever-so-tasty retro dish) needs medium-weight reds with prominent acidity. The texture of medium rare liver is relatively delicate but the flavour is rich and pure, and the wine's acidity cuts through this intensity with style. Loire reds made from Cabernet Franc are your first port of call; Saumur-Champigny, Chinon, St Nicolas de Bourgueil and Bourgueil are all relatively inexpensive (sub-tenner) and a perfect match. Personally I wouldn't look any further but, if you need a larger choice, then head to northern Italy to some well known and other less so names – Valpolicella, Teroldego from Trentino, Lagrein, Marzemino and Cabernet (Franc or Sauvignon – sometimes Italians don't specify which you're getting). You could even head to Austria and give a Blauer Zweigelt a welcome day out. These all have the required fruit richness with the balancing acidity, freshness and grip needed for this task. *Liver and bacon* needs a touch more spice in a red wine, but not much more weight, so move to a warmer part of France or Italy (i.e. head further south or look for a hot vintage). Red Bordeaux and Chianti would be ideal, but this is likely to push the price up a few pounds.

Meat *Balls* – yes, say it loud! – (see 'Pasta'), *pies* (see 'Beef') and *loaf* (see 'Terrines').

Mexican *Fajitas, enchiladas, tortillas, quesadillas, tacos, burritos* (my tummy is rumbling – actually it's pleading deafeningly) – these are all loaded with chilli and salsa, and lead to the consumption of copious quantities of lime-stuffed (*so* yesterday) beer. It may have excellent thirst-quenching properties but it's got bugger-all flavour. If you are partial to a glass of wine, you must go in search of ripe, fruity, chillable red grapes like Nero d'Avola, Negroamaro and Primitivo (from southern Italy), Carmenère and Merlot from Chile, inexpensive Zinfandel from California and Cabernet or Merlot cheapies from Oz. As for whites – they are likely to get bashed up no matter what you choose, so find inexpensive, New World, mildly oaked Chardonnay or Semillon (or a blend of the two), chilled down to sub zero. Interestingly, *Cajun* cooking follows a similar pattern to Mexican when it comes to wine styles, because cayenne, paprika, oregano, garlic and thyme all cook up a storm and need to be tempered with similarly juicy whites and reds.

Mezze (or *Meze*) This is the chance for dry Greek whites to shine, and there are enough out there of sufficiently high quality to really hit the mark. If you are unable to track them down, then try dry Muscat, Pinot Blanc or Sylvaner from Alsace, New Zealand Sauvignon Blanc or Argentinian Torrontés. You could always try to find dry Muscat from Australia, Spain or Portugal, too. Albariño from northwestern Spain and good old Vinho Verde from Portugal also work well. Greek reds still lag behind the whites in terms of overall quality – some cheapies are fine, if a little coarse, but I would avoid spending more than a tenner as you will be hard-pushed to justify it. I would head off to the Mediterranean instead for more joy.

Mixed grill A vital part of every modern man's cooking repertoire, mixed grill is the dish of choice for superheroes the world over. You need a rich, robust red and there is nothing more macho than a feisty southern Rhône (see the Gazetteer for top performers) or its New World counterpart, a 'GSM' blend (Grenache, Shiraz and Mourvèdre in any combo). To infinity and beyond!

Moroccan/North African The most important factor to remember when matching this intriguing style of food with wine, is the level of spicing involved in the dish. Once you have gauged this, you can do one of two things – either choose fresh, clean, neutral whites that sit in the background and let the food do the talking, or go head-to-head with the flavours and drink a stunning aromatic white. Spain, Italy and France are the most obvious and geographically closest ports of call and, within these three great wine nations, my favourite aromatic white styles would be Albariño (from Galicia in northwestern Spain), Viognier (south of France) and Ribolla Gialla, Traminer, Tocai, Lugana and richer Pinot

Grigios (northeast and northwest Italy). Other Italian whites that would be a little more intriguing and competitive with the food are Grillo from Sicily, and Falanghina, Fiano and Greco from southern Italy. Cool reds that work well are Rioja or similar-style Tempranillo/Garnacha blends (Spain), chilled and ripe Côtes-du-Rhône (France), and Nero d'Avola, Aglianico or Primitivo (southern Italy and Sicily). If you want to go down the neutral route, choose Beaujolais as a red, or Alsace Pinot Blanc or Loire Sauvignon Blanc as a white. If you feel the need to stray further from the Med, aim for more Sauvignon Blanc, this time from Chile or South Africa, for its herbal, lime-juice characters, and Barossa Valley Bush Vine Grenache (South Australia) for its pure red-berry fruit and herbal, smoky nose.

Mushrooms I am happy to forgo my rampaging carnivorous tendencies if mushrooms form the backbone of an evening's cooking. The inbuilt 'meatiness' in field mushrooms or the intensity, flavour and texture of wild mushrooms really work their wonders for me. Clearly the mushroom family is a diverse one and you can cook them in every way imaginable, so this is a pretty long entry. When matching wine to mushrooms, ignore the fact that they are fungi and look at the task they are employed to do. *Baked* or *grilled* mushrooms usually retain their essence, moisture and flavour, and cellar temperature reds (i.e. chilled a touch) should allow them to express themselves fully, losing nothing in translation. Make sure that you choose relaxed, fruit-driven reds with low tannins – simple Grenache blends, Gamay or Pinot Noir, for example. *Creamy sauces* are always difficult; if you overdo the cream, a robust, oaked Chardonnay or Semillon is needed, but if the cream features only in a supporting, 'folded-in' role, then refreshing red grapes such as Merlot, Trincadeira, Bonarda and Barbera would be superb. *Mushroom omelettes* and *mushroom tarts* are both classic examples of how a mushroom can hold its own in the competitive egg world – here, again, light, fruit-driven reds and smart, dry rosés must mobilise forces. *Wild mushrooms* can be intensely scented, gamey and foresty, so look to my 'Game' entry and trade down in terms of muscle (and cash). *Mushrooms on toast* are ever-so fashionable again (we've been waiting too long) – good news, as there is nothing better for setting up your palate. This is one of the easiest dishes to make at home and, even if you splash out on fancy bread (Poilâne is surely the best in the world) and top shrooms, it is still dead cheap. Wine-wise, look to the main course you are preparing and downsize the wine a touch for your starters. If you are having a double serving as a stand-alone dish, then try Barbera or Dolcetto from northern Italy, for their truffley, black-cherry aromas and flavours. *Stuffed mushrooms* depend on what they are stuffed with. I know that sounds obvious, but cheesy or veggie ones work well with lighter reds. If you lose the cheese, rich whites are in with a shout – medium-sized Chardonnays and Rieslings are ideal. For *mushroom risotto* see 'Risotto'.

Mustard Make sure you turn up the volume on any red or white wine if you are contemplating a mustard sauce/dressing or an accompanying dish with a strong mustardy theme. You do not need to go too far in terms of size or style, but a notch up in quality and flavour is needed to accommodate the flavour intensity – this will probably mean you'll have to spend a pound or two more on your bottle.

Olives See 'Apéritif Wine Styles' if you are restricting your intake to pre-dinner olives. But, if you're cooking with olives, say in a lamb recipe, take care not to pour in the liquor (water, brine or oil) from the jar or can, as it is very pungent (and often not of the highest quality) and can cast too strong an influence over the final taste of the dish. This, of course, would affect you and your wine's chances of happiness. As usual, the trick is to look to the main ingredient in the recipe and make sure that your chosen wine can be enjoyed alongside a sliver of olive (munch on one and taste the wine as a road test). *Tapenade* is a funny old thing – totally unfriendly when it comes to wine (unless you find refuge in a bracingly dry sherry), so it is best to go for very dry whites from cooler-climate regions, for example Frascati, Gavi, Soave, Lugana, Greco, Falanghina, Grillo and Vernaccia (all Italian), or Sauvignon de Touraine, Cheverny, Muscadet, Bergerac Sec, Jurançon Sec or Pacherenc de Vic Bihl (all French).

Onion As the leading ingredient in a dish, onion is at its best in a classic *French onion tart,* and Alsatian Riesling is the only true wine to drink with this noble offering. If you must stray from this advice (more fool you), Clare Valley Rieslings from South Australia would work beautifully. Occasionally you see *caramelised onions* offered as a side dish – watch out! They are often delicious, intensely sweet (of the same order as a treacle tart) and, although you can moderate this by combining mouthfuls with the other elements of your meal, they are a real danger to a glass of dry wine so don't bother drinking anything serious when you eat them. My advice is to munch enthusiastically and sip cautiously. For *French onion soup* see 'Soups'.

Oysters see 'Seafood'.

Paella Not worthy of its own listing, really, if it weren't for the fact that it is such a desperately incongruous mix of ingredients. The answers to this gastronomic quandary are as follows – chilled, ripe Cabernet Franc (red Loire), Albariño or Godello (Spanish white grapes) or French Grenache-based/Spanish Garnacha-based light reds and rosés. All you need now is a dustbin lid in which to start cooking.

Pasta The trick with pasta-and-wine matching is to consider what you are serving over, under, around or in it. Stuffed styles such as *cannelloni*, *agnolotti*, *cappelletti*, *tortellini* or *ravioli* can contain veg, cheese, meat and all sorts, so think inside out and select accordingly. *Spinach and ricotta tortellini* soaks up juicy Italian reds like Freisa, Dolcetto and Barbera from Piedmont, and young, simple Chianti, Franciacorta, Bardolino and Valpolicella. *Seafood* pasta dishes, including the all-time favourite *spaghetti vongole* (clams), love serious, crisp Sauvignon Blanc (from anywhere), decent Frascati (over £5 if you can find it!), Soave (again, break over the fiver barrier please), Lugana, Fiano di Avellino, Verdicchio, Greco di Tufo, Inzolia from Sicily and Vernaccia di San Gimignano. *Meatballs*, *spaghetti Bolognese*, *lasagne* and *meaty sauces* all respond well to juicy reds. Keep the budget down and head for expressive, fruit-driven examples that work in harmony with the dish, as opposed to trying to dominate it. Consider all of Italy and many New World regions, but steer clear of overly alcoholic wines (read the label and stay under 13.5%). And, this may sound like heresy, anything bright and juicy made from Tempranillo or Garnacha from Spain would also be delicious. *Roasted vegetables* often pop up in pasta dishes, allowing you to choose between richer whites and lighter reds. *Pesto* may be a classic pasta partner but it is remarkably argumentative on the wine front. Oil, pine nuts, Parmesan and basil seem innocent enough, but put them together and there's trouble – you are forced into lean, dry whites for safety. Go to the famous Italian regions of Friuli, Alto Adige or Veneto as your guide. Sauvignon Blanc is made here, so at least you can rely on that stalwart grape but, otherwise, Pinot Grigio, Riesling, Picolit, Tocai Friulano, posh Soave and Pinot Bianco are all good bets. *Red pesto* is a funny old fish (not literally, of course). This time go for light red wines and keep their temperature down (15 minutes in the fridge) to focus the fruity flavours. *Cheesy* and *creamy sauces* tend to be more dominant than the ingredients bound therein, so Bardolino and Valpolicella (both from Veneto), Dolcetto, Freisa and Barbera (all from Piedmont), Montepulciano (from Marche) and medium-weight Chianti or Vino Nobile (from Tuscany) are all accurate. If, for some reason, you want to stray from Italy's idyllic shores (I wouldn't – there is so much choice and the wines are great value and widely available), there is plenty to be found – medium-weight reds and dry whites are everywhere. Just remember not to overshadow the dish, particularly with higher-alcohol wines. For *tomato sauce*, see 'Tomatoes'. For *mushroom sauce*, see 'Mushrooms'.

Pâté Regardless of its main ingredients, pâté is, perhaps surprisingly, keen on white wines. The only reds that really work are featherweights such as Beaujolais, Dornfelder (I can't believe I have just recommended this comedic grape) or Bardolino. In the white world, you need to hunt down fruity, aromatic wines from any decent estate in my Gazetteer. The crucial character you are searching for, in terms of taste, is a degree of sweetness (not much, just a hint). All styles from the technically dry (but still ripe and fruity) Riesling, Gewürztraminer, Muscat, Chenin Blanc and so on, up to genuine rich/sweet wines can be considered. Pâté is usually served as a starter, so pouring a sweet wine at the beginning of the meal might seem a little strange. But if you are serving pudding or cheese later on in the proceedings (make sure you plan this carefully beforehand), you can happily open a bottle of sweet wine, serve a few small glasses for starters and finish it off later. Many sweet wines are sold in half (37.5cl) or 50cl bottles, so even if it's a small gathering, anything up to six, you'll not waste a drop. *Chicken liver* pâté favours dry to medium-dry German Riesling, Alsace Riesling, Pinot Blanc or mildly sweet white Bordeaux styles (Loupiac or Saussignac) and older Aussie Rieslings (Eden and Clare Valleys). *Country* pâté, a clumsy catch-all term that often hints at a coarser texture pâté of indeterminate origin, similarly suits light white wines with a degree of sweetness – Riesling usually – or a pint or two of real ale. If you are pushed into choosing from a short wine list or are confronted with an undernourished offie, then play safe, buy a dry white and hope for the best. But if you have the luxury of choice, then Alsace is a great region to start hunting. Riesling and Tokay-Pinot Gris are the plum picks here. Head to the New World and you'll find Riesling in abundance in Australia, while Chilean Gewürztraminer is an unusual but rewarding style. With *duck* pâté and *foie gras* (*goose liver* pâté), we are firmly in sweet wine territory – Sauternes, Loire and Alsace sweeties, Aussie botrytised Riesling and Semillon, or, on a tighter budget, Monbazillac, Ste-Croix du Mont, Loupiac, Cadillac and Saussignac (Sauternes' taste-alike neighbours). If you have never tasted this heady food-and-wine combo, you are in for a very pleasant surprise. *Parfait*, the smoother, creamier, Mr Whippy version of pâté, tends to reveal its covert brandy ingredient more than a coarse pâté, so make sure your wine is rich enough to cope with this. If you don't want to sip a sweet wine, then nearly sweet whites from Alsace also work. Vendange Tardive (late-picked) wines offer richness without cloying, sugary sweetness and will appease the non-sweet wine fans. Grapes to consider are Tokay-Pinot Gris, Muscat,

Gewürztraminer and Riesling. *Smoked salmon* pâté and other *fish* pâté incarnations are well served by dry aromatic whites (see 'Fish'). One thing to remember with pâté dishes is that occasionally *chutney* (or *onion confit/marmalade*) is served on the side, providing an intense, sweet-fruit or veg explosion of flavour, which may confuse the wine. Alsatian Vendange Tardive wines, mentioned above, have tons of spice and richness of fruit, and they will simply cruise through these added flavours – dry wines will choke. I have already talked about *gherkins* and *capers* in the 'Charcuterie' section, so keep them well marshalled.

Peppers Fresh, crunchy, *raw* peppers crackle with zingy, juicy, healthy flavours. It should come as no surprise, then, that Sauvignon Blanc (from almost anywhere in the solar system) is the best grape for them – 'capsicum' is a recognised tasting note for this variety. It is a marriage made in heaven, but if you want to try something different, then dry Chenin Blanc from South Africa or Italian Pinot Grigio would also be splendid. *Piemontese* peppers are a favourite Saturday lunch dish of mine and, with the olive oil, garlic, black pepper and tomato ingredients, dry whites are required, especially if the traditional anchovy fillets are criss-crossed on top of the shimmering orbs. Assertive Sauvignon Blanc is the best option, although Verdicchio, Orvieto, Greco, Fiano, Arneis and Gavi (or a less expensive, Cortese-based Piedmont white) would be appropriate. A *stuffed* pepper depends more on its stuffing than the pepper itself, so look to the filling for your inspiration. Generally speaking, meat or cheese stuffings go well with light Italian reds. Peppers *marinated in olive oil* love any dry white wines – Italy would be the best fit, so find some Soave, Frascati or Friuli single varietals such as Pinot Grigio, Pinot Bianco, Traminer or Sauvignon Blanc. For *gazpacho* see 'Soups'.

Picnics You simply must find screwcap-sealed bottles for picnics – thank goodness there are so many out there these days. The benefits are numerous – there is no need for a corkscrew, you can reseal the bottle with ease and you also don't have to worry about anyone knocking it over. Your first port of call for all-round, picnic-matching skills has to be rosé. It is multitalented when it comes to all manner of cold food dishes, and if you chill the bottles down ice cold before departure, it will drink like a fresh white early on and, as the day hots up (cross fingers), it will behave more like a red. This should cunningly coincide with your move through the courses, from crudités and dips, via smoked salmon, to rare roast beef and finally some good cheese. Other varieties that enjoy *al fresco* food are Sauvignon Blanc for whites and Beaujolais for reds. Once again, chill all of your wines right down prior to departure and drink them in order from white, via rosé to red, and bring some ice if you can.

Pigeon see 'Game' but spend less.

Pizza I adore pizza and, if prepared well, there is nothing to touch it for taste-bud satisfaction and that warm, pudgy-tummy thing afterwards (or is that just me?). Heroic pizzas rarely allow white wines enough space to be heard. However, I suppose a simple *vegetable* or *seafood* pizza might need a weedy, dry white wine. Assuming you have a tomato (or red pepper – much tangier) base and some mozzarella cheese on top, the real point of a pizza is the unlimited number of toppings that you lob on board – *mushroom*, *onion*, *anchovy*, *caper*, *olive*, *beef*, *ham*, *egg*, *pepperoni* and, crucially, *chillies*. A real man's pizza has these and more, so you will have to find a feisty red and cool it down. My all-Italian, pizza-wine line-up includes: whites – Arneis, Soave, Bianco di Custoza, Verdicchio, Pinot Bianco,

Pinot Grigio and Orvieto; chillable reds – Sardinian Cannonau, Freisa, Barbera and Dolcetto from Piedmont, Marzemino and Teroldego from Trentino, Bardolino and Valpolicella from Veneto and Chianti, Montepulciano d'Abruzzo, Morellino di Scansano, Sangiovese di Romagna, Primitivo di Puglia, Nero d'Avola di Sicilia, Negroamaro and Aglianico all from further south.

Pork The noble hog has so many different gastronomic guises that I have given the gallant sausage its own section. And, no doubt, *pâté* and *terrine* lovers are delighted that these two dishes warrant their own headings, too. I have also dealt with *charcuterie*, *cassoulet*, *bacon*, *full English breakfast* and *ham* in other sections – it just gets better! Here, though, I endeavour to cover the porcine dishes not otherwise mentioned. First the princely *pork pie* and its less exciting, ever-so-slightly-unnaturally-orange-coloured, asteroid cousin, the *Scotch egg*. A good pork pie is a real treat and, while I'm sure that a pint of Shepherd Neame's Bishop's Finger ale is the ideal partner, a glass of Cru Beaujolais is also a perfect fit. The Scotch egg crops up in pub and picnic cuisine more than at the dinner table and bitter is the only sensible choice – but you wouldn't be putting a foot wrong by ordering a juicy Merlot either. If you like a dollop of Branston or piccalilli on the plate, then expect the wine to be sent into a momentary tailspin. *Chorizo* and *salami* fall into the aforementioned 'Charcuterie' section, but remember that the spicier the salami, the greater the need for a cool red wine. A plate of chorizo is excellent with dry sherry – manzanilla and fino are the two best styles. Next on the menu, *spare ribs*. Whether drenched in barbecue sauce or not, these are prehistoric fare, so Palaeolithic reds are needed to slake your thirst. Juice and texture are the essential ingredients, so head to the New

World in search of Argentinian Sangiovese, Malbec, Bonarda or Tempranillo, Chilean Carmenère or Australian Cabernet/Shiraz blends. Californian Zinfandel would also work well, although it might be disproportionately expensive. *Rillettes*, which can also be made from duck or rabbit, expose one of pork's lighter sides. This mild, oddly fondanty, hiccupy dish is often served as part of a plate of cold meats. White wine is called for, with Pinot Blanc, Sylvaner and Riesling from Alsace all working well. As usual, world-beating Aussie dry Rieslings will find this a doddle, too. I have left the big daddy to last – *roast* pork. There are a number of ways to serve this so, when it comes to matching it to wine, the brief is fairly open. One thing is certain – if you are going to serve a red, make it light (Pinot Noir is best). Pork is far more excited by white wine, particularly if there is apple sauce sidling up to your plate. Classy, unoaked Chardonnay from Chablis or Burgundy would be exact, although New World Chardonnays can hack it so long as they are not overtly oaky. Riesling (dry and luxurious), Condrieu (the super-dear northern Rhône Viognier), Vouvray (make sure it says 'sec' on the label) and southern Rhône whites (thin on the ground but a lot of bang for your buck) are all worth a substantial sniff.

Quiche (and posh tarts) see 'Eggs'.

Rabbit *Rillettes* made with rabbit meat love a little more musk and exoticism in their wines than plain pork rillettes, so Marsanne, Roussanne and Viognier from anywhere in the world (Rhône is your starting point, with perhaps California, Eden Valley or Victoria next), or Pinot Blanc and Riesling (the richer styles from Alsace) would be mouth-wateringly spot on. For all other bunnies, bounce along to 'Game'.

Risotto Generally, the richness and texture of a risotto needs to be 'cut' with the acidity of a clean, dry, white wine, but check what else you have folded in. It is these magic ingredients that matter the most when finding the perfect wine to counter the creamy, cheesy rice, particularly if you've whacked a spot of grated Parmesan, mascarpone and butter in with the stock! Light reds can work with *wild mushroom* risotto but I prefer scented, cool, classy whites. *À la Milanese*, with saffron, can force a light, dry white into submission unless it has enough fruit and 'oomph' – Arneis or Gavi from Piedmont are worth a go, as is Riesling from a good Australian or Alsatian producer. *Chicken and mushroom* risotto likes Chardonnay and light Pinot Noirs, just as a non-risotto-style dish might. *Primavera* favours fresh, zingy, green whites – Sauvignon Blanc, anyone? Finally, *seafood* risotto – here dry Italian wines including decent Frascati, Vernaccia di San Gimignano, Arneis, Verdicchio Classico, Greco and Fiano, along with South African Sauvignon Blanc and Chenin Blanc make a rather delicious combination. Remember that Chilean Sauvignon is often cheaper than both South African and New Zealand versions, so if you are having a big risotto party then look here for a decent volume purchase.

Salads This is a huge subject that just needs a moment's common sense. Basic *green* or *mixed* salad without dressing is virtually tasteless, as far as wine is concerned. Be careful if it's dressed, though – particularly if vinegar is involved, because this changes all the rules (see 'Vinaigrette'). *Seafood* salad enjoys the white wines that go well with seafood (obvious, I know, see 'Seafood'); *Niçoise* likes tangy Sauvignon Blanc, Sauv/Sem blends and neon green Margaret River or Hunter Valley Semillons (Australia); *chicken* salad works well with Rhône whites and middleweight

Chardonnays; *feta* salad, not surprisingly, is perfect with dry Greek whites; *French bean and shallot* salad likes lighter, inexpensive Alsace Tokay-Pinot Gris and Pinot Blanc; *tomato and basil* salad is best matched with rosé or anything fresh, dry, keenly acidic, white and Italian; *Caesar* salad is great with Sauvignon Blanc, Grüner Veltliner (Austria) or Gavi; *Waldorf* salad needs softer, calmer white grapes like Pinot Blanc and Sylvaner (Alsace), or South African Chenin Blanc; *pasta* salad can get a little stodgy so uplifting, acidity-rich, dry whites are essential. Every country in the wine world makes salad-friendly wines, even the UK, where the better dry white grapes like Bacchus, Reichensteiner and Seyval Blanc, in the right hands, can be a joy (you know where to look!).

Sausages (Meaty ones, please, not the fish or veggie kind, otherwise you're out!) Any sausage dish, including *toad-in-the-hole* and *bangers and mash*, needs manly, robust, no-buggering-around reds. Cahors, Garnacha blends from Tarragona, Shiraz or Cabernet from Western Australia, Victoria, Clare or McLaren Vale, Malbec from Argentina, any Languedoc or southern Rhône reds, Barbera from northern Italy, Primitivo from southern Italy, and Chinon or other red Loires are all suitable. Zinfandel, Merlot and Cabernet from California would also be awesome, as would a bottle of plain old red Bordeaux. Hurrah for sausages and their hands-around-the-world, global compatibility with red wine! They're not fussy and nor should you be.

Seafood Muscadet, Cheverny, Menetou-Salon, Sauvignon de Touraine, Quincy, Pouilly-Fumé and Sancerre (all white Loire wines), Chenin Blanc (South Africa), Albariño (Spain), Lugana, Verdicchio, Soave and Pinot Grigio (Italy) and any buttock-clenchingly dry, unoaked New World whites are all perfect with seafood. *Squid* and *octopus* both need very dry whites with aromatic fruit, like Sauvignon Blanc, northern Italian or Penedès (Spain) whites, and resinous Greek whites if the dish is served in its ink. The curious, springy texture of both squid and octopus does not embrace wine in the same way fish does, so concentrate on the method of cooking and the other ingredients to help you make your final choice. Aussie Riesling is a must if you have a spicy dipping sauce. *Crevettes grises* (the little grey/brown shrimps) eaten whole as a pre-dinner nibble, are stunning with Muscadet or Sauvignon Blanc from the Loire, Australia or New Zealand. *Crayfish* and *prawns* are lovely with dry English whites, simple, dry Riesling, and Sauvignon or Semillon/Sauvignon Blanc blends. If you are a *prawn cocktail* fiend (a capital dish if ever there was one), then decent Sauvignon Blanc (no need to spend over £8) is dry and sharp enough to wade through the livid pink Marie Rose sauce. *Lobster*, the noblest of all crustaceans, served cold or in a salad, should tempt you to delve into the deepest, darkest corners of your cellar and uncork the finest of whites. Burgundy (no upper limit), Australian (ditto) and Californian Chardonnay (only the best – not too oaky) and Viognier (from its spiritual birthplace in Condrieu) will all set you back a fortune but, hey, you've already bought lobster, so go off half cocked – finish the job properly. *Lobster thermidor* is not my favourite dish, since I think lobster loses its magical texture and elegant flavour when served hot, but you can easily uncork richer (but less expensive) whites like older Aussie Semillons or oaky South American Chardonnays. If you feel like a slice of lobster class, but for a slightly reduced price, then *langoustines* (or *bugs/ yabbies* if you're mad for crustacea and on hols in Australia) are the answer. Lobster-wines are perfect here, but just adjust the price downwards by a few quid. *Dressed crab* is a fabulous dish and, once again, Loire whites like Muscadet (only £5 for a good bottle) are spot on. Dry whites such as Ugni Blanc from Gascony, Jurançon Sec and 'village' Chablis are also excellent, but again Sauvignon Blanc is probably the pick of the grapes (isn't it always?). Don't just look at the Loire, though, as the white wines from Bordeaux and Bergerac often have a fair slug of Sauvignon in them and, of course, Sauvignon is grown all over the world. *Mussels* probably do best in *gratin* or *marinière* form when dry Riesling, Barossa or Hunter Valley Semillon, New Zealand Pinot Gris and New World Sauvignon Blanc are all worthy contenders. *Scallops* require a little more weight in a white wine (mildly oaked Sauvignon Blanc; for example, Fumé Blanc from California). They can even handle a spot of light red or rosé (chilled). *Scallops sauté Provençal* (with tomatoes and garlic) and *scallops wrapped in bacon* are wicked with smarter rosé. *Scallops Bercy* (with shallots, butter, thyme, white wine, parsley and lemon juice) are superb with top Sancerre, Menetou-Salon or Pouilly-Fumé – spend up, it will be worth it. *Oysters* are traditionally matched with Champagne – but not by me. I prefer a simple dry white like Muscadet, with its salty tang, or a 'village' Chablis or Sauvignon de St-Bris. A *plateau de fruits de mer* involves all of the above, plus *whelks* (yuk) and *winkles* (bleuch), and only needs a first-class bottle of Sauvignon de Touraine or Muscadet. You'll thank me when you receive the bill for this mountainous platter of seafood – you'll only have spent a fraction on a bottle of chuggable wine. For *clams*, see 'Pasta'.

Side dishes see 'Vegetables'.

Snails see 'Garlic'.

Soups Dry sherry is often quoted as soup's ideal soul mate but it seems a little ludicrous to crack open a bottle of fino every time you fancy a bowl of broth. And, what's more, it's not always the best wine for the job. The soup dynasty is a diverse collection of oddballs – no one wine can expect to cover all of the flavours. *Minestrone*, with its wonderful cannellini bean base, and *ribollita* (the stunning, next-day minestrone incarnation – re-boiled with cabbage and bread thrown in for extra body) like to keep things Italian, with chilled Teroldego or Marzemino from Trentino and Valpolicella being superb candidates. If you want to hop over the mountains to France, then simpler southern Rhônes (a well-made C-de-R would do) make a refreshing and accurate alternative. *Spinach and chickpea* soup goes well with bone-dry whites like those from Orvieto, Frascati, Greco, Verdicchio (Italy), Penedès or Rueda (Spain), or Sauvignon Blanc from New Zealand, South Africa or Chile. *Vichyssoise* (chilled leek and potato soup) needs creamy, floral whites, such as straightforward Alsatian Riesling, Australian, South American or French Viognier, or light, white Rhônes. *Lobster* or *crayfish bisque* has a creamy texture coupled with a deceptive richness, so dry sherry could conceivably make an appearance here. If you don't fancy that, then youthful white Burgundy is best. *Bouillabaisse with rouille*, the serious fish, garlic, tomatoes, onion and herb broth with floating toasty crostinis topped with garlic, chilli and mayo, is a mighty dish and yet it only needs very simple whites like our old favourites Muscadet and Sauvignon de Touraine. *Consommé* is a definite Fino sherry dish (at last). *Gazpacho* (chilled tomato, cucumber, onion, pepper and garlic soup) likes nothing more than Spanish new-wave Viura (unoaked for goodness sake) or cheeky Verdejo from Rueda. *Mushroom* soup is another dry sherry candidate (you might use some in the recipe), while *French onion* soup goes well with dry Riesling from Alsace or South Australia. *Oxtail* demands hearty reds – rustic, earthy inexpensive southern

French bruisers like St-Chinian or Minervois. *Lentil and chestnut* and *lentil and bacon* soups both crave dry sherry (this time trade up from a fino to an amontillado, for complexity and intensity). *Clam chowder* is basically a fishy soup with cream (and sometimes potato), so Sauvignon Blanc, Chenin Blanc and all seafood-friendly whites are perfect. With *vegetable* soup, rustic reds at the bottom of the price ladder are needed. *Tomato* soup is a strange one. Always avoid oak. I favour light reds or dry whites – Gamay (Beaujolais or Loire) or Sauvignon Blanc (Pays d'Oc, Loire, South Africa or Chile) all do the job admirably.

Sweetbreads With *butter* and *sorrel, sauce ravigote* (mustard, red wine vinegar, capers and tarragon) or *sauce gribiche* (like ravigote but with chopped hard-boiled eggs and parsley as well), sweetbreads demand aromatic, decadently textured, luxurious, self-confident whites. Alsatian or South Australian Riesling (Clare or Eden Valley) with a bit of age would be my first choice. If you can't find any, then try creamy, oily, nutmeg- and peach-scented Rhône whites. All of these are dear, but there's no way around this quandary, as this is a demanding sector of the food repertoire. *Ris de veau aux morilles* (veal sweetbreads with a very rich, creamy wild mushroom sauce) needs the most intense Rhône whites or Alsatian Rieslings.

Tapas Sherry and dry white wines, preferably Spanish and avoiding oak, are perfect partners for these addictive Spanish snacks.

Terrines A terrine is a more robust, often hearty pâté, generally served in slices. So what's good enough for a pâté is often perfect with terrine. One of the classics is *ham and chicken,* and this loves white Burgundy or elegant, non-

French, mildly oaked Chardonnays. Another white Burgundy lover is *jambon persillé*, the sublime parsley, jelly and ham dish. This is not surprising, as it is a Burgundian recipe in the first place. I would dive in with a youthful, inexpensive Bourgogne Blanc from a reputable Domaine, or head south to Rully, Mercurey, Montagny, Pouilly-Fuissé or a crisp Mâconnais wine for a match. Even smart Aligoté would do. Beaujolais, Alsatian Gewürztraminer, Riesling and Tokay-Pinot Gris love *rabbit*, *hare* and *game* terrines, particularly if there are prunes lurking within. *Fish* terrines follow the lead of fish pâtés and mousses with Sauvignon Blanc, Riesling, clean, fresh Chardonnays like Chablis, Fiano di Avellino from Campania in southern Italy and finally the enigmatic Spanish stunner, Albariño.

Thai Along the same lines as Vietnamese and other 'Asian but not overtly so' styles of cuisine, it is best to look to the main ingredient and then concentrate on appropriate southern hemisphere, fruit-driven wines. Likely candidates are: Australian or New Zealand Riesling, Viognier, Semillon, Verdelho, Pinot Gris and Sauvignon Blanc. New World sparkling wines in general work well, as do dry Muscats from Portugal and Pinot Gris, Torrontés or Viognier from Argentina.

Tomatoes Strangely, tomatoes are pretty fussy when it comes to wine matching (see 'Soups'). Pinot Noir works well and New World versions perform better than their Old World counterparts, as they often have more fruit expression and lower acidity. Other reds, like Sicilian Nero d'Avola, Aglianico, Primitivo (all southern Italy) and any juicy, warm-climate Merlot or Zinfandel would be accommodating. When *raw*, as in a salad, rosé or Sauvignon Blanc is a good choice. A *tomato sauce* demands dry, light whites and Italy is the best place to look for these, as they are often ripe and cheap. *Ketchup,* while delicious, is so sweet and vinegary that it gives wine a hard time. Use sparingly on your burger if you like drinking fine wine but drench it if you're gunning down a cheap glugging red.

Truffles Foresty, feral and musky – hoorah! Choose similarly scented wines to match this unusual life form – Burgundian Pinot Noir, Piedmont's magnificent Nebbiolo and Barbera, and Syrah (French and serious, please). If you want to cook chicken or fish with truffles, then vintage Champagne or top Alsatian or Australian Riesling would be spectacular (or go crazy and find some vintage rosé Champs).

Turkey The thing to watch out for with *roast* turkey is the cranberry sauce and an excess of gravy. Often a fresh, young Crianza Rioja or juicy New World Pinot Noir complements this outlandish red-fruit flavour. At Christmas, Aussie Grenache or Rioja is again a winner as mountains of cocktail sausages, bacon, sprouts and the rest take the flavour spotlight away from the turkey. If you are feeling very brave, totally ahead of your time, or just a little barking mad, then take leave of your senses and wade into a sparkling Shiraz from Australia (you can get a superb example for as little as £7) would be fantastic, celebratory and original. *Cold* turkey – see 'Chicken'.

Turkish I have already covered lamb kebabs (with lashings of chilli sauce) in the 'Lamb' section but, generally, Turkish food is best with Greek wines as the cuisine styles are linked and the resinous, aromatic whites and purple, earth- and violet-scented reds are spot on.

Veal There are some mightily good dishes in this section but, sadly, there is no hard and fast rule as to what to follow on the wine front. In general, veal prefers to keep the company of grown-up white wines and classy, lighter reds. *Saltimbocca*, the terrific veal, sage and prosciutto dish, needs Pinot Nero (Italian Pinot Noir), but is hard to find and often a little dear. If your search is unsuccessful, try another unusual wine – Trincadeira from Portugal would be an inexpensive and inspirational substitute. Otherwise, just relax into some red Burgundy. *Vitello tonnato*, a phenomenal dish of contrasting flavours, using thinly sliced, braised veal and served cold, drizzled in a sauce made from marinated tuna, lemon juice, olive oil and capers, is one of the world's most sumptuous starters. Taking the tuna and anchovy (used in the braising stage) as your lead, fresh, sunny, seaside whites like Verdicchio, Greco and Vernaccia work especially well. If you are snookered for decent Italian whites, then go for a Kiwi Sauvignon. *Wiener schnitzel*, fried veal in egg and breadcrumbs, can often taste a little on the dry side, so see what else is on the plate. If there is nothing of enormous character to deflect your mission, give it the kiss of life with a juicy, mildly oaked Chardonnay. *Blanquette de veau*, the French classic with a creamy sauce, is definitely a white wine dish. Again, Chardonnay will do but for perfection go for Viognier, Roussanne or Marsanne blends from the Rhône or Victoria in South Australia. *Osso bucco*, veal shin with wine, tomatoes, parsley, garlic and zesty gremolata, is a lighter, yet headier stew than most. Tasmanian, Yarra Valley, Adelaide Hills (Aussie), New Zealand or Oregon Pinot Noir would be great, as would huge, full-on Chardonnays from anywhere in my Gazetteer.

Vegetables Vegetables (served on their own or as an accompaniment) taste, on the whole, relatively neutral.

But, depending on how they are cooked, they can require a moment or two's thought on the wine front. Any *gratin* (vegetables baked with cheese) or *dauphinoise* (thinly sliced potato baked with cream and garlic) dish needs light reds or firm, self-confident whites. *Beetroot* is a tad tricky, but Alsatian whites and cool, juicy reds generally have the texture and flavour to make it through. *Cabbage*, *leeks*, *spinach*, *parsnips*, *cauliflower*, *sprouts*, *courgettes*, *carrots*, *peas* and *potatoes* are usually innocent so don't worry about them, but *gnocchi* (plain or flavoured with spinach) needs juicy, fruit-driven wines with perky acidity to cut through their weird texture. *Marinated* vegetables and *polenta* both love Italian whites – Pinot Grigio, Soave, Verdicchio etc. *Lentils* often dry the palate out and rustic, earthy reds are essential. Look to French Country wines for an endless supply of candidates or to Chile and Argentina for Malbec or Syrah/Shiraz. *Corn on the cob* is a dead ringer for New World Sauvignon Blanc. Open a bottle and, with some wines, you may actually detect a canned sweetcorn aroma! *Celeriac* is a stunning accompaniment to a dish and it has a pretty strong aroma and flavour, so make sure your wine is forceful enough to cope.

Vegetarian If you are a strict vegetarian or vegan, look at the label (usually the one on the back), as most organic and vegan associations have stickers or a logo to let you know the contents and production techniques of the wine. If you are still unsure, ask your wine merchant.

Vinaigrette A passion killer for wine, vinegar is strongly flavoured and makes any wine taste flat for a few seconds. This can give your palate an annoying stop-start sensation. Dressing made with lemon juice and oil is more wine-friendly – and healthier, too!

Vinegar See above! Balsamic vinegar seems to be more accommodating than most (perhaps because you tend to use less), and it is more winey in depth and flavour.

Welsh rarebit Ah – what a delightful note to finish on! Whether you make these toasties for late-night nibbling or as a traditional savoury to serve after pudding, you deserve a meaty, rustic red swimming alongside. Anything from the south of France, southern Italy or Spain would be a delicious match – make sure it is not too dear. And if you are really broke, pop over to Australia for a chunky, inexpensive Shiraz.

PUDDINGS

It is pretty obvious that port drinking has taken something of a hit recently in the after-dinner-drinking stakes. Fashion is a cruel thing. Many of my friends now prefer to end a feast on a sweet wine, as it enlivens the palate and wakes you and your taste buds up. For my part, there is nothing better than finishing off dinner with a glass of sweet wine, particularly if it accompanies a tasty pudding. Thankfully there is only one rule to remember when matching wine to sweet dishes – you must make sure the wine is at least as sweet as the pudding, otherwise it will taste dry. Most wine shops have a few sweet wines lurking on the racks, but sadly not as many as one would like. You may have to find a decent independent merchant to get a good selection of sweeties so check out the Directory on page 217 for a merchant near you. But also run through my Top 250 for a serious list of sweet wines that, between them, cover every dish in this decadent section.

Almond tart Despite its heavenly flavour and fantastic texture, this dish needs careful handling on the wine front, as an overbearing sweet wine would crush the delicate almondy nuances. Lighter, youthful sweeties like Muscat de Beaumes-de-Venise, Muscat de Rivesaltes, Moelleux (sweet) Loire whites and Jurançon Moelleux would all be spot on. Stick to these styles if your almond tart has fresh fruit on top. *Bakewell tart*, while perhaps not as elegant as a fresh fruit tart, likes these sweeties, too, but you'd be well advised to go for a little more age on a sweet Loire wine or head to Australia for similarly styled botrytised Semillon or Riesling.

Apple *Strudels*, *pies*, *fritters* and *crumbles* all come with varying degrees of nutty, cinnamony, buttery pastry and burnt-brown-sugar flavours. These overlay the intrinsic fruitiness of the filling and, therefore, demand a richer, heavier style of pudding wine than you might expect. Having said that, we are still in the foothills of sweetness! German Riesling (of at least Auslese status), late-picked Muscat or Riesling from Australia, classic French Sauternes (don't blow too much dosh) or New World botrytised Semillon and lighter, youthful Hungarian Tokaji (a lower number of puttonyos, say 4) are all runners. *Baked* apples (assuming they are served warm/hot) ought to have ice-cold, light, fresh German or Austrian Riesling (Spätlese or Auslese level) and clean, light Muscats. This will give your palate a marvellous and invigorating sauna then plunge-pool sensation every time you take a sip. If they are served cold, don't bother with wine. See below for *tarte tatin*.

Apricot A sensationally accurate apricot match is Vendange Tardive (late-picked) Condrieu (from the northern Rhône) so look there for apricot *crumble*. Unfortunately this wine is extremely rare and exceedingly expensive (best to buy it on hols in the Rhône). Where else should you look? Australia makes some good copies and they taste great and are less expensive. Another answer is sweet Jurançon (Moelleux), bursting with tropical quince and peach flavours, or Monbazillac or Saussignac – a friendlier-priced Sauternes-style offering from southwest France.

Bananas *Banoffee pie*, the fugly offspring of a sticky toffee pudding and rampant banana, can only be tamed by the most outrageous of sweet wines – Hungarian Tokaji (although I wouldn't waste it), Australian liqueur Muscat and Malmsey Madeira (I might even turn up if this was served). With banana *splits*, the candied sprinkles, hundreds and thousands and ice cream flavours are more dominant than the castrated banana, so watch out on the wine front – I'd head straight for the Aussie liqueur Muscat – all men would, I think you'll find.

Berries *Black, Chuck* (joke), *goose, blue, rasp, logan, huckle, straw, mul, cran, bil* and *damson* bounce around in many different recipes. Whether they are served *au naturel*, in a juicy *compote*, or appear in a *summer pudding*, they all love the talented sweet wine superhero Semillon and his trusty sidekick Muscat. Track down these grapes from France – Sauternes, Saussignac, Monbazillac, Loupiac and Cadillac all fall neatly into the Semillon camp; while Muscat de Rivesaltes, de Beaumes-de-Venise, de Frontignan and de Lunel all advertise Muscat on the label, so are easier to spot on the shelves. Aussie late-picked Muscats are all great and inexpensive, but watch out for liqueur Muscats, as they are wildly different and will destroy a delicate *fruit purée*. Not that you'd care if you were drinking that, as you'd be a giggling wreck in the corner!

Biscuits/Biscotti (and proper shortbread)
Vin Santo is the top choice for the extended biscuit family.

Sweeter Madeira styles and good old cream sherry also work very well, counter-pointing the crumbly texture, butter and fruit or nut ingredients well. None of these wines need be served in large quantities (unless you are feeling particularly frisky), as they are all sipping styles. Sauternes (heady, sweet white Bordeaux) or New World botrytised Semillon (exactly the same style but better value) come in a worthy second. Other lighter biscuits enjoy the company of simple sweet wines – I would still stick to Semillon- or Chenin-Blanc-based French versions.

Brandy snaps I love brandy snaps (Ma Jukesy is Yoda when it comes to making these). Once again, try Australian liqueur Muscat, you'll love it – just stop when you've got through the first batch and bottle, otherwise you'll be drunk, fat and lock-jawed in no time.

Bread and butter pudding You need wines with a bit of power and acidity to stand up to a traditional B & B pudding. Weightier Muscat-based wines are just the job – Moscatel de Setúbal from Portugal and Moscato or Passito di Pantelleria from the volcanic island off the south of Sicily would be there or thereabouts. Take it steady, though, as these are addictive, gloriously moreish and hugely alcoholic. Saddle up for a late night.

Cakes What's wrong with a cup of tea? Well, quite a lot, really, when you could be enjoying an elegant glass of cream sherry or a schooner of Aussie liqueur Muscat with your *coffee* cake, Bual or Malmsey Madeira with *Dundee* or *Battenberg*, Maury or Banyuls with *brownies* or a traditional *fruitcake*, or demi-sec Champagne with *Victoria* or *lemon sponge*. For the perfect sugar hit try *doughnuts* with ice-cold Asti – and invite a very pretty friend.

Cheesecake Whether it is cherry or any other style, the 'cheesiness', not the fruit, controls the choice of wine. Botrytised Semillon and Riesling from the New World, Coteaux du Layon and other sweet Loire wines, Austrian Beerenauslese and Alsatian Vendange Tardive Riesling and Tokay-Pinot Gris all work. The trick is to keep the sweetness intense and fruit-driven, without resorting to heavyweight styles of high alcohol/fortified wines.

Cherries In *pie* form, cherries behave like berries and prefer the company of mid-weight sweet wines. Served with *chocolate* in a *marquise* or *Black Forest gâteau*, though, and they can handle a much richer wine. Try Amarone, the wickedly intense red Valpolicella from Veneto in Italy, Maury or Banyuls from Roussillon (France) or really juicy Californian Zinfandel for a bizarre match. Your guests might think you're a course late with the red but it works, honest.

Chocolate A deluxe choccy *cake* can, if it's not too intense, retreat into lighter Muscats and botrytised Rieslings. Chocolate *mousse* (knock off the antlers), *petits pots au chocolat* and chocolate *soufflé* all head towards Orange Muscat, with its wonderful pervading aroma and flavour of orange blossom. This is one of the finest food-and-wine combinations of all, as orange and chocolate are natural partners (remember the adverts?). Australia and California make two examples that I know of, so well done Brown Bros and Andrew Quady respectively, your places in the choccy hall of fame are guaranteed. If these wines are too hard to find, then you could – dare I say it? – open a bottle of Asti Spumante! Chocolate *pithiviers*, the single most decadent dish in the pudding repertoire, need unctuous fortified wines with a touch of burnt nuttiness – Banyuls or Maury (Roussillon, France), liqueur Muscat or liqueur Tokay

(Australia). Match any of these ridiculously insane dishes with the following list of Olympically serious wines – Passito di Pantelleria (for its mind-boggling orange zest aroma), Tokaji, black Muscat (intergalactic – get ready for re-entry), liqueur Muscat, PX (short for Pedro Ximénez, the boozy, black, teeth-rottingly sweet turbo-sherry), botrytised Semillon from the New World, Maury and Banyuls (the mega, port-like sweet Grenache wines from the south of France) and, finally, young, punchy, underrated, tawny port.

Christmas pudding During the festive period, it is useful to have a wine that lasts well once opened – you've got to make it all the way from Christmas Eve to New Year's Day, after all. Top-quality tawny port and liqueur Muscat or Tokay from Australia, as well as heady Malmsey Madeira, all fit the bill. You can squeeze twelve glasses out of a bottle without short-changing anyone. Not bad, hey, and these are not expensive wines by any stretch of the imagination. See my Top 250 for this year's best versions.

Cinnamon rolls A heavenly creation – but ever so wicked. You need considerable levels of sweetness and toffeed aromas in the wine to cope with the intensity of sugar. Vin Santo, Hungarian Tokaji, liqueur Muscat and old oloroso sherry would be stunning. Old-fashioned *lardy cakes* are hard to find these days, sadly, but, if you do know a dealer, stick to Malmsey Madeira – it fits with the image as well as being a great flavour combination.

Crème brûlée As I only like the crunchy, caramelised bit on the top, as opposed to the silky, creamy bit, I have asked some pals for their advice on this one. The general consensus is that you need to aim somewhere between my almond tart and cheesecake wines. As Loire sweeties, made from Chenin

Blanc, appear in both sections, they must be spot on –
Coteaux du Layon (and that extended family), Vouvray
Moelleux, Bonnezeaux (pronounced 'Bonzo') and Quarts de
Chaume are your choices. You could always look for some
South African Chenin Blanc sweet wines, as the grape is
widely planted down there and they are stunning value.

Crème caramel Sadly, this is another pud that you
won't get me near (it's the slipperiness – I get goose bumps
just thinking about it), but I have it on good authority that
light, delicate sweeties are required. German Auslese
Rieslings from the Mosel and youthful, fairy-light Muscats
are apparently spot on.

Crêpes Suzette Clairette de Die, the little-known
sparkling wine from the Rhône, or Asti (Italy's frothy
Moscato) would be cheap but worthy options, with demi-sec
Champagne being the grown-up, expensive choice.

Custard As soon as you start waving custard around, you
are giving your palate much more to think about. Intense
creaminess craves acidity in a wine. Since custard is the
ultimate in eggy creaminess, the big guns like Malmsey
Madeira, liqueur Muscat and Tokaji must be got.

Doughnuts see 'Cakes'.

Figs Cold shower time again, sorry readers! I simply lose
control at the very sight of one. See the fig entry (ooh er) in
the Starters and Main Courses section for recommendations.

Fruit *Raw* fruit of any kind has a much lighter flavour than
you would expect when pitted against a sweet wine. So stay
with dainty Asti, German or Austrian Spätlese Rieslings,

demi-sec Champagne, fresh, clean Muscats, Italy's Recioto di Soave, Spain's Moscatel de Valencia or very light, young Sauternes. But if you fancy a *lychee*, then find a sweet Gewürztraminer, as it has remarkable lychee characteristics on the nose and palate. *Poached* fruit, like *peaches* or *apricots*, picks up sweetness from the added sugar and can be pretty intense, so tread carefully. You may need a rich Coteaux du Layon from the Loire to see you through.

Fruitcake see 'Cakes'.

Gingerbread A wonderful creation that, along with *ginger cake* and *ginger biscuits*, is made even better when accompanied by a glass of good-quality cream sherry, Bual or Malmsey Madeira.

Gooseberry fool A heavy, oleaginous sweet wine would trample all over this refreshing, palate-primping pudding. What you need is a young, botrytised Semillon, like Sauternes, Saussignac, Monbazillac or Loupiac, or Asti or demi-sec Champagne. Try to keep the price down, as more expensive wines will usually taste finer and more intense. Or grab a bottle of fresh, young Riesling Auslese (Mosel, Germany) for a fruit-cocktail, grapey flavour – it will also be much cheaper.

Ice cream If you want to play safe then *vanilla*, *chocolate*, *rum and raisin*, *coffee*, *chubby-hubby* and *cookie-dough* ice creams all love Pedro Ximénez. You could always try sweet liqueur Muscats from Australia as well. If you have a *fruity* ice cream or *sorbet*, just leave it alone – you need a few minutes without a goblet in your hand occasionally! If you want to ignore me then go crazy and experiment, but you're on your own.

Jam tart You need a very sweet wine. This is the only rule, as you can't get sweeter than jam. Icewine from Canada might be a relatively inexpensive way of tackling this dish. Other than that, you are looking at a monstrous price tag (Trockenbeerenauslese from Germany, for example) and, you have to ask yourself, is the tart worth it?

Jelly Light, sweet German Riesling would be all right. Hang on a second – are you really flicking through this majestic tome looking for the 'wine with jelly' entry!?

Lemons *Lemon meringue pie* works well with German or Alsatian Riesling. Make sure it's sweet but not too cloying. Recioto di Soave (Italian) or youthful sweet Loire Chenin Blanc (Coteaux du Layon) would also handle this citrus theme very well. The good thing is that these styles of wine are relatively inexpensive and pretty easy to come by. *Tarte au citron*, my preferred choice in the lemon/pastry arena, is also stunning with Coteaux du Layon.

Meringue Flying solo, meringues are virtually tasteless (and dusty) so forget it, you're on your own. For *pavlova*, it's the fruit that you need to worry about so see 'Fruit'.

Mince pies I generally follow the Christmas pud/ Christmas cake lead of rich, sweet Madeira, youthful tawny port and blindingly brilliant Australian liqueur Muscats. It will save you another trip to the shops and all of these brews are big enough to wrestle with an unleaded brandy butter.

Pastries Belonging in the same school as tarts and cakes, I am not really convinced you need a wine recommendation for this wholesome family fare. Are you really going to crack open a bottle of wine for a *pain au chocolat*? It's too early, surely? Well, don't let me stop you – demi-sec Champagne, Coteaux du Layon, Muscat de Beaumes-de-Venise, Saussignac and Monbazillac are France's best efforts. Botrytised Riesling from Australia and New Zealand, or sweet Muscat from California might also work well. Otherwise, try a German Spätlese Riesling but remember to keep the price down – and please wait until midday!

Peach melba Botrytised Riesling does the peachy thing well, as you should be able to detect peach notes in the wine – head Down Under or to Germany. Alternatively, a late-picked Viognier from the Rhône would be stunning, but they are hard to come by and mightily dear. If all else fails, grab a bottle of Sauternes, the most multi-talented of sweet wines.

Pecan pie A great dish that craves the company of Australian wines. Not sure why but this is exactly the right fit and you should search for a liqueur Muscat of Tokay. If this sounds a little too much like globetrotting, stick with a posh-tasting but inexpensive Malmsey Madeira.

Pineapple upside-down pudding This deserves a mention as one of the classic and most irresistible menu items of all time (well, I think so anyway!). The caramel and pineapple team up to form a supremely exotic partnership and smart Sauternes would give a real result here. If you are keeping an eye on expenses, then Australian botrytised Semillon would also work wonders.

Plums Of the *crumble* family, plum is up there with blackberry and apple as one of the mightiest. A degree of concentrated sweetness is needed here, so head off to Canada for decadent Riesling Icewines, Hungary for sexy Tokaji, or Italy for heroic Vin Santo.

Rhubarb A relative lightweight compared to plum crum, rhubarb *crumble* takes it easy on the wine front. Exotically sweet Riesling from just about anywhere has rhubarby notes on the nose and palate, so this is the one and only grape to follow with rhubarb–based puddings (including *fool*, *compote* and *ice cream*).

Rice pudding Still nothing to add to this note. I haven't eaten rice pudding since school, and don't intend to.

Rum baba As its name suggests, a rum baba has a bit of a kick to it. Underneath the mild, genial exterior, a sweet-wine-thumping freak is itching to get out. This is the Hannibal Lecter of the pudding world and you have to go for a fortified wine to stand a chance of survival – tawny port, Bual or Malmsey Madeira and liqueur Muscat. Go get 'em boys.

Sorbet see 'Ice cream'.

Steamed puddings I am a devout fan of steamed puddings. The greatest syrupy, toffeed, old-fashioned ones (*spotted dick*, *treacle sponge* and *suet pudding* included) deserve the most regal sweet wines. I don't care that suet is a beastly ingredient and that these recipes don't involve any tricky cooking techniques. Here we go – top-flight botrytised Semillon (from anywhere), decadent Madeira, Tokaji (spend up by as many puttonyos as you can afford), Vin Santo (see the Gazetteer) and liqueur Muscat (from any one of the top Victorian or South Australian specialists in Australia).

Strawberries Top quality strawberries love Asti and Moscato d'Asti (Italy), demi-sec Champagne and Clairette de Die (Rhône, France). These are all fizzy or frothy, with the faintest touch of grapey sweetness.

Tarte au citron see 'Lemon meringue pie'.

Tarte tatin This is another of the greatest dishes of all time. I haven't put it into the apple section – not because these days tatin is made with pear and all manner of other fruit, but because the tatin method of cooking is the influencing factor. The rich, toffee/caramel gooeyness is what preoccupies the palate and, for that reason, honeyed Loire sweeties like Coteaux du Layon are right on the money. New World botrytised Semillons would be great as well, and Sauternes would be a real treat.

Tiramisù If you must eat this sickly dish, try Vin Santo (to knock the flavour out) or Marsala (to knock you out).

Treacle tart Treacle tart, particularly if you have included lemon zest in the recipe, is not as stodgy as you might expect. You could try Sauternes but, if in any doubt, Hungarian Tokaji, Vin Santo or youthful liqueur Muscat would probably be safest. Love it!

Trifle German Riesling Beerenauslese is my top choice but any sweet Riesling would be lovely. Likewise, Sauternes and the family of worldwide sweet Semillons all love this dish. If you are going to pour in a bit of booze (sherry is traditionally used), a good quality cream sherry is probably best. The grand, old English creation must be delighted to have so many options on the wine front.

Zabaglione Passito di Pantelleria, from an island off Sicily, is the only wine to accompany this creamy concoction – unless the Marsala you use in the recipe is of drinking quality. If it is, then you can cover two bases with one wine – and that must be the epitome of food-and-wine matching.

CHEESE

The old 'red-wine-with-cheese' adage is downright wrong. When pondering which wine to drink with your chosen cheese, keep an open mind as, surprisingly, almost anything goes – white, red, sweet, dry and fortified. Try to keep your cheese board simple to limit the number of flavours and, therefore, wines needed – and watch out for chutney as its pungent flavour tends to trip wines up.

Fresh cheese (*Cream cheese, feta, ricotta* and *mozzarella*) These usually pop up in salads or simple cooking and their flavours are not dominant, so drink what you fancy. Whites would be best but make sure they have some cleansing acidity on board.

Natural rind cheese (*Goats' cheese – Crottin de Chavignol, Sainte-Maure de Touraine, Saint-Marcellin* and *Selles-sur-Cher*) Sauvignon Blanc from the Loire Valley in France is the benchmark wine to drink with goats' cheese, and the stunning bottles from Sancerre are the pick of the crop (Chavignol is one of the finest wine villages in Sancerre and the home of the famous Crottin de Chavignol cheeses). If you're caught short, though, any dry, fresh, unoaked white would be fine. If you feel like drinking red, then Gamay, Beaujolais or Loire Cabernet Franc work perfectly well.

Soft white cheese (*Camembert, Brie de Meaux, Pavé d'Affinois, Chaource, Bonchester, Pencarreg, Explorateur, Boursault, Gratte-Paille* and *Brillat-Savarin*) Once again, Sauvignon Blanc works terrifically well here. Although, if you want more palate 'oomph', head to Marlborough in New Zealand, Elim in South Africa or Adelaide Hills in Australia. Remember that the richer the cheese, the bigger the white, so Chardonnay can be considered, too. For reds try Pinot Noir (either red Sancerre or lighter red Burgundies), fresh young Syrah/Shiraz from the Rhône or McLaren Vale in Oz, and rosé Champagne. Gratte-Paille and Brillat-Savarin traditionally go well with youthful, inexpensive red Bordeaux – stick to my favoured wine makers in the Gazetteer section or wines in the Top 250.

Washed rind cheese Milder examples like *Chaumes*, *Port Salut* and *Milleens* need nothing more than dry, fruity reds – light Loire, inexpensive red Bordeaux or New World Merlots. Smellier cheeses, including *Epoisses*, *Chambertin* (from Chablis in the north all the way down to Mâcon in the south), Alsace Riesling or Tokay-Pinot Gris, and other controlled (i.e. not too oaky) Chardonnays from further afield. *Munster* loves Alsatian Gewürztraminer and *Vacherin Mont d'Or* loves red Burgundy, Beaujolais and lighter red Rhônes.

Semi-soft cheese Try the following combinations: *Livarot* – Alsatian Tokay Pinot-Gris; *Maroilles* – Roussanne or Marsanne from the Rhône; *Pont-l'Evêque* – Viognier, also from the Rhône; *Raclette* (assuming you are reading this halfway up a mountain in the Alps, you lucky thing) – anything from the Savoie region, red or white; *Gubbeen* – Pinot Blanc or Sylvaner from Alsace; *Edam* – light whites and reds or whatever, it's not fussy; *Morbier* – Rhône whites; *Fontina* – light, Alpine Gamay or Valpolicella; *Reblochon* – this outstanding cheese likes much richer Gamay (smart Cru Beaujolais) and also red Burgundy; *Saint-Nectaire* – another heroic cheese, particularly the wild, farmhouse version, likes the same again, plus meaty red Côtes-du-Rhônes; *Tomme de Savoie* – Rhône whites or lighter reds; *Bel Paese* and *Taleggio* – Lombardy whites such as Lugana and reds like Dolcetto, Barbera and Franciacorta.

Hard cheese This is the largest category of all, ranging from mild, via medium and strong, to extra-strong cheeses. As a starting point get an idea of the strength and age of your chosen cheese (a small taste in the shop is recommended) and this will help your wine selection. Cheeses in this group are, among others – *Cheddar, Gruyère, Cheshire, Parmigiano-Reggiano, Pecorino, Cornish Yarg, Double Gloucester, Lancashire, Caerphilly, Gouda, Beaufort, Manchego, Cantal, Etorki, Comté, Emmenthal, Jarlsberg* and *Mimolette.* Listing wines in order from those for mild cheese all the way to wines for the extra strong: whites – Alsace Pinot Blanc, Chablis, Jurançon Sec, white Burgundy, white Rhônes, New World Semillons and, lastly, New World Chardonnays; reds – Loire reds, Chilean Merlot, Côtes-du-Rhône, spicy Italian reds like Primitivo, Old World Cabernet from Bordeaux or Margaret River (Australia), Shiraz from Frankland, Barossa Valley, McLaren Vale and Clare Valley (Australia), Vino Nobile di Montepulciano and Chianti (Italy), and Zinfandel (California); fortified – port (tawny, LBV and vintage), Madeira, Banyuls and Maury (both from France), and old oloroso sherries.

Blue cheese For *Stilton,* look no further than rich, nutty Madeira, tawny port, LBV or vintage port; *Roquefort* and *Fourme d'Ambert,* however, prefer sweet Sauternes, Monbazillac or Saussignac; *Gorgonzola* likes Amarone della Valpolicella; *Chashel Blue* needs sweet whites; *Dolcelatte* is a bit of a lightweight and, because of its unusual sweet flavour and texture, I never eat it so I can't help you; and, finally, *Beenleigh Blue* needs a pint of authentic, hazy scrumpy cider (drink it in a field with a wench or a milkmaid – if you can find one!).

GAZETTEER

GRAPE VARIETIES

Before I launch into my definitive list of the finest wineries in the world, I have compiled a short Albariño-Zinfandel of the most important white and red grape varieties in the world. These are the players responsible for most of the wines in this guide and you will see their names mentioned in many of the write-ups in my Top 250. These extra tasting notes should give you an idea of some of the vast array of flavours you will find in the wines.

WHITES

Albariño/Alvarinho (Al-ba-reen-yo/Al-va-reen-yo)

A top-notch example will have a faint, peachy aroma like Viognier and a floral, spicy, lime-juice palate like Riesling. The best ones also have a tangy, bone-dry, refreshing finish, often with a touch of spritz.

Aligoté (Alee-got-ay)

Aligoté produces dry, lean apéritif styles of wine with a fairly neutral palate, designed for drinking within the first year or so of release.

Chardonnay (Shar-dunn-ay)

Ranging in style from pale, neutral and characterless to exotic, rich and golden – you should detect honey, freshly baked pâtisserie, hazelnuts, vanilla, butterscotch, orange blossom and fresh meadow flowers in full-on Chardonnays. Many are fermented and matured in oak barrels, so oaky nuances are woven into this panoply of flavours.

Chenin Blanc (Shuh-nan Blon)

Chenin Blanc is an underrated grape that makes clean, zippy, dry, apéritif wines; medium-dry, textured, food-friendly styles; and rich, honeyed, succulent, peach-flavoured sweeties dripping in unctuous, mouth-filling richness.

Gewürztraminer (Guh-vurz-tram-inner)

'Gewürz' has the most distinctive aroma of any grape variety.

Pungent lychee, spice and rose-petal notes abound on the nose, and the palate is usually oily, rich and intense. The finish varies from bone dry to just off-dry, and they often have the unusual knack of smelling sweet but tasting dry.

Manseng (Man-seng)

Both Gros and Petit Manseng wines have a complex nose of quince, peach and lemon curd, and a citrusy, floral palate usually accompanied by a shockingly firm, crisp finish. Although pretty rare, these grapes are also used to make celestial sweet wines with juicy, tropical, honeyed flavours.

Marsanne (Marce-ann)

Plump, rich, vaguely floral, peachy and always oily, Marsanne makes rather hefty, foody wines and likes to be blended with the more elegant grapes like Roussanne.

Muscat (Muss-cat)

Muscat wines vary from the lightest, fizziest soda-siphon of grapey juice, to the deepest, darkest, headiest liqueur that looks like a rugby player's liniment and tastes like knock-out drops. Muscat is the only grape variety that in its simplest form actually smells and tastes 'grapey'.

Pinot Blanc/Pinot Bianco (Pee-no Blon/Pee-no Bee-anko)

Almost all PBs worldwide are unoaked, dry and relatively inexpensive. They taste vaguely appley, creamy and nutty. Most are dull but every now and again a delicious one comes along with more weight, length and intrigue.

Pinot Gris/Pinot Grigio/ Tokay-Pinot Gris (Pee-no Gree/Pee-no Gridge-ee-oh/ Tock-eye Pee-no Gree)

The flavour of Pinot Gris is somewhere between that of Pinot Blanc and Gewürztraminer. The distinctive nose of this grape is one of spice, fruit and honey. It does not have the rose-petal, perfumed element of Gewürz and tends to be drier, like Pinot Blanc. Italy's Pinot Grigio is more akin to Aligoté, as it usually makes a light, spritzy, dry, apéritif style of wine.

Riesling (Rees-ling)

One of the truly great white varieties, Riesling produces a vast array of wine styles, from aromatic, bone-dry apéritifs, through structured, lime-juice-scented, foody beauties, via long-lived, complex, off-dry stunners, and ending up at heart-achingly beautiful sweeties. Rhubarb, petrol, honey, citrus, honeysuckle, toast and spice are there in varying degrees throughout this cornucopia of guises – heavenly.

Roussanne (Roo-sann)

Generally lean, leggy and hauntingly aromatic with hints of apricot and honey. When on top form, Roussanne takes well to oak barrels, ages well and can provide a welcome change for Chardonnay drinkers.

Sauvignon Blanc (So-veen-yon Blon)

'Sauv' Blanc is an up-front, brazen, aromatic, happy-go-lucky style, with an asparagus, fresh herb, lemon and elderflower scent, and refreshing, zesty, dry, citrusy fruit on the palate. Sauvignon is the definitive apéritif grape variety – it's a proven crowd-pleaser.

Sémillon (Sem-ee-yon)

The dominant aromas in dry Sémillon are honey and lime juice, and sometimes creamy vanilla and toasty oak elements creep in, depending on the style of wine. But Sémillon also makes incredible, unctuous sweet wines, tasting of tropical fruit, honey, honey and more honey.

Viognier (Vee-yon-yay)

In the best examples, Viognier offers a mind-blowing perfume of peach kernels, wild honey and apricot blossom, followed by an ample, curvaceous body with plenty of charm and a lingering, dry aftertaste.

REDS

Cabernet Franc (Cab-er-nay Fron)

Often used in a blend with Cabernet Sauvignon and Merlot,

Cabernet Franc gives an aromatic dimension to this threesome. On its own it has firm acidity, oodles of black-fruit flavours and a wonderful violet element coupled with green, leafy notes on the nose.

Cabernet Sauvignon (Cab-er-nay So-veen-yon)

Age-worthy Cabernet Sauvignon forms the backbone of many sturdy, lusty reds. Its hallmarks are deep colour, blackcurrant flavour, with occasional cigar-box, fresh leather or cedarwood notes. When it's on top form, a smooth, velvety, dark-chocolate texture and flavour emerge from the glass.

Gamay (Ga-may)

Gamay is a jolly fellow that makes underrated, early-drinking wines ranging in taste from chillable, frivolous, summery, strawberry-juice concoctions to wintry, foody, black cherry, damp earth and cracked-pepper styles.

Grenache/Garnacha (Gre-nash/Gar-natch-ah)

Grenache is usually blended with Syrah (Shiraz) among others. It is a meaty, earthy, red- and black-fruit-drenched variety, often with high-ish alcohol and a garnet hue. It often parades a wild herbal scent not dissimilar to aromatic pipe smoke.

Malbec (Mal-beck)

This brutish grape is inky black in colour and loaded with dense, macerated black-fruit flavours and earthy spice, often enhanced by a dollop of well-seasoned oak. Malbec is one of the biggest, brawniest red varieties on the block. Also known as Cot in Cahors.

Merlot (Mer-low)

Merlot is a juicy red grape, with supple, smooth, silky, blackberry, plum, red-wine-gum and fruitcake flavours. It happily flies solo but loves the company of Cabernet Sauvignon in a blend. As Merlot is usually oak aged, the fruit flavours are often accompanied by a touch of sweet, wood-smoke barrel nuances.

Mourvèdre/Monastrell/Mataro (More-veh-dr/Mon-ah-strell/Mat-are-oh)

This rich, plum- and damson-flavoured variety is often made into powerful, earthy, long-lived wines. It is not the most charming variety in its youth but ages gracefully, picking up more complex aromas and flavours along the way. It also likes to be blended with Grenache and Syrah.

Nebbiolo (Neb-ee-olo)

A tough grape that often needs five years in the bottle to soften to drinkability. A great Nebbiolo can conjure up intense plummy flavours with leathery, spicy, gamey overtones and a firm, dry finish.

Pinotage (Pee-no-tahge)

Pinotage is an earthy, spicy, deeply coloured grape with tobacco and plums on the nose, crushed blackberry fruit on the palate and a hearty, full, savoury finish. A speciality of South Africa.

Pinot Noir (Pee-no Nw-ar)

When on form, the Pinot Noir nose is often reminiscent of wild strawberries, violets and redcurrants, with a black-cherry flavour on the palate. There can be a degree of oakiness apparent, depending on the style. As these wines age, they may take on a slightly farmyardy character and the colour fades to pale, brick red.

Sangiovese (San-gee-o-vay-zee)

This grape has red- and black-fruit (mulberry, cherry, plum, blackcurrant and cranberry) nuances on the nose with a whiff of fresh-cut herbs and leather for good measure. Famous for making Chianti, there is usually an oaky element tucked into the wine, and it always has an acidic kick on the finish.

Syrah/Shiraz (Sirrah/Shirraz)

Syrah invokes explosive blackberry and ground-pepper aromas with vanilla, smoke and charred-oak nuances. In the

New World, big, inky-black Shiraz (the Syrah synonym) often has high alcohol and a mouth-filling prune, chocolate, raisin and spice palate.

Tempranillo (Temp-ra-nee-yo)

Ranging in flavour from vanilla- and strawberry-flavoured early-drinking styles, to dark, brooding, black-cherry reds, Tempranillo is Spain's noblest red grape, and the main grape variety in Rioja and countless other serious Spanish wines.

Zinfandel (Zin-fan-dell)

'Zin' tastes like a flavour collision between turbo-charged blackberries, a handful of vanilla pods and a fully stocked spice rack. These wines generally have luxurious, mouth-filling texture and often pretty impressive alcohol levels.

WINE REGIONS OF THE WORLD

In this crucial chapter I have taken twenty years of tasting notes and whittled them down to just the very best Bodegas, Châteaux, Domaines, Estates, Tenutas and Wineries. This year, as always, I have augmented this list with brand new finds. I have also subjected this roll call of heroes to a thorough inspection – kicking out any who are not performing at the highest level and downgrading those who have slipped a little over the last twelve months. Each and every entry has had to fight for its place in this elite list, and this year it's the biggest yet – a good sign that more people are making better wine than ever before.

If a favourite winery of yours is missing, it is either because I haven't yet tasted their wines or, sadly, they have not quite made the cut. Please do drop me a line if you have a hot tip (see address on page 218) and I will track down the wines and make sure I have a go at them before next year's edition. There are no one-hit-wonder estates in this list, only top-quality, talent-rich, hard-working wine-making experts, whose bottles have set my palate alight with wonder and enthusiasm. These are the producers you can rely on day in, day out, when you are shopping for home drinking, eating out in a restaurant, travelling the globe on business or holiday, or buying a gift for a wine-smart friend.

Occasionally you'll spot a producer or winery whose name is in bold. These are specially selected estates that are truly outstanding and every wine in their entire portfolio is first class. If a producer is both in bold and has a £, it means that its wines are on the expensive side (£25 plus). These titanium-plated names make money-no-object wines, for those of you with a no-upper-limit mentality. This doesn't mean that every wine they make is out of reach – far from it. Their flagship wine may be dizzily dear, but their other labels may still be brilliant but significantly cheaper, so do take note. The bold estates without a £ make more affordable wines (somewhere between £5 and £25), so keep an eye out for them – this is where I do virtually all of my everyday drinking.

This year I have introduced a new feature – my dream estates. These are my personal favourites from the bold list and they are my desert-island/lottery winning wines – they are highlighted in *red bold italic*. I am always asked what my favourite handful of wine producers in the world are – now you know.

ARGENTINA

Under new PR direction in the UK (hopefully), Argentina will finally start to move forwards at the pace at which it deserves. In the past I have been bored by the muddy, over-oaked, macho reds and amateurish, hit-and-miss whites, but signs of improvement are starting to come thick and fast. You will see from my list of recommended estates that there aren't very many who make the grade. But, believe me, this is more than enough to keep you happy during the course of the year. There is no doubt that in the £5 to £10 mark Argentina makes some hearty reds. The Malbec and Bonarda grapes are two very good reasons to go shopping in this section of your offie. Cabernet and Syrah, too, is starting to look good. But, beyond these, there is massive competition out there for the other international white and red grapes. As far as whites are concerned, I still favour Chile's wines unless you fancy a glass of the intriguing, indigenous Torrontés grape. People always think I am hard on Argentina, but I can see the potential there. Argentina needs to raise its game to be taken more seriously on a world stage. How many do you drink in the year? As I type this I have only one bottle of Argentinian wine in my cellar – surely they can do better than that?

The best Argentinian estates are – **Anubis**, **Argento**, **Bodega Noemía de Patagonia**, **Catena Zapata (Catena)**, **Chacayes (Lurton)**, **Clos de los Siete**, **Familia Zuccardi**, Finca El Retiro, Lurton, **Norton**, **Santa Julia**, Terrazas, **Val de Flores**, Valentin Bianchi and Weinert.

AUSTRALIA

I make no bones about the fact that I consider Australia to be the most exciting wine-producing country in the world today. Granted Australia lacks true Burgundy and Champagne regions, and, while we're at it, it would be nice to have a Jerez (sherry) and a Douro (port), too. But you can't have everything, and you have to admit that they are doing a bloody good job already with what they've got.

I visit Australia more than any other winemaking country in the course of my work – shame it's so far away, but I am not complaining about my air miles! On each and every trip I discover more and more shockingly exciting wines. I recently judged the Royal Sydney Wine Show and managed to have a go at some 2,100 wines in the course of four days – it was amazing. Gone are the days of sweaty, oaky Chadonnays – hello fit, new-style, lithe, balanced Chardonnays. High alcohol, monstrous reds are on the way out, too. The overall winner of the show was a cool climate Paringa Shiraz from Mornington Peninsula in Victoria – fresh, crunchy tannins and pure aromatic fruit winning through. The sparklers looked great and the dry Rieslings and Semillons are among the finest on the planet. Red blends are well-judged and these award-winning wines were coming in at all price points. These are my barometers of excellence and over the past year Australian wines have passed every test with flying colours.

The vast majority of Australian wines sold in the UK are everyday drinking bottles at below the £5 mark. Australia is very good (if not the best) at making these wines. There is a huge over-supply of wine in Australia, and British supermarkets are exploiting this remorselessly – this is all well and good for the average drinker, but it is holding everyone back from finding the real gems available. The UK wine lover barely realises that there is a world of wine beyond these entry-level wines – and they compete head on with those from France and the rest of the world. My aim is to drag the average wine lover up the ladder to where I think Australia really rules the roost – £6.99 to £12.99. With the exception of very few grape varieties, Australian wines are shoulder to shoulder with the very best in the world at this level, and it is these wines that we should start to embrace. In sheer value for money terms I think that it is very hard to beat the Aussies at this game. There are, of course, exceptions, and you will find loads in the Top 250 but, as a nation, they are fast becoming the model to which all others have to aspire.

Why is this? I think that the main answer lies with the people working within the business. The passion, excitement, determination, business acumen, palate awareness and their sheer finger-on-the-pulse-of-modern-society mentality is nothing short of phenomenal. Add to that world-class viticulture and cutting-edge technical wizardry (embracing screwcaps so quickly is a perfect example of how Australia and New Zealand lead the world) and the picture becomes clearer. But the final element, which tips the scales in favour of this enchanting land, is the liberal dusting of fun that you find in the bottle, and also in everything these winemakers do. This simple yet fundamental ingredient is something that a vast chunk of the rest of the wine world simply fails to realise is key to making great wine. It is Australia's recipe for success.

From the big brands at the bottom of the ladder, who make some of the most popular wines on our shelves, to the more serious offerings featured in this book and beyond, Australia is making terrific in-roads into our cellars. Being number one is not good enough, though. Australians are continually striving to make better and better wines – this should send a shiver down competitors' spines. I don't see this hunger for improvement anywhere else. It is not all success, of course. Part of this development is a willingness to admit defeat if something goes wrong and then to have the determination to start again immediately, developing a new label, flavour or concept.

This positive momentum does not just happen on a winery-by-winery basis. It happens in a very big way, too, as each region has its own generic body promoting its wines and sharing its hard-earned knowledge among its members. This collaborative mentality means that everyone benefits and they move forward together. This is one of the reasons Italy, Spain and France have lost out to Australia of late. They not only find it hard to work with their neighbours but, in most cases, they actively don't want to!

The fact is I have a higher hit rate of stunning bottles in Australia than in any other country in the world. This is an irrefutable fact. And I also drink more Aussie wine at home than any other country, too.

There is an entire world of wine to be discovered in Australia (it has so many regions and styles at its fingertips) and this is the definitive list of awesome wineries. Not one of these producers will let you down – the next few pages are gold dust!

WESTERN AUSTRALIA
The top producers are – Alkoomi, Amberley, Ashbrook Estate, Brookland Valley, **Cape Mentelle**, *Cullen*, Devil's Lair, Evans & Tate, Ferngrove, Forrest Hill, **Frankland Estate**, Garlands, Goundrey, **Houghton**, Howard Park, Juniper Estate, *Leeuwin Estate*, Millbrook, **Moss Wood**, **Picardy**, **Pierro**, Plantagenet, **Suckfizzle Augusta (Stella Bella)**, Vasse Felix, **Voyager**, West Cape Howe, Wignalls, Willow Bridge and Xanadu.

SOUTH AUSTRALIA
The top producers in each region are:
Clare Valley – Annie's Lane, Cardinham, Clos Clare, Crabtree, **Eldredge**, *Grosset*, Jeanneret, **Jim Barry**, **Kilikanoon**, Knappstein, *Leasingham*, **Mitchell**, **Mount Horrocks**, **Neagles Rock**, **O'Leary Walker**, Paulett, **Petaluma**, **Pikes**, Reilly's, Sevenhill, Skillogalee, Taylors (Wakefield in the UK), *Tim Adams*, Two Fold and **Wendouree £**.
Barossa Valley – Barossa Valley Estate, Burge Family Winemakers, Charles Cimicky, **Charlie Melton**, Chateau Tanunda, Craneford, Elderton, **Fox Gordon**, *Glaetzer*, **Grant Burge**, **Greenock Creek**, **Haan**, **Heritage**, **Hobbs**, **Kaesler**, **Kalleske**, **Leo Buring**, Massena, Murray Street Vineyards, **Orlando (Jacobs Creek)**, *Penfolds*, Peter

Lehmann, Rockford, Rolf Binder Wines, Rusden, St Hallett, Saltram, Schwarz, Seppelt, **Spinifex**, *Standish Wine Co.*, **Teusner**, Thorn-Clarke, Tin Shed, *Torbreck £*, Turkey Flat, **Two Hands**, Willows, Wolf Blass and *Yalumba*.

Eden Valley – Heggies (Yalumba), **Henschke**, Irvine, **Mesh (Grosset & Hill Smith)** and **Pewsey Vale** (Yalumba).

Adelaide Hills – Ashton Hills, **Barratt**, Chain of Ponds, **Geoff Weaver**, *The Lane & Off The Leash (Edwards Family)*, Nepenthe, Petaluma, Shaw & Smith and TK (Tim Knappstein Lenswood Vineyard).

Adelaide Plains – Primo Estate and Wilkie.

McLaren Vale – **Bosworth**, Cascabel, **Chalk Hill**, **Chapel Hill**, Chateau Reynella (Hardys), Clarendon Hills, **Coriole**, d'Arenberg, Fox Creek, **Gemtree**, Geoff Merrill, **Hardys Tintara**, **Hastwell & Lightfoot**, Hoffmann's, **Kangarilla Road**, *Kay Brothers Amery*, Koltz, **Linda Domas**, Mitolo, Noon, Oliver's Taranga, Pertaringa, Pirramimma, Richard Hamilton, Rosemount (McLaren Vale), Simon Hackett, Tatachilla, **Ulithorne**, *Wirra Wirra* and Woodstock.

Coonawarra – *Balnaves*, Bowen, Brand's, Highbank, **Hollick**, Jamiesons Run, **Katnook**, Ladbroke Grove, **Leconfield**, Lindemans, **Majella**, **Parker**, **Penley**, Redman, **Wynns** and **Yalumba**.

Miscellaneous – Ballast Stone (Currency Creek), Bleasdale (Langhorne), Brothers in Arms (Langhorne), **Heartland** (Limestone Coast/Langhorne), **Tapanappa** (Wrattonbully) and Zonte's Footsteps (Langhorne).

VICTORIA

The top producers are – **All Saints**, **Baileys**, Balgownie, **Bannockburn**, **Bass Phillip**, Battely, **Best's Great Western**, **Bindi**, By Farr, *De Bortoli (Yarra Valley)*, Brown Brothers, **Campbells**, Castagna, *Chambers Rosewood*, Cobaw Ridge, **Coldstream Hills**, Craig Avon, **Craiglee**, **Crawford River**,

Curlewis, *Dalwhinnie*, David Traeger, Diamond Valley Vineyards, **Domaine Chandon (Green Point)**, **Domaine Epis**, Dromana Estate, **Gembrook Hill**, *Giaconda £*, Hanging Rock, Heathcote Winery, Jasper Hill, **Kooyong**, McPherson, Main Ridge, Métier Wines, **Mitchelton**, **Morris**, Mount Ida, **Mount Langi Ghiran**, *Mount Mary*, Passing Clouds, **Paringa Estate**, Pondalowie, Provenance, Redbank, **Savaterre**, Scorpo, **Scotchmans Hill**, **Seppelt Great Western**, Shelmerdine, Sorrenberg, Stanton & Killeen, **Stonier**, **Tahbilk**, Tallarook, Taltarni, Virgin Hills, Water Wheel, Wild Duck Creek, Yarra Burn, **Yarra Yering**, **Yeringberg** and **Yering Station**.

TASMANIA
The top producers are – Andrew Pirie, Apsley Gorge, **Bay of Fires**, **Clover Hill**, **Craigow**, *Domaine A (Stoney Vineyard)*, Elsewhere, **Freycinet**, Grey Sands, Jansz, No Regrets, **Pipers Brook (Ninth Island)**, Providence, Spring Vale, **Stefano Lubiana**, **Tamar Ridge** and Touchwood.

NEW SOUTH WALES
The top producers are – Allandale, Benwarin, Bimbadgen, Bloodwood, Brangayne, **De Bortoli (Riverina)**, **Brokenwood**, **Chatto**, **Clonakilla**, **Cumulus**, **De Iuliis**, First Creek, Glenguin, **Keith Tulloch**, **Lake's Folly**, Lark Hill, Lillypilly, Lindemans, Logan Wines, Margan, McGuigan, *McWilliam's/ Mount Pleasant*, Meerea Park, Pyramid Hill, Rosemount (Hunter Valley), Simon Gilbert, SmithLeigh, **Tempus Two**, **Tower Estate** and **Tyrrell's**.

AUSTRIA
Austria continues to ride a wave of popularity in the UK. Our wine journalists have jumped on the wines and seemingly cannot let go. Now I don't want to pee on

anyone's bonfire, but while I love many of the funky Rieslings and zesty Grüner Veltliners that have infiltrated our wine shops, I do baulk at having to spend well over a tenner for the pleasure of taking them home. There are a handful of wines that have emerged over the last twelve months from decent producers under the tenner mark, but is this enough? In this respect Austria is light years behind the competition. You only have to look to Australia for dry Riesling and there are ten times the number of wines available, with decent nationwide distribution, too.

Having said that, I am certain, the Austrians will continue to do well. My advice is to stick to my list below and mind out for the inevitable nose-bleed price-dizziness.

The top producers are – Alois Kracher, **Bründlmayer**, **Emmerich Knoll**, **Feiler-Artinger**, *Franz Hirtzberger*, Fred Loimer, Freie Weingärtner Wachau, Graf Hardegg, G & H Heinrich, Helmut Lang, Hiedler, Höpler, Josef Pöckl, Jurtschitsch, **Kurt Angerer**, **Manfred Tement**, Nittnaus, Paul Achs, **F.X. Pichler**, Polz, **Prager**, Salomon, Schloss Gobelsburg, Sepp Moser, Velich, Wieninger, Willi Opitz and Dr Wolfgang Unger.

CANADA

It has been yet another year of soporific inactivity from the Canadians and, to be honest, you would have go there on holiday to find a decent list of wines because, in the UK, we only ship wine from a handful of estates.

The best estates are – **Burrowing Owl**, **Cave Springs**, **Château des Charmes**, Daniel Lenko, Henry of Pelham, **Inniskillin**, **Mission Hill**, **Osoyoos Larose**, Paradise Ranch, Quails' Gate, Southbrook, Spring Cellars, **Sumac Ridge** and Tinhorn Creek.

CHILE

We have benfitted from a more dynamic Chilean drive over the last eighteen months and this has led to more choice and more success for their sector of the market. The only problem is that this expansion in labels seems to have been at the upper end (£7.99+ where very few sales occur). These wines are also, on the whole, 'tricked up', with masses of oak, higher alcohol and low yields etc. This is not the way to impress the worldwide audience. A uniqueness and 'sense of place' is what we are after.

I know that the Chileans are working hard, and results are starting to come through with more regularity, but with all of the competition on the international stage, they need to focus their attention in the right direction. The solution to this problem is to emphasise what they have that no one else does – the land and climate of Chile. This will happen, in time, but I am surprised that they are making such a hash of it in the medium term.

As a source of reliable, sub-£5 red and white wine Chile works well – but this is not the tag line that this country deserves.

The best Chilean estates are – **Alvaro Espinoza**, **Amayna**, Anakena, **Antiyal**, **Araucano**, **Casa Lapostolle**, **Casa Marin**, **Concha y Toro (Casillero del Diablo, Marqués de Casa Concha, Terrunyo, Trio, Don Melchor)**, Cousiño-Macul, **De Martino**, Michel Laroche & Jorge Coderch, **Miguel Torres**, San Pedro, Santa Rita, **Seña**, Valdivieso, **Veramonte**, **Viña Errázuriz**, **Viña Haras de Pirque**, Viña Leyda, **Viña Montes**, **Viña MontGras**, Viña Morandé, **Viña Pérez Cruz**, **Ventisquero** and **Viñedos Organicos Emiliana**.

FRANCE
BORDEAUX

I realise that most top-end red Bordeaux falls into the head-spinningly scary price bracket (there are £ signs everywhere in this section) and they usually need a decade in the cellar to really start cruising up their drinking curve, but there is no getting away from the fact that this is one of the most important and influential wine regions in the world. When these Châteaux get it right (i.e. the weather is kind and there's no rain at harvest – 2000, 2001, 2002ish, 2003, 2004 and 2005, for example), the wines are hard to beat. I am always sadistically tough on this list each year, as I have no time for charlatans or fashion-conscious, emperor's-new-clothes styles of wine. The bottles that rock my boat are from the stellar estates, whose wines can't be copied anywhere else on the planet and whose flavours transport your palate to a different dimension. Bordeaux is the home to the majestic red grapes Cabernet Sauvignon, Merlot and Cabernet Franc. The percentages of each grape variety in the final blend vary from Château to Château, depending on the sub-region, soil and winemaker. The wines will also have spent eighteen months or so maturing in smart, French oak barrels. This classic recipe is the model for red wines around the globe. *Bonne chance mes amies!*

RED WINES
THE LEFT BANK

Graves Bahans-Haut-Brion £, **Carmes-Haut-Brion**, Chantegrive, **Domaine de Chevalier**, de Fieuzal, Haut-Bailly, *Haut-Brion £*, La Garde, **La Mission-Haut-Brion £**, Pape-Clément, Picque-Caillou and Smith-Haut-Lafitte.
Haut-Médoc and (**Bas**) **Médoc** Arnauld, **Belgrave**, Cambon la Pelouse, Cantemerle, Clément-Pichon,

d'Agassac, de Lamarque, Malescasse, Patache d'Aux, **Potensac**, Rollan de By, **Sociando-Mallet**, Tour du Haut-Moulin and Villegeorge.

Margaux d'Angludet, Brane-Cantenac, Cantemerle, **Durfort-Vivens**, Ferrière, d'Issan, **La Lagune**, *Margaux £*, **Palmer £**, **Pavillon Rouge du Château Margaux** and Rausan-Ségla.

Moulis and **Listrac** Chasse-Spleen, Clarke, Fourcas Loubaney and **Poujeaux**.

Pauillac Batailley, **Les Forts de Latour**, **Grand-Puy-Lacoste**, Haut-Bages-Libéral, Haut-Batailley, **Lafite-Rothschild £**, *Latour £*, Lynch-Bages, Mouton-Rothschild £, **Pichon-Longueville Baron £**, **Pichon-Longueville-Comtesse de Lalande £** and *Pontet-Canet*.

St-Estèphe Beau-Site, Le Boscq, **Calon-Ségur**, **Cos d'Estournel £**, Cos Labory, Haut-Marbuzet, La Haye, Lafon-Rochet, Marbuzet, *Montrose £*, Les-Ormes-de-Pez, de Pez and Ségur de Cabanac.

St-Julien Clos du Marquis, Ducru-Beaucaillou £, Gruaud-Larose £, Lagrange, Langoa-Barton, *Léoville-Barton £*, *Léoville-Las-Cases £*, **Léoville-Poyferré £**, St-Pierre and Talbot.

THE RIGHT BANK

Canon-Fronsac and **Fronsac** Canon-Moueix, **de Carles**, **Fontenil**, du Gaby, Hervé-Laroque, Mazeris, Moulin-Haut-Laroque and La Vieille-Cure.

Castillon Cap de Faugères, **d'Aiguilhe** and Puyanché.

Côtes de Bourg and **Blaye** Haut-Sociando, **Roc des Cambes** and Tayac.

Lalande-de-Pomerol Bel-Air, Belles-Graves, **La Fleur de Boüard** and Laborde.

Pomerol Beauregard, **Bon Pasteur**, **Certan Marzelle**, Certan-de-May, **Clinet £**, Clos de Litanies, Clos du Clocher,

Clos René, **La Conseillante £**, La Croix-St Georges, Domaine de l'Eglise, **l'Eglise-Clinet £**, l'Enclos, **l'Evangile £**, La Fleur de Gay, La Fleur-Pétrus, Le Gay, Gazin, **Hosanna**, **Lafleur £**, Lafleur-Gazin, Latour à Pomerol, Nenin, Petit Village, **Pétrus £**, Le Pin, **Trotanoy £** and **Vieux-Château-Certan £**.

St-Emilion Angélus £, L'Arrosée, **Ausone £**, Beau-Séjour Bécot, Beauséjour Duffau-Lagarosse, Belair, Canon-La-Gaffelière £, Le Castelot, **Cheval Blanc £**, Clos Fourtet, **Dassault**, La Dominique, **Figeac**, Larmande, Magdelaine, Monbousquet, Pavie, Tertre-Rôteboeuf £, La Tour-du-Pin-Figeac, **Troplong-Mondot £** and Valandraud £.

DRY WHITE WINES
Carbonnieux, **Clos Floridène**, **Domaine de Chevalier £**, de Fieuzal, **Haut-Brion Blanc £**, Laville-Haut-Brion £, **Pavillon Blanc de Château Margaux**, Smith-Haut-Lafitte and La Tour Martillac.

SWEET WHITE WINES
Sauternes and **Barsac** d'Arche, Bastor-Lamontagne, Broustet, **Climens £**, **Coutet £**, Doisy-Daëne, Doisy-Dubroca, Doisy-Védrines, de Fargues, Filhot, **Gilette**, **Guiraud**, Les Justices, **Lafaurie-Peyraguey £**, de Malle, Nairac, Rabaud-Promis, **Raymond-Lafon £**, Rayne-Vigneau, **Rieussec £**, **Suduiraut £**, La Tour Blanche £ and **d'Yquem £**.

BURGUNDY
This is my favourite wine region in the world! It is home to the most incredible Chardonnays and Pinot Noirs on the planet. I visit Burgundy several times a year – for work and for pleasure, and I always get goosebumps on the motorway as I get closer and closer. Burgundy

encapsulates in one small region what the mystique, allure and fascination of wine is all about. I simply adore the wines, the food and the people. But – and this is very important – just because this is the most hallowed turf in the wine world, it doesn't mean that some reprobates don't make some dross here! Unless you have this failsafe list of top Domaines in your hand, you could very seriously (and very expensively) lose your way.

Burgundy is a veritable minefield of tiny vineyards and thousands of producers – French inheritance law at its peak of confusion! Pick carefully, using my vintage table at the back of this guide, and you will be fine. I promise. Every other estate in the world tries to reach the heights of Pinot Noir and Chardonnay perfection that they achieve here in Burgundy. They can't – this soil and setting are unique. Some come close, but these vineyards are extremely special – one visit and you'll see why. It is easy to get hooked! You will also find the zippy white grape Aligoté and the underrated red variety Gamay (Beaujolais) in Burgundy ably support the two aforementioned super-grapes. Stick to these chaps and you can eat and drink without busting the bank but head back to Pinot Noir and Chardonnay for dinner and special occasions! What follows is worth its weight in Grand Cru Pinot Noir – remember me with a smile and a 'Santé' when you gaze into your next glass of celestial Burgundy!

CHABLIS
Chablis (white) **Billaud-Simon**, A & F Boudin, **Christian Moreau**, Daniel Dampt, des Genèves, Jean Durup, **Jean-Paul Droin**, **Laroche**, **Laurent Tribut**, Louis Michel, **Raveneau £**, **René & Vincent Dauvissat** and William Fèvre.
St-Bris-le-Vineux and **Chitry** (white) Jean-Hugues Goisot.

CÔTE DE NUITS
Marsannay-la-Côte and **Fixin** (mainly red) Bruno Clair, Charles Audoin, Fougeray de Beauclair and René Bouvier.
Gevrey-Chambertin (red) *Armand Rousseau*, Bernard Dugat-Py, **Claude Dugat**, *Denis Mortet*, Drouhin-Laroze, *Fourrier*, Géantet-Pansiot, Joseph Roty and **Sérafin**.
Morey-St-Denis (red) **Dujac**, Hubert Lignier, **des Lambrays**, *Ponsot* and **Virgile Lignier**.
Chambolle-Musigny & **Vougeot** (red) Christian Clerget, **Comte Georges de Vogüé**, *Ghislaine Barthod*, Jacques-Frédéric Mugnier, Pierre Bertheau, *G. Roumier* and **de la Vougeraie**.
Vosne-Romanée and **Flagey-Echézeaux** (red) **Anne Gros**, **Emmanuel Rouget**, **Jean Grivot**, Lamarche, **Leroy £**, *Méo-Camuzet £*, Mongeard-Mugneret, **René Engel**, **Robert Arnoux**, *de la Romanée-Conti £* and Sylvain Cathiard.
Nuits-St-Georges (red) Alain Michelot, Bertrand Ambroise, **J-C Boisset**, Daniel Chopin-Groffier, Daniel Rion, Dominique Laurent, Faiveley, Henri Gouges, Jean Chauvenet, Jean-Jacques Confuron, Lécheneaut, **Nicolas Potel** and **Robert Chevillon**.

CÔTE DE BEAUNE
Ladoix (mainly red) Edmond Cornu.
Aloxe-Corton and **Ladoix-Serrigny** (mainly red) Michel Voarick.
Pernand-Vergelesses (red and white) *Bonneau du Martray (Corton-Charlemagne) £*, Dubreuil-Fontaine and Maurice Rollin.
Savigny-lès-Beaune (red and white) Chandon de Briailles, **Jean-Marc Pavelot** and Maurice Ecard.
Chorey-lès-Beaune (red) Germain and **Tollot-Beaut**.
Beaune (mainly red) Bouchard Père et Fils, A-F Gros &

François Parent, Joseph Drouhin, **Louis Jadot** and
Maison Champy.
Pommard (red) **Comte Armand, de Courcel,** *Jean-Marc Boillot* and Parent.
Volnay (red) Coste Caumartin, **de Montille, Marquis d'Angerville, Michel Lafarge** and Roblet-Monnot.
Monthelie (red and white) **Annick Parent** and Denis Boussey.
Auxey-Duresses (red and white) **Claude & Catherine Maréchal** and Jean-Pierre Diconne.
St-Romain (mainly white) d'Auvenay and Christophe Buisson.
Meursault (white) **des Comtes Lafon £,** Henri Germain, *Jean-François Coche-Dury £,* Jean-Michel Gaunoux, **Jean-Philippe Fichet,** Marc Rougeot, Michel Tessier, **Patrick Javillier,** *Roulot* and **Vincent Bouzereau.**
Puligny-Montrachet (white) *Domaine Leflaive £,* **Etienne Sauzet £,** *Louis Carillon,* Olivier Leflaive and Paul Pernot.
Chassagne-Montrachet (white) **Bernard Morey,** Blain-Gagnard, Fontaine-Gagnard, Gagnard-Delagrange, Guy Amiot, Jean-Noël Gagnard, Lequin-Colin, **Marc Colin, Marc Morey,** Michel Colin-Deléger, **Michel Niellon** and **Ramonet £.**
St-Aubin (red and white) Gérard Thomas, Henri Prudhon and Hubert & Olivier Lamy.
Santenay (red and white) Vincent Girardin.

CÔTE CHALONNAISE
Rully (red and white) Eric de Suremain, de la Folie, Paul & Henri Jacquesson and Vincent Dureuil-Janthial.
Montagny (white) Stéphane Aladame.
Mercurey (red and white) Antonin Rodet, **Bruno Lorenzon,** Luc Brintet, Michel & Laurent Juillot and

J. & F. Raquillet.
Givry (red and white) François Lumpp, Joblot and **Michel Sarrazin**.

MÂCONNAIS
Mâcon, Pouilly-Fuissé, St-Véran and **Viré-Clessé** (mainly white) **André Bonhomme**, **Château de Beauregard**, **Château des Rontets**, Château Fuissé (Jean-Jacques Vincent), Daniel Barraud, de Roally, **des Deux Roches**, Fagot, Goyard, **Guillemot-Michel**, Héritiers du Comte Lafon, **Jeandeau**, Jean Thévenet, la Croix Senaillet, la Sarazinière, Marc Jambon, **Michel Forest**, Robert-Denogent, Talmard and Verget (Guffens-Heynen).

BEAUJOLAIS
Producing mainly red wines, the most highly regarded sub-regions in Beaujolais are the ten 'Cru' Villages: Brouilly, Chénas, Chiroubles, Côte de Brouilly, Fleurie, Juliénas, Morgon, Moulin-à-Vent, Régnié and St-Amour.

The top producers are – *Alain Passot*, André Cologne, Aucoeur, Bernard Mélinand, **F & J Calot**, Champagnon, **Château de Pierreux**, *Coudert*, J.-L. Dutraive, J.-F. Echallier (des Pins), Hélène & Denis Barbelet, Henry Fessy, Jacky Janodet, **Jean-Charles Pivot**, **Jean Foillard**, **Louis Jadot (Château des Jacques)**, **Marcel Lapierre**, Maurice Gaget, Michel Chignard, Pascal Granger, Patrick Brunet, **Paul Janin** and **Vissoux**.

CHAMPAGNE
Each year I try not to list too many non-vintage Champagnes in my Top 250 because they tend to vary so much in flavour – bottle age and storage conditions make such a difference. So the idea with this section of the

guide is to use it as a pointer to the best makers of consistently excellent NV and vintage Champagne. I have also included a stunning list of smaller Champagne houses for you to track down when you are on holiday in France or if you are eagle-eyed and find them in the UK. These are all terrific estates whose wines rival the big boys in every department except for price tag, so save some cash and head 'off piste'.

FAMOUS NAMES

Billecart-Salmon *NV* Brut Réserve, Brut Rosé, Blanc de Blancs and Demi-Sec. *Vintage* Blanc de Blancs, Le Clos Saint-Hilaire, Cuvée Nicolas-François Billecart, Elisabeth Salmon Rosé and Grande Cuvée.

Bollinger *NV* Special Cuvée. *Vintage* Grande Année, RD and Vieilles Vignes Françaises Blanc de Noirs.

Deutz *Vintage* Blanc de Blancs and Cuvée William Deutz.

Gosset *NV* Brut Excellence, Grande Réserve Brut and Grand Réserve Rosé. *Vintage* Célébris and Grande Millésime Brut.

Alfred Gratien *Vintage* Brut.

Charles Heidsieck *NV* Mise en Cave and Rosé. *Vintage* Brut Millésime.

Jacquesson *Vintage* Avize Grand Cru Blanc de Blancs, Dégorgement Tardive and Grand Vin Signature.

Krug £ *NV* Grande Cuvée. *Vintage* Vintage and Clos du Mesnil.

Laurent-Perrier *NV* Cuvée Rosé Brut, Grand Siècle 'La Cuvée' and Ultra Brut.

Moët & Chandon *Vintage* Brut Impérial and Cuvée Dom Pérignon Brut.

Pol Roger *NV* Brut 'White Foil'. *Vintage* Brut Chardonnay, Brut Rosé, Brut Vintage and Cuvée Sir Winston Churchill.

Louis Roederer *NV* Brut Premier. *Vintage* Blanc de Blancs, Brut Millésime, Brut Rosé, Cristal and Cristal Rosé.
Ruinart *Vintage* Dom Ruinart Blanc de Blancs and 'R' de Ruinart Brut.
Salon £ *Vintage* Blanc de Blancs.
Taittinger *NV* Brut Réserve and Prélude. *Vintage* Comtes de Champagne Blanc de Blancs.
Alain Thiénot *Vintage* Brut and Grande Cuvée.
Veuve Clicquot *NV* Brut 'Yellow Label' and Demi-Sec. *Vintage* La Grande Dame Brut, La Grande Dame Rosé and Vintage Réserve.

SMALLER HOUSES – A-V
Albert Beerens, André Jacquart, Ayala, Bertrand Robert, Château de Boursault, Claude Carré, Delamotte, J. Dumangin, Edouard Brun, Egly-Ouriet, Fernand Thill, Fleury, Gatinois, Gérard Dubois, J-M Gobillard, D. Henriet-Bazin, Jacques Selosse, Larmandier-Bernier, Leclerc Briant, Legras, A. Margaine, Le Mesnil, Paul Déthune, Pertois-Moriset, Pierre Gimonnet, Pierre Moncuit, Pierre Vaudon, Roger Brun, G. Tribaut and Vilmart.

ALSACE
Alsace continues its run of spot-on vintages and you really should be making it your mission to track down a few Alsatians over the next twelve months. In general, they are under-priced, over-performing, food-friendly, aromatic, white beauties. From apéritif-style palate soothers and mid-weight, haute-cuisine-matching wines, to decadently sweet pud-style sweeties, this region covers a lot of ground. You will have to look to the smaller, independent wine merchants for most of the following names, as they are all fairly small operations. The main grape varieties to imbibe enthusiastically are Gewürztraminer, Riesling, Tokay-Pinot

Gris, Muscat, Pinot Blanc and Sylvaner. I personally wouldn't bother with reds (skinny Pinot Noirs) and fizzies!

The best producers are – Albert Boxler, Albert Mann, André Kientzler, André Rieffel, **André Thomas**, Bott-Geyl, Ernest Burn, Frédéric Mochel, **Hugel**, **Josmeyer**, Marc Kreydenweiss, **Marcel Deiss**, Mittnacht-Klack, Ostertag, Paul Blanck, Rolly Gassmann, Schlumberger, Schoffit, Stoeffler, **Trimbach**, *Weinbach* and **Zind-Humbrecht**.

THE LOIRE VALLEY

This rather fragmented but comprehensive list of wines follows the Loire river inland from the Atlantic, picking out the greatest estates from the key areas in this elongated, inexpensive, yet essential wine region. Sauvignon Blanc and Chenin Blanc are the main white grapes grown here. The Sauvignons are nearly always dry, whereas the Chenins can be fizzy, dry, medium-sweet or full-on sweeties. The serious reds are made from Cabernet Franc, with Gamay and Pinot Noir stepping in for lighter styles.

Muscadet (white) Château de Chasseloir, Chéreau, Luc Choblet, Couillaud, de la Mortaine and **de la Quilla**.
Savennières (white) **des Baumard**, **Clos de la Coulée de Serrant** and La Roche-aux-Moines.
Coteaux du Layon, **Coteaux de l'Aubance**, **Bonnezeaux** and **Quarts de Chaume** (white sweeties) des Baumard, Château de Fesles, *Château Pierre-Bise*, Didier Richou, Moulin Touchais, de la Roulierie and Vincent Lecointre.
Saumur (sparkling) Bouvet-Ladubay.
Saumur and **Saumur Champigny** (red and white) du Hureau, *Filliatreau*, Langlois-Château and **Nerleux**.
Chinon (mainly red) *Bernard Baudry*, Charles Joguet,

Couly-Dutheil, **Desbourdes** and **Philippe Alliet**.
St-Nicolas de Bourgueil (red) Jean-Paul Mabileau and
Max & Lydie Cognard-Taluau.
Bourgueil (red) Joël Taluau, Lamé-Delille-Boucard, **de la
Lande (Delaunay)** and **Pierre-Jacques Druet**.
Vouvray (white) Bourillon-Dorléans, **Gaston Huet**,
Philippe Foreau and Vincent Rimbault.
Montlouis (white) Deletang, Stéphane Cossais and **Taille
aux Loups**.
Sauvignon de Touraine (white) **Alain Marcadet**.
Gamay de Touraine (red) Henry Marionnet.
Jasnières (white) Jean-Baptiste Pinon and Joël Gigou.
Cheverny (white) de la Gaudronnière and Salvard.
Sancerre (white, rosé and red) Alain Gueneau, **Alphonse
Mellot**, André Dézat, **André Vatan**, Bailly-Reverdy,
Christian Lauverjat, *Cotat*, **Daulny**, **Henri Bourgeois**,
Henri Natter, Merlin-Cherrier, *Pascal & Nicolas Reverdy*,
Philippe de Benoist, **Serge Laloue**, **Sylvain Bailly**,
Vacheron and **Vincent Delaporte**.
Pouilly-Fumé (white) André Dézat (Domaine Thibault),
Cédrick Bardin, **Château du Nozet (de Ladoucette)**,
Château de Tracy, **Didier Dagueneau**, Hervé Seguin,
Jean-Claude Chatelain, **Michel Redde**, Serge Dagueneau
and Tabordet.
Menetou-Salon (mainly white) de Chatenoy, **Henry Pellé**
and **Jean Teiller**.
Quincy (white) Jacques Rouzé.

THE RHÔNE VALLEY

The Rhône Valley is home to a cornucopia of great French
wines. It makes some of the most spectacular reds and
beguiling whites on the planet, while at the same time
giving us amazing bargains. The Rhône has never
commanded the prices that top Burgundy and Bordeaux

seems to, so make the most of it. It is here that Syrah, Grenache and Mourvèdre rule the reds. Viognier commands the whites in the north, while Roussanne and Marsanne are in charge in the south. If you take the time to get to know this region well, you can drink smartypants wine for very little expenditure.

THE NORTHERN RHÔNE
FROM NORTH TO SOUTH

Côte Rôtie (red) Bernard Burgaud, Chapoutier, **Clusel-Roch £**, **David & Benjamin Duclaux**, *E. Guigal (and Château d'Ampuis) £*, Guy Bernard, **Jamet**, Jean-Michel Gerin, Marius Gentaz-Dervieux, **Patrick & Christophe Bonnefond**, **Pierre Gaillard**, René Rostaing, Yves Cuilleron and **Yves Gangloff**.

Condrieu (white) **André Perret**, Christian Facchin, **Christophe Pichon**, **François Villard £**, *Georges Vernay*, Louis Cheze, Robert Niero and *Yves Cuilleron £*.

St-Joseph (red and white) Bernard Faurie, **Bernard Gripa**, Delas, **Jean-Louis Chave**, Jean-Louis Grippat and **Pierre Gonon**.

Hermitage (red and white) **Chapoutier £**, Delas, Grippat, *Jean-Louis Chave £*, Michel Ferraton, **Paul Jaboulet Ainé £**, Sorrel and Tardieu-Laurent £.

Crozes-Hermitage (mainly red) *Alain Graillot*, Albert Belle, Combier, du Colombier, Domaine Pochon, **Gilles Robin**, **Les Chênets** and Olivier Dumaine.

Cornas (red) **Alain Voge**, **Auguste Clape**, Jean Lionnet, Noël Verset, **Robert Michel**, Thierry Allemand and **du Tunnel (Stéphane Robert)**.

THE SOUTHERN RHÔNE

Côtes-du-Rhône and **-Villages** (red) **Brusset**, Château du Trignon, **Clos Petite Bellane**, **Coudoulet de Beaucastel**,

Domaine Gramenon, E. Guigal, **Marcel Richaud**, Piaugier, Rayas (Fonsalette) and **Tardieu-Laurent**.

Cairanne, **Lirac**, **Rasteau**, **Tavel** and **Vacqueyras** (red) **Château des Tours**, Clos des Cazaux, des Espiers, de la Mordorée, **de l'Oratoire Saint-Martin**, **La Soumade**, **Le Sang des Caillou** and **du Trapadis**.

Gigondas (red) Château du Trignon, Font-Sane, R. & J.-P. Meffre (Saint-Gayan), **Raspail-Ay**, **Saint-Cosme** and Santa-Duc.

Châteauneuf-du-Pape (red and white) *Château de Beaucastel*, Les Cailloux, Chapoutier, de la Charbonnière, **Charvin**, **Clos du Caillou**, **Clos des Papes**, de Ferrand, Fortia, **de la Janasse**, de Marcoux, **de la Mordorée**, du Pegaü, **Rayas**, des Saumades, Versino and Le Vieux Donjon.

Muscat de Beaumes-de-Venise (sweet white) Chapoutier, **Domaine de Durban** and Paul Jaboulet Aîné.

FRENCH COUNTRY

This may be the most dishevelled (visually) section in this chapter (Italy is a close second), but if you take it slowly you'll find some amazing, handcrafted wines here, that don't cost a bomb and deliver amazing amounts of authentic, Gallic flavour. 'French Country' is an old-fashioned term that really just means 'the rest of France's wine regions'. Years ago this would be a jumbled mass of funky, artisan estates, some of which made passable wines, and others that bumbled along selling their bottles to their friends and local restaurants. How things have changed! There is nothing other than exceptionally professional, totally committed producers, world-class expertise in this list, making some of the most remarkable and unique wine in the whole of France. The New World gave France a kick up the arse ten years ago when they started stealing French slots on wine merchants' shelves. The 'classic' regions ignored this threat, and are paying the price. French Country regions responded quickest and are now offering us some truly fascinating and delicious wines for us to savour. Many of these are impossible to copy abroad which further demonstrates their worth.

SOUTHWEST FRANCE
Bergerac (red and white) de la Jaubertie, **Moulin des Dames** and **La Tour des Gendres**.
Cahors (reds) de la Berangeraie, **du Cèdre**, **Clos Triguedina**, Lagrezette and **Les Laquets**.
Jurançon (dry and sweet whites) Bellegarde, **Cauhapé**, **Charles Hours**, Clos Guirouilh, **Clos Lapeyre**, Clos Uroulat, de Lahargue and Lapouble-Laplace.
Madiran (reds) d'Aydie, **Alain Brumont (Bouscassé and Montus)** and Domaine Pichard.
Monbazillac (sweet white) **de l'Ancienne Cure**, la Borderie and **Tirecul La Gravière**.
Saussignac (sweet white) Château Richard and Clos d'Yvigne.

LANGUEDOC-ROUSSILLON
Banyuls (fortified) and **Collioure** (red) de la Casa Blanca, Château de Jau, **du Mas Blanc** and de la Rectoire.
La Clape (red and white) **Camplazens**, **Château de Capitoul**, **de l'Hospitalet**, de la Negly and Pech-Redon.
Corbières (mainly red) **La Baronne**, des Chandelles, Château de Sérame, Château les Palais, Château Vaugélas, Etang des Colombes, **de Lastours**, **Meunier St Louis** and **Pech-Latt**.
Costières de Nîmes (red, white and rosé) des Aveylans, de Belle-Coste, Grande-Cassagne, Mourgues-du-Grès and **de Nages**.

Coteaux du Languedoc (red and white) Abbaye de Valmagne, d'Aupilhac, Les Aurelles, **Mas d'Azelon**, Mas de Chimères, Font Caude, Mas Jullien, **Mas Mortiès**, Peyre Rose, Puech-Haut, **Roc d'Anglade** and La Sauvagéonne.

Faugères (mainly red) **Alquier**, **de Ciffre** and des Estanilles.

Minervois (red and white) **Borie de Maurel**, **Le Cazal**, **Clos Centeilles**, Fabas, de Gourgazaud, **Lignon** and d'Oupia.

Pic St-Loup (mainly red) Cazeneuve, Ermitage du Pic St-Loup, **de l'Hortus**, de **Lascaux**, Lascours and Mas Bruguière.

St-Chinian (red and white) **Canet-Valette**, **Cazal-Viel**, Coujan, des Jougla, des Terres Falmet, Mas Champart and **Moulinier**.

Miscellaneous estates of excellence (and where to find them): **de l'Aigle** – Limoux; **Bégude** – Limoux; **Cazes** – Rivesaltes; *Clos des Fées* – Côtes de Roussillon-Villages; **Domaine de Baruel** – Cévennes; *Domaine Gardiés* – Côtes de Roussillon-Villages; **Domaine des Ravanès** – Coteaux de Murveil; **Elian da Ros** – Côtes du Marmandais; *de la Granges des Pères* – l'Hérault; **Mas Amiel** – Maury; **Massamier la Mignarde** – Côteaux de Peyriac, **Mas de Daumas Gassac** – l'Hérault.

PROVENCE

Bandol (red) **de la Bégude**, Château Jean-Pierre Gaussen, **de Terrebrune**, Lafran-Veyrolles, La Laidière, Mas de la Rouvière, Maubernard, de Pibarnon, **Pradeaux**, **Ray-Jane**, Souviou, **La Suffrène** and *Tempier*.

Les Baux-de-Provence (mainly red) Hauvette, des Terres Blanches and *de Trévallon £*

Bellet (red, white and rosé) Château de Crémat.

Cassis (mainly white) Clos Ste-Madeleine.

Côtes de Provence (mainly red) **Château de Roquefort, de la Courtade**, Gavoty, de Rimauresq and de St-Baillon. **Palette** (red, white and rosé) **Château Simone**.

GERMANY

Germany is making better wines than ever before – although they never really dropped the ball. You really must start drinking them if you aren't already because the exceptional Rieslings that hail from these historic vineyards are life-changing. Forget Black Tower, Lieb and Blue Nun (although apparently this brand is having a full makeover!?) as German wine is nothing to do with these eighties headaches. German Riesling is a fundamental cornerstone of everyone's wine diet. The new, drier styles of Riesling are simply spellbinding. The long-awaited Riesling revolution is here – join in! What follows is the hit list of some of the finest exponents of this grape variety on the planet. All you have to do is find them. Independent merchants will help in this quest.

The best producers are – Balthasar Ress, **J.B. Becker**, Dr Bürklin-Wolf, J.J. Cristoffel, Daniel Vollenweider, Deutschherren-Hof, Dönnhoff, **Egon Müller**, Heymann-Löwenstein, F**ritz Haag**, Karl H Johner, Koehler-Ruprecht, Künstler, J.L. Wolf, **Josef Leitz**, **Freiherr Langwerth von Simmern**, H. & R. Lingenfelder, *Dr. Loosen*, Müller-Cattoir, *J.J. Prüm*, **Reichsgraf von Kesselstatt**, **Max Ferd. Richter**, Reichsrat von Buhl, Reinhold Haart, **Robert Weil**, Schloss Lieser, Schloss Reinhartshausen, Seehof, **Selbach-Oster**, **von Schubert-Maximin Grünhaus**, **St. Urbans-Hof**, **Dr. H. Thanisch Erben**, Weingut Kerpen, *Weingut Karthäuserhof* and Willi Schaefer.

GREAT BRITAIN

English winemakers are starting to look to the future with some optimism. And they can thank global warming for some of this positivity. If you believe the papers, then even the French are looking to invest in sparkling wine operations in the south of England! Sparklers and dry whites are where you should be spending your money. It is a shame, though, that we still have to pay duty to the government on our purchases of English wine. If you took £2 or so off every bottle of English wine on the shelves, it might encourage us to make more and better wines, at the expense of boring Cava from Spain and lacklustre dry whites from France, Germany or the Loire. Now there's a thought! Lobby your local MP, please. Remember prices are lowest if you buy direct and also almost all UK wineries welcome visitors – see www.englishwineproducers.com.

The chosen few are – Biddenden, **Camel Valley**, **Chapel Down (Curious Grape)**, Clay Hill, Coddington, **Davenport**, Nyetimber, RidgeView and Shawsgate.

ITALY

Italy is home to the most disorganised wine industry on the planet (although, Spain is desperately trying to grab this crown, for some reason). Hundreds of obscure, indigenous grape varieties and many thousands of different bottles of wine are made by thousands of producers. It is such a muddle, but somehow they still manage to serve up some delicious wines. This is a bang-up-to-date list of the best Italian producers available in the UK. Italy happens to make a fair few of the finest value wines on the shelves today and if you are tempted to venture up the price ladder, you'll find they also make seriously brilliant wines around the £10 to £15 pound mark, too. But, like most of my serious wines, you will probably have to go to top-quality independent wine merchants to find the majority of the estates listed below.

NORTHWEST
PIEDMONT
Barolo, **Barbaresco**, **Barbera**, **Dolcetto** and **other reds** – Aldo Conterno, *Angelo Gaja £*, **Ascheri**, **Bruno Rocca**, **Ca' Rossa**, Ceretto, Cigliuti, Conterno Fantino, Domenico Clerico, **Elio Altare**, **Fontanafredda**, Giacomo Conterno, Giuseppe Mascarello, **Luciano Sandrone**, **Paolo Scavino**, **Parusso**, E. Pira, **Roberto Voerzio** and *La Spinetta*.
Moscato (fizzy, sweet white) **Fontanafredda** and **La Spinetta**.
Gavi (dry white) **La Giustiniana**, Nicola Bergaglio and **La Scolca**.
Roero Arneis (red and dry white) **Bric Cenciurio**, **Matteo Correggia** and Carlo Deltetto.
LOMBARDY
Red and white – **Bellavista** (Franciacorta), **Ca' del Bosco** (Franciacorta), **Ca' dei Frati** (Lugana), **Fratelli Muratori** (Franciacorta) and **Nino Negri** (Valtellina).

NORTHEAST
TRENTINO
All styles – Bossi Fedrigotti, Endrizzi, **Ferrari**, **Foradori**, Letrari, Pojer & Sandri, **San Leonardo**, Vigneto Dalzocchio and **La-Vis**.
ALTO ADIGE
All styles – Alois Lageder, *Colterenzio*, **Franz Haas**, Hofstätter and **San Michele Appiano**.
VENETO
Soave (white) Ca' Rugate, Gini, *Pieropan*, Prà and

Roberto Anselmi.
Valpolicella (red) Allegrini, Ca' del Pipa, Dal Forno,
Giuseppe Quintarelli £ and Masi.
Miscellaneous estates of excellence – (fizz) **Ruggeri**
(Valdobbiadene); (reds and sweeties) **Maculan**
(Breganze).
FRIULI-VENEZIA GIULIA
Mainly white – **Dario Raccaro**, Davide Moschioni,
Giovanni Puiatti, Girolamo Dorigo, **Lis Neris (Alvararo
Pecorari)**, Livio Felluga, Meroi, Mario Schiopetto, Miani,
Ronco del Gnemiz, **Roncùs**, Tercic, Villa Russiz, **Vinnaioli
Jermann** and **Visintini**.

CENTRAL
TUSCANY
Chianti (red) P. Antinori, Carobbio, **Castello di Brolio**,
Castello di Fonterutoli, Felsina Berardenga, Le Filigare,
Fontodi, **Isole e Olena**, **La Massa**, **Il Molino di Grace**,
Poggerino, **Querciabella**, Selvapiana and Villa Caffagio.
Brunello di Montalcino (red) Altesino, *Argiano*, Case
Basse, Ciacci Piccolomini d'Aragona, **Collosorbo**, Corte
Pavone, **Costanti**, Donatella Cinelli Colombini, **Fanti San
Filippo**, Fuligni, La Gerla, Lisini, **Mastrojanni**, Pietroso,
Poggio Antico, **Il Poggione**, Sesti, Silvio Nardi and
Uccelliera.
Vino Nobile di Montepulciano (red) **Dei**, Il Macchione,
Poliziano and Villa Sant'Anna.
Carmignano (red) Ambra and Tenuta di Capezzana.
Super-Tuscans (red) **Il Borro**, Il Bosco (Manzano),
Brancaia, Camartina (Querciabella) £, Campora (Falchini),
Il Carbonaione (Poggio Scalette), **Casalfero (Barone
Ricasoli)**, Cepparello (Isole e Olena) £, Cortaccio (Villa
Caffagio), Flaccianello della Pieve (Fontodi), Fontalloro
(Felsina Berardenga), Ghiaie della Furba (Capezzana),

Lupicaia (Tenuta del Terricio) £, Masseto (L. Antinori), Nambrot (Tenuta di Ghizzano) £, Ornellaia (Frescobaldi) £, Palazzo Altesi (Altesino), Paleo Rosso (Le Macchiole), Le Pergole Torte (Montevertine), Saffredi (Le Pupille) £, Sammarco (Castello dei Rampolla), Sassicaia (Marchesi Incisa della Rochetta) £, Siepi (Fonterutoli) £, Solaia (P. Antinori) £, Solengo (Argiano) £, Tassinaia (Tenuta del Terriccio) and Tignanello (P. Antinori).

Maremma and Morellino (mainly red) Costanza Malfatti, Lohsa (Poliziano), Le Pupille and Tenuta di Belguardo & Poggio Bronzone (Mazzei).

Vernaccia di San Gimignano (white) Montenidoli, Panizzi, Pietraserena and Teruzzi & Puthod.

Vin Santo (sweetie) Avignonesi £, *Isole e Olena £*, Selvapiana and Villa Branca.

MARCHE

Red and white – Coroncino, Saladini Pilastri, Le Terrazze and Umani Ronchi.

UMBRIA

Red and white – Arnaldo Caprai, La Carraia, Castello della Sala, La Fiorita Lamborghini, Luigi Bigi, Lungarotti, Palazzone and Sportoletti.

LAZIO

Red and white – Castel De Paolis, Falesco and Pallavincini.

ABRUZZO AND MOLISE

Red and white – Edoardo Valentini, Di Majo Norante, Podere Castorani and Valle Reale.

SOUTHERN AND ISLANDS – (ALL STYLES)

PUGLIA

Angelo Rocca, Apollonio, Botromagno, Cosimo Taurino, Francesco Candido, Tenuta Rubino and Vallone.

CAMPANIA

Colli di Lapio, Feudi di San Gregorio, Luigi Maffini,

Mastroberardino, **Montevetrano** and **Taburno**.
BASILICATA
D'Angelo, Basilisco and Paternoster.
CALABRIA
Librandi and San Francesco.
SICILY AND PANTELLERIA
Abbazia Santa Anastasia, **Abraxas**, De Bartoli, Cusumano,
Inycon, **Maurigi**, **Morgante**, *Planeta*, Salvatore Murana
and Tasca d'Almerita.
SARDINIA
Agricola Punica (Barrua), Argiolas, **Gallura**, Giovanni
Cherchi, **Santadi** and Sella & Mosca.

NEW ZEALAND
They don't shout about it, but the Kiwis are doing a great
job. With their championing of screwcaps (the best thing
to happen to winemaking in the last decade), brilliant
viticulture (the growing side) and inspirational vinification
(the making side), they are winning friends far and wide.
The UK is New Zealand's number one export market at
40% of total exports. More estates' wines are available
in the UK than ever before. Sauvignon Blanc has always
been the main fodder for punters, but Pinot Noir is looking
good these days, too, and don't forget about Chardonnays,
Rieslings (and other aromatics) and even Cabernets,
Merlots and Syrahs, now that Hawke's Bay has got its
collective eye zeroed in on the target. It has been painful
waiting for this to happen – I've been waiting for twenty
years. I like a healthy bit of sport on wine shop shelves
and so I am delighted that New Zealand finally wants to
join in with the rest of the world.

The best estates – Akarua, Alana Estate, Allan Scott,
Alpha Domus, Amisfield, Astrolabe, *Ata Rangi*, Auntsfield,

Babich, **Blind River**, Borthwick, Cable Bay, **Carrick**, Chard Farm, **Cloudy Bay**, *Craggy Range*, *Dog Point*, **Dry River**, Esk Valley, *Felton Road*, **Forrest Estate**, Foxes Island, Framingham, Fromm, Giesen, Goldwater Estate, Gravitas, Grove Mill, Highfield, **Huia**, **Hunter's**, **Isabel Estate**, **Jackson Estate**, Kathy Lynskey, Kim Crawford, **Kumeu River**, Lawson's Dry Hills, **Martinborough Vineyard**s, Matahiwi, **Matakana Estate**, Mills Reef, Montana, **Mt Difficulty**, Mount Edward, Mount Michael, **Mountford**, Mud House, Murdoch James, Nautilus, Neudorf, Ngatarawa, Olssens, **Palliser Estate**, Passage Rock, **Pegasus Bay**, **Peregrine**, Pisa Range, Quartz Reef, Rippon, Rockburn, Sacred Hill, **Saint Clair**, **Seresin**, Sileni, Sleeping Dogs, Solstone, Southbank, Spy Valley, **Stonecroft**, **Stonyridge**, Te Awa, Te Karainga, Te Mata, **TerraVin**, *Te Whare Ra*, The Crossings, The Ned, Tohu, Trinity Hill, **Two Paddocks**, **Unison**, Valli, **Vavasour**, **Vidal**, **Villa Maria**, Wairau River, West Brook and *Wither Hills*.

PORTUGAL

Portugal will always make two of the finest fortified wines in the world – Port and Madeira. These two tremendous creations are staggeringly serious in the right hands. Unfortunately they suffer from being a little out of fashion. Please buck the trend and discover just how wonderful these two historic styles of wines are (see my Top 250 for some senior examples). In addition to this, I have also compiled a list of the fine purveyors of non-fortified wines. I must admit that I don't drink much Portuguese wine at home, and I haven't been out there for a few years either, but things are moving forward smoothly and the future is bright. I will make a massive effort with Portugal, its wines and its people this year – I am looking forward to it enormously.

PORT

The best special-occasion port houses are – **Dow**, **Fonseca**, *Graham*, **Quinta do Noval Nacional**, *Taylor* and **Warre**.

The less famous overachievers are – Churchill, *Niepoort*, **Quinta do Portal**, Quinta Roriz, **Quinta do Vesuvio**, Quinto do Infantado, **Ramos-Pinto** and **Senhora da Ribeira**.

MADEIRA

The top producers are – **Blandy's**, **Cossart Gordon** and **Henriques & Henriques**.

THE REST OF PORTUGAL

Here's a short hit list of fine winemakers in the better regions.

Alentejo Canto Décimo, **Cortes de Cima**, Quinta de Cabriz, Quinta do Carmo, **João Portugal Ramos** and Segada.

Bairrada Manuel dos Santos Campolargo, Caves São João and **Luis Pato**.

Beiras Caves Aliança.

Dão Alvaro Castro, Conde de Santar, Quinta da Cabriz, Quinta dos Carvalhais and **Quinta dos Roques**.

Douro Duas Quintas, **Niepoort**, **Quinta do Crasto**, Quinta da Gaivosa, Quinta do Infantado, *Quinta do Portal*, **Quinta de Roriz**, Quinta de la Rosa, Quinta do Vale da Raposa and **Redoma**.

Estremadura Palha Canas, **Quinta da Boavista** and Quinta de Pancas.

Ribatejo Quinta da Lagoalva.

Terras do Sado João Pires, José-Maria da Fonseca, Pasmados, Periquita and **Quinta de Camarate**.

Vinho Verde Palácio da Brejoeira and **Quinta do Ameal**.

SOUTH AFRICA

2006 saw another Cape Wine Expo in South Africa and journalists from all over the world tasted every wine that South Africa makes over a hectic week of touring around. It is clear to me that this country and its wines are moving at high speed. It is amazing to think that in the space of only a decade or so, this archaic industry has reinvented itself and come out fighting. Sauvignon, Chenin Blanc and Chardonnay are the white grapes to watch, and I suspect that Syrah and clever Rhône blends will end up being the strong suit with regard to reds. But don't forget the Cabernets, Merlots and Cape blends, which utilise local favourite Pinotage to its best effect. South Africa has arrived with a bang on the world market and it is here to stay. This is the longest list of star estates I have ever compiled. Get stuck in.

The top producers are – Allée Bleue, Ataraxia, Avondale, Beaumont, **Beyerskloof**, *Boekenhoutskloof (including Porcupine Ridge)*, Boschendal, **Bouchard Finlayson**, Brahms, La Bri, **Cape Point**, Cederberg, **Chamonix**, Coleraine, *Columella (Sadie Family)*, De Grendel, **De Toren**, De Trafford, De Wetshof, **Diemersfontein**, Dornier (Donatus in the UK), **Ernie Els Wines (including Guardian Peak), Fairview, Flagstone (including Jack & Knox, The Berrio), Glen Carlou, Graham Beck**, Grangehurst, Groot Constantia, **Hamilton Russell**, Hartenberg, Hidden Valley, Idiom, *Iona*, **Jean Daneel**, Joostenberg, **Jordan**, Kanonkop, *Ken Forrester*, Klein Constantia, Kleine Zalze, **Lammershoek**, Land's End, Lindhorst, Linton Park, Longridge, **Luddite**, Meinert, Mischa, Mont Rochelle, **Mont du Toit**, Môreson, Morgenhof, Morgenster, La Motte, **Neil Ellis**, Nelson's Creek, Newton Johnson, L'Ormarins, **Paul Cluver**, **Phileo**,

Raats, Remhoogte, **Rijk's**, Robertson Winery, Rudera, **Rupert & Rothschild**, *Rustenberg (including Brampton)*, Rust en Vrede, **Scali**, Signal Hill, Simonsig, Southern Right, **Spice Route**, **Springfield**, Stark-Condé, Steenberg, Stellenzicht, Stormhoek, Thelema, **Tokara**, Uva Mira, Veenwouden, **Vergelegen**, **Vilafonté**, Viljoensdrift, Villiera, **Warwick Estate**, **Waterford (including Kevin Arnold)**, Waterkloof and Wildekrans.

SPAIN

I have listed my Spanish wines by region first and then by producer. Spain is still woefully under represented in the UK at the top end but, bit by bit, Spanish companies are encouraging us to understand and accept their new wines. There is so much development and modernisation going on that, in the next ten years, I think it will become a real force to be reckoned with worldwide. For the time being it is a chaotic mess, or are they just keeping all of the best wines for themselves?!

ANDALUCÍA
Jerez (sherry) *Emilio Lustau*, **Fernando de Castilla**, **González Byass**, Hidalgo, Osborne and *Valdespino*.

ARAGÓN
Calatayud Marqués de Aragón and San Gregorio.
Campo de Borja Bodegas Borsao.
Somontano Blecua (Viñas del Vero) and Enate.

CASTILLA Y LEÓN
Bierzo Descendientes de J. Palacios.
Ribera del Duero Alión, **Cillar de Silos**, Condado de Haza, **Dominio de Pingus**, Pago de Carraovejas, **Pesquera**, Tarsus, Valduero and *Vega Sicilia £*.

Valladolid Mauro.
Rueda Agrícola Castellana and **Bodegas Dos Victorias**.
Toro Alquiriz (Vega Sicilia) and Viña Bajoz.
Arribes del Duero Durius Alto Duero (Marqués de Griñon).

CATALUÑA
Conca de Barberá Josep Foraster and **Miguel Torres**.
Empordà-Costa Brava Mas Estela.
Penedès Albet I Noya, Can Ràfols dels Caus, Jean Léon, **Marquès de Monistrol**, Miguel Torres and Puig i Roca.
Tarragona-Montsant and Priorat Celler de Capçanes, **Clos Mogador £**, Clos de L'Obac, **Dits Del Terra**, **L'Ermita** and **Finca Dofi (Alvaro Palacios)**, Laurona, Mas d'en Compte, Mas Igneus, **Mas Martinet** and **Scala Dei**.
Terra Alta Bàrbara Forés and Xavier Clua.

EXTREMADURA, CASTILLA-LA MANCHA AND MADRID
Almansa Piqueras.
Castilla-La Mancha Dominio de Valdepusa.
Valdepeñas Los Llanos.

ISLANDS
Mallorca Anima Negra.

LEVANTE
Jumilla Casa de la Ermita.
Valencia Dominio Los Pinos.

NORTHERN COASTAL SPAIN
Rías Baixas Fillaboa, **Lagar de Cervera**, Lagar de Fornelos, *Lusco do Miño*, Martín Codax, **Pazo de Barrantes**, *Pazo Señoráns*, Valdamor and Valmiñor.

Bizkaiko and Getariako Txacolina Bodegas Ametzoi and Txomín Etaniz.

RIOJA AND NAVARRA
Rioja Artadi, Barón de Ley, **Contino**, **CVNE**, Lopez de Heredia, **Marqués de la Concordia**, **Marqués de Griñon**, **Marqués de Murrieta**, **Marqués de Vargas**, Muga, Navajas, Remelluri, La Rioja Alta, **Roda**, Urbina and Viña Salceda.
Navarra Agramont, Guelbenzu, Julián Chivite, Ochoa, Príncipe de Viana and **Vega del Castillo**.

USA
CALIFORNIA
While there is still the band of ridiculously narcissistic micro-wineries flogging their wares to like-minded mugs at astronomical prices, the majority of winemakers in the USA look at the wine market with level heads. This means there are plenty of wines for us to choose from at reasonable prices – and this category will continue to grow. The main problem is that this huge industry has no trouble in selling its wines locally and so they are understandably lazy about their export markets. Comparing like for like in the New World arena, California has many wines to be proud of, but value for money is still an issue. New Zealand (with Pinot Noir), Australia (with Cabernet, Shiraz/Syrah and Chardonnay) and South America (with Bordeaux blends) are the countries that take chunks out of it below the £10 mark but, as you drift upwards, California has some real gems worth tracking down. Also, whenever you need a hit of Zinfandel (and we all do from time to time), this is the place to come – it is California's only truly unique offering.

I have arranged the wineries in order of wine style, rather than by region.

Cabernet Sauvignon/Merlot/Cabernet Franc Araujo, **Arietta £**, Beringer, **Bryant Family £**, Cain, **Caymus £**, Clos LaChance, **Corison**, **Dalle Valle £**, Diamond Creek £, Dominus £, **Duckhorn**, Dunn, **Etude**, Flora Springs, Forman, **Frog's Leap**, **Harlan Estate £**, Havens, Hess Collection, **Joseph Phelps £**, Justin Vineyards, Lail Vineyards, Matanzas Creek, **Moraga**, **Niebaum Coppola**, **Newton £**, **Opus One**, Pahlmeyer, **Paradigm £**, Paul Hobbs, **Peter Michael £**, Philip Togni, **Quintessa £**, *Ridge £*, Robert Mondavi, St Francis, *Shafer £*, Silver Oak, *Spottswoode £*, *Stag's Leap Wine Cellars £* and **Viader £**.
Chardonnay Arrowood, **Au Bon Climat**, Beringer, Clos LaChance, *David Ramey*, Frog's Leap, **Hanzell £**, **Kistler £**, *Kongsgaard £*, **Landmark £**, **Lymar £**, Morgan, Paul Hobbs, **Peter Michael £**, **Shafer £** and Sinskey.
Sauvignon Blanc Beringer, Carmenet, **Frog's Leap**, Matanzas Creek and **Robert Mondavi**.
Pinot Noir Au Bon Climat, *Calera £*, Cinnabar, *Etude £*, Gary Farrell, **Hanzell**, **Kistler £**, Marimar Torres, **J. Rochioli £**, Saintsbury, Sinskey and Talley Vineyards.
Rhône Rangers Alban, Au Bon Climat, Bonny Doon, Cline, Jade Mountain, JC Cellars, **Qupé**, **Sean Thackrey**, **Tablas Creek £**, **Turley £** and Wild Hog.
Zinfandel Biale, **Cline**, **Elyse**, **Doug Nalle**, De Loach, *Ravenswood*, Renwood, **Ridge £**, Rosenblum, *Seghesio* and **Turley £**.
Sparkling Domaine Carneros, **Domaine Chandon**, Mumm Napa, **Roederer Estate** and **Schramsberg**.
Inexpensive estates Avila, Bogle, **Concannon**, Estancia, **Fetzer Bonterra**, Gallo, Hahn, Kendall-Jackson, J. Lohr, Marietta Cellars, **Ramsay**, Seventh Moon and **Wente**.

PACIFIC NORTHWEST
Wines from Oregon and Washington State are still very

hard to get hold of in the UK and are, therefore, expensive. Good luck with your search, but don't get too excited – while these producers all make sensational wines, you'll probably have to get on a plane to find them.

Oregon's best estates – **Adelsheim**, Archery Summit, Beaux Frères, Bethel Heights, **Cristom**, **Domaine Drouhin £**, Duck Pond, **Evesham Wood**, King Estate, Ponzi and Rex Hill.
Washington State's best estates – **Andrew Will £**, Château Ste-Michelle, DiStefano, **L'Ecole No 41**, **Leonetti Cellar £**, **Pepper Bridge**, **Quilceda Creek £**, Snoqualmie, **Woodward Canyon** and **Zefina**.

THE REST OF THE WORLD

Once again, in the interests of keeping things relatively sane and ordered, I have skipped out a load of less important (yes, I've said it – I don't mind causing a riot) winemaking countries and regions in the main body of the chapter. I know that the Jura, Savoie and Corsica were missed out of the French section, but I haven't drunk any bottles from these regions this year that have stopped me in my tracks. While Austria warrants its own mini-listing, Switzerland's fine wines fail to register on my Richter scale. This might be because the Swiss drink all of their wine in their own country, but maybe not!

Eastern Europe still leaves me cold, but it has to be said that Nagyréde and Riverview from Hungary are good operations, and Blueridge from Bulgaria manages to make passable wine, too. I don't drink them though – if you have a fiver to spend I can give you a load of fantastic wines in my Top 250 to spend it on. Having said that, someone must enjoy them somewhere. Tokaji from Hungary is widely regarded as the greatest wine from Eastern Europe, and if you haven't experienced this incredible burst of honeyed, luxurious, tropical fruit before, you should find a bottle immediately. They are, admittedly, all pretty expensive (around £20 for a 50cl bottle – but they go a long way). Look out for these producers – Disznókö, Oremus and the Royal Tokaji Wine Company.

Château Musar is still the Lebanon's most famous wine and Israel is apparently making some half decent wine, too, but I haven't seen any samples recently. Greek wines are continuing to improve, with Boutari, Gaia Estate, Gerovassiliou, Kir-Yanni, Nikos Lazaridis, Tsantali and Tselepos my favourite estates. I have thankfully managed to avoid Cypriot wine and the irresistable charms of Tenerife's finest this year, too. North African wines, from Tunisia and Morocco, are occasionally seen on UK shelves. There are some pretty chunky Carignans around, but nothing that can't be trumped by Sicilian Nero d'Avola or Primitivo from Puglia. Mexican, Bolivian and Peruvian wines are still a mystery to me (thank goodness) and I have not repeated last year's near fatal brush with Chinese wine (a Merlot that could have blinded me, I am sure). Uruguay is trying hard to excite but only Filgueria, Juanicó and Preludio, to date, have made swallowable wines – check out their Tannats. The Hatten winery in Bali is still going strong, as are the impressive Monsoon Valley wines from Thailand and the fascinating Sula Vineyard project in India. Rajeev Samant from Sula is a very passionate man and he will put his wines on lists up and down the country – watch out for them, they are pretty good. If the quality is up there (and some bottles look OK), we should be able to drink truly authentic, indigenous wines with our Asian and Indian cuisine in the near future. On that cheery note, I will say, 'Hoorah and mine's a large one!'

DIRECTORY
OF UK WINE
MERCHANTS

If your favourite wine shop isn't here, or if you're a brand new wine merchant and want to be included in next year's list, then drop me a line:
The Wine List, c/o Headline Book Publishing, 338 Euston Road, London, NW1 3BH

Subject to a thorough grilling, I will put you in next year's book!

KEY
✪ = Jukesy-rated wine merchant worthy of particular note
C = Wine sold by the case (often mixed) of twelve bottles
M = Mail order company, usually with no retail premises
F = Fine wine sales/wine broker/good range of expensive stuff!

RECOMMENDED LARGER CHAIN STORES AND SUPERMARKETS (PLUS ABBREVIATIONS)

Asda (Asd) 350 stores 0500 100055 www.asda.co.uk
E.H. Booth & Co., of Lancashire, Cheshire, Cumbria and Yorkshire (**Boo**) 26 stores 01772 251701 www.booths-supermarkets.co.uk ✪
Co-operative Group CWS (Coo) 1,750 stores 0800 068 6727 www.co-op.co.uk
Majestic Wine Warehouses (Maj) 127 stores and Majestic Fine Wine 12 stores 01923 298200 www.majestic.co.uk ✪C
Marks & Spencer (M&S) over 400 stores 020 7935 4422 www.marksandspencer.com ✪
Wm Morrison (Mor) more than 400 stores 01924 870000 www.morereasons.co.uk
Oddbins (Odd) 227 stores and **Oddbins Fine Wine shops** (**OFW**) 8 stores 0800 917 4093 www.oddbins.com
Sainsbury's (Sai) 728 stores 0800 636262 www.sainsburys.co.uk ✪
Somerfield Stores (Som) 1,000 stores 0117 935 6669 www.somerfield.co.uk

Tesco Stores (Tes) 1,224 stores 0800 505555
www.tesco.com ✪
Thresher Group – including **Thresher (Thr)** and **Wine Rack
(WRa)** around 2,000 stores 01707 387200
www.threshergroup.com ✪
Waitrose (Wai) 175 stores 0800 188 884
www.waitrose.com ✪
Wine Cellar (WCe) 187 stores 0800 838251
www.winecellar.co.uk

RECOMMENDED INDEPENDENT RETAIL SPECIALISTS, SMALL CHAINS, WINE BROKERS AND MAIL ORDER WINE COMPANIES SORTED ALPHABETICALLY

A & A Wines, Cranleigh, Surrey 01483 274666
aawines@aol.com **C**
A & B Vintners, Brenchley, Kent 01892 724977
info@abvintners.co.uk ✪**MC**
Abbey Wines, Melrose, Roxburghshire 01896 823224 ✪
Adnams Wine Merchants, Southwold, Suffolk 01502
727200 wines@adnams.co.uk ✪
Albion Wine Shippers, London 020 7242 0873
sales@albionwineshippers.co.uk
Ameys Wines, Sudbury, Suffolk 01787 377144 ✪
Amps Fine Wines of Oundle, near Peterborough,
Northamptonshire 01832 273502
info@ampsfinewines.co.uk ✪
Arkell Vintners, Swindon, Wiltshire 01793 823026
wines@arkells.com
John Armit Wines, London 020 7908 0600
info@armit.co.uk ✪**MCF**
W.J. Armstrong, East Grinstead, West Sussex 01342 321478
www.wjarmstrong.com
Arnolds, Broadway, Worcestershire 01386 852427

Arriba Kettle & Co., Broadway, Worcestershire
 01386 854700 arribakettle@aol.com **C**
Australian Wine Club, Slough, Berkshire 0800 8562004
 orders@australianwine.co.uk ✪**MC**
Averys, Bristol 0117 921 4146 ✪

William Baber Wines, Bath 01225 463 392
 office@tastingroom.co.uk
Bacchanalia, Cambridge 01223 576292 ✪
Bacchus Wine, Warrington, Buckinghamshire
 01234 711140 wine@bacchus.co.uk ✪**C**
Bakers & Larners, Holt, Norfolk 01263 712323
 ctbaker@cwcom.net
Stanley Ball, Crawley, West Sussex 01293 525777
 stanley_ball@msn.com
Ballantynes, Cowbridge, Vale of Glamorgan 01446 774840
 enq@ballantynes.co.uk ✪
Balls Brothers, London 020 7739 1642
 wine@ballsbrothers.co.uk **MC**
Georges Barbier, London 020 8852 5801
 georgesbarbier@f2s.com ✪**MC**
Barrels & Bottles, Sheepbridge, Chesterfield 01246 453399
 sales@barrelsandbottles.co.uk
Bat & Bottle, Oakham, Rutland 0845 108 4407
 post@batwine.com ✪
Beaconsfield Wine Cellar, Beaconsfield, Buckinghamshire
 01494 675545 info@beaconsfieldwinecellars.com
Bedales, London 020 7403 8853 info@bedalestreet.com ✪
Bella Wines, Newmarket, Suffolk 01638 604899
 sales@bellawines.co.uk ✪**M**
Bennetts Fine Wines, Chipping Campden, Gloucestershire
 01386 840392 enquiries@bennettsfinewines.com ✪
Bentalls, Kingston-upon-Thames, Surrey 020 8546 1001
Bergerac Wine Cellar, St Helier, Jersey 01534 870756

Berkmann Wine Cellars, London 020 7609 4711
  info@berkmann.co.uk ✪M

Berry Bros. & Rudd, London 0870 900 4300
  www.bbr.com ✪F

Best Cellars, Ashburton, Devon 01364 652546
  sales@bestcellars.co.uk

Bibendum Wine Ltd, London 020 7449 4120
  sales@bibendum-wine.co.uk ✪MCF

Bideford Wines, Bideford, Devon 01237 470507

Bintwo, Padstow, Cornwall 01841 532022
  david@bintwo.com ✪

Le Bon Vin, Sheffield 0114 2560090
  sales@lebonvin.co.uk

Bonhote Foster, Bumpstead, Suffolk 01440 730779
  info@bonhotefoster.co.uk **M**

Booths of Stockport, Heaton Moor, Stockport
0161 432 3309 johnbooth@lineone.net

Bordeaux Index, London 020 7253 2110
  sales@bordeauxindex.com ✪MF

The Bottleneck, Broadstairs, Kent 01843 861095
  sales@thebottleneck.co.uk

Bowland Forest Vintners, Clitheroe, Lancashire
01200 448688 milescorish@aol.com

Brinkleys Wines, London 020 7351 1683
  www.brinkleys.com

Burgundy Shuttle, London 07771 630826 **MC**

Burgundy Wines, Brighton, East Sussex 01273 330012
  md@BurgundyWines.co.uk

Butlers Wine Cellar, Brighton, East Sussex 01273 698724
  henry@butlers-winecellar.co.uk ✪

Anthony Byrne Fine Wines, Ramsey, Cambridgeshire
01487 814555 sales@abfw.co.uk **MC**

D. Byrne & Co., Clitheroe, Lancashire
  01200 423152 ✪

Cadman Fine Wines, Northampton, Northamptonshire
0845 1214011 sales@cadmanfinewines.co.uk

Cairns & Hickey, Bramhope, Leeds 0113 267 3746
pcairns@c-hwines.fsnet.co.uk

Cambridge Wine Merchants, Cambridge 01223 568 989
info@cambridgewine.com

Cape Wine & Food, Staines, Middlesex 01784 451860
capewineandfood@aol.com

Carley & Webb, Framlingham, Suffolk 01728 723503

Carringtons, Manchester 0161 466 2546

Castang Wine Shippers, Pelynt, Cornwall 01503 220359
sales@castang-wines.co.uk MC

Catchpole & Frogitt, Orsett, Essex 01375 892788
info@catchpoleandfrogitt.co.uk

Cave Cru Classé, London 020 7378 8579
enquiries@ccc.co.uk ✪MCF

Les Caves du Patron, Stoneygate, Leicester 0116 221 8221
wines@lescavesdupatron.com

Les Caves de Pyrene, Guildford, Surrey 01483 538820
sales@lescaves.co.uk ✪

Ceci Paolo, Ledbury, Herefordshire 01531 632976
www.cecipaolo.com

The Cellar Door, Overton, Hampshire 01256 770 397
info@thecellardoor.co.uk ✪

Cellar Door Wines, St Albans, Hertfordshire 01727 854488
sales@cellardoorwines.co.uk

The Champagne & Wine Cellar, Winchcombe,
Gloucestershire 01242 603514
grape.expectations@btinternet.com

Andrew Chapman Fine Wines, Abingdon, Oxfordshire
0845 458 0707 info@surf4wine.co.uk ✪

The Charterhouse Wine Co., Spalding, Lincolnshire
01775 720 300 info@charterhousewine.co.uk

Cheers Wine Merchants, Swansea 01792 403895

andrewcheers@hotmail.com

Cheshire Smokehouse, Wilmslow, Cheshire 01625 540123
sales@cheshiresmokehouselimited.co.uk

Chiltern Cellars, High Wycombe, Buckinghamshire
01494 526212

Chippendale Fine Wines, Bradford, West Yorkshire 01274
582424 mikepoll@chippendalewine.free-online.co.uk **MC**

Church House Vintners, Compton, Berkshire 01635 579 327
chv@saqnet.co.uk **MC**

Clarion Wines, London 020 8747 2069
info@clarionwines.co.uk

Clifton Cellars, Bristol 0117 973 0287
clifton@cellars.freeserve.co.uk

Coad Wine Cellars, Plympton, Devon 01752 334970
brian.coad@berkmann.co.uk ✪**MC**

Cockburns of Leith, Edinburgh 0131 346 1113
sales@winelist.co.uk

Colombier Vins Fins, Swadlincote, Derbyshire 01283 552552
colombier@colombierwines.co.uk **MC**

Compendium, Belfast 028 9079 1197
info@compendiumwines.com

Connolly's, Birmingham 0121 236 9269
chris@connollyswine.co.uk ✪

Constantine Stores, Falmouth, Cornwall 01326 340226
andrew@drinkfinder.co.uk

Cooden Cellars, Eastbourne, East Sussex 01323 649663
cooden@lineone.net ✪

Corks, Cotham, Bristol 0117 973 1620 sales@corksof.com ✪

Corkscrew Wines, Carlisle, Cumbria 01228 543033
corkscrewwines@aol.com

Corney & Barrow, London 020 7265 2400
wine@corbar.co.uk ✪**F**

Crane River Fine Wines, Middlesex 020 8891 4343
craneriviera@aol.com **MC**

Creber's, Tavistock, Devon 01822 612266
Croque-en-Bouche, Malvern Wells, Worcestershire
  01684 565612 mail@croque.co.uk ❂MC

Dartmouth Vintners, Dartmouth, Devon 01803 832602
  bill@dartmouthvintners.fsnet.co.uk
Andrew Darwin Fine Wines, Kington, Herefordshire
  01544 230534 darwin@kc3.co.uk
Davy's Wine Merchants, London 020 7407 9670
  jdavy@davy.co.uk
Decorum Vintners, London 020 8969 6581
  admin-decvin@decvin.com ❂MC
deFINE Food and Wine, Sandiway, Cheshire 01606 882101
  office@definefoodandwine.com ❂
Rodney Densem Wines, Crewe 01270 212200
  sales@rdwines.com
F.L. Dickins, Rickmansworth, Hertfordshire
01923 773636
Direct Wine Shipments, Belfast 028 9050 8000
  enquiry@directwine.co.uk ❂
Direct Wines, Theale, Reading 0870 444 8383
  orders@laithwaites.co.uk ❂MF
Dodici Wines, Harpenden, Hertfordshire 01582 713004
  info@dodici.co.uk
Domaine Direct, London 020 7837 1142
  mail@domainedirect.co.uk ❂C
The Dorchester Wine Centre at Eldridge Pope,
  Dorchester, Dorset 01305 258266
  wineshopdorchester@eldridge.pope.co.uk ❂
Dunells Premier Wines Ltd, St Peter, Jersey 01534 736418
  dunells.wines@jerseymail.co.uk ❂

Eagle's Wines, London 020 7223 7209
East Coast Wines, Grimsby, N E Lincolnshire 01472 827207

M = Mail order company, usually with no retail premises
F = Fine wine sales/wine broker/good range of expensive stuff!

sales@the winewarehouse.net
Edencroft Fine Wines, Nantwich, Cheshire 01270 629975
sales@edencroft.co.uk
Ells Fine Wines, Portadown 028 3833 2306
rrwines@hotmail.com
El Vino, London 020 7353 5384 all@elvino.co.uk
English Wine Centre, Alfriston Roundabout, East Sussex
01323 870164 bottles@englishwine.co.uk
Eton Vintners, Windsor 01753 790188
sales@etonvintners.co.uk M
Evertons, Abberley, Worcestershire 01299 890113
sales@evertonswines.co.uk
Evingtons Wine Merchants, Leicester 0116 254 2702
evingtonwine@fsbdial.co.uk
Execellars, Kennford, Exeter, Devon 0800 0838075
andy@execellars.co.uk

Farr Vintners, London 020 7821 2000
sales@farrvintners.com ✪MF
Fine & Rare Wines, London 020 8960 1995
wine@frw.co.uk ✪MF
Fine Cheese Co., Bath 01225 483407 sales@finecheese.co.uk
Fine Wines of New Zealand, London 020 7482 0093
sales@fwnz.co.uk ✪M
Irma Fingal-Rock, Monmouth, Monmouthshire 01600
712372 tom@pinotnoir.co.uk
Flagship Wines, St Albans, Hertfordshire 01727 841968
info@flagshipwines.co.uk ✪
Le Fleming Wines, Harpenden, Hertfordshire 01582 760125
MC
Rodney Fletcher Vintners, Horsmonden, Kent 01892
723084 wine@rfvintners.co.uk
The Flying Corkscrew, Hemel Hempstead, Hertfordshire
01442 412311 sales@flyingcorkscrew.com ✪

Forge Wines, Marksbury, Bath 01761 472349
wine@laforgewines.com MF

Fortnum & Mason, London 020 7734 8040
info@fortnumandmason.co.uk ✿

Four Walls Wine Company, Chilgrove, West Sussex
01243 535360 fourwallswine@aol.com ✿MF

Friarwood, London 020 7736 2628 sales@friarwood.com

FWW Wines, London 020 8567 3731
sales@fwwwines.demon.co.uk ✿MC

Gallery Wines, Gomshall, Surrey 01483 203795
info@thegomshallgallery.net

Garland Wine Cellar, Ashtead, Surrey 01372 275247
stephen@garlandwines.co.uk

Garrards, Cockermouth, Cumbria 01900 823592
admin@garrards-wine.co.uk

Gauntleys, Nottingham 0115 911 0555
rhone@gauntleywine.com ✿

General Wine Company, Liphook, Hampshire 01428
727744 sales@thegeneralwine.co.uk ✿

Genesis Wines, London 020 7963 9060
mattw@genesiswines.com ✿

Goedhuis & Co., London 020 7793 7900
sales@goedhuis.com ✿MCF

Gourmet Vintners, Billingshurst, West Sussex
01403 784128 sales@gourmetvintners.co.uk

Peter Graham Wines, Norwich, Norfolk 01603 598910
louisa@petergrahamwines.com

Richard Granger Fine Wine Merchants, Newcastle-upon-
Tyne 0191 281 5000 sales@richardgrangerwines.co.uk

The Grape Shop, London 020 7924 3638
dp@thegrapeshop.com ✿

The Great Grog Wine Co., Edinburgh 0131 662 4777
www.greatgrog.co.uk

Great Northern Wines, Ripon, North Yorkshire
01765 606767 info@greatnorthernwine.com ✪M
Great Western Wine Company, Bath 01225 322800
wine@greatwesternwine.co.uk ✪
Peter Green, Edinburgh 0131 229 5925
shop@petergreenwines.com
The Grogblossom, London 020 7794 7808
Patrick Grubb Selections, Oxford 01869 340229
patrickgrubbselections@btinternet.com ✪
Gunson Fine Wines, Hastings, East Sussex 01424 445777
dion@gfwl.co.uk ✪MC

H & H Bancroft Wines, London 020 7232 5450
sales@bancroftwines.com ✪MC
Alexander Hadleigh, Locks Heath, Southampton 01489
885959 info@ahadleigh-wine.com
Hailsham Cellars, Hailsham, East Sussex 01323 441212
wine@hailshamcellars.com
Halifax Wine Company, Halifax, West Yorkshire 01422
256333 andy@halifaxwinecompany.com ✪
Hall & Woodhouse Ltd, Blandford, Dorset 01258 452 141
admin@hall-woodhouse.co.uk
Handford Wines, London 020 7221 9614
wine@handford.net✪F
Hanslope Wines, Milton Keynes, Buckinghamshire
01908 510262 charles@hanslopewines.co.uk
Roger Harris Wines, Weston Longville, Norfolk
01603 880171 sales@rogerharriswines.co.uk ✪MC
Harrods, London 020 7730 1234 ✪F
Harrogate Fine Wine, Harrogate, North Yorkshire
01423 522270 enquiries@harrogatefinewine.co.uk
Harvey Nichols & Co., London 020 7201 8537
wineshop@harveynichols.com ✪
Richard Harvey Wines, Wareham, Dorset 01929 481437

harvey@lds.co.uk MC

The Haslemere Cellar, Haslemere, Surrey 01428 645081
info@haslemerecellar.co.uk ❂

Haynes, Hanson & Clark, London 020 7259 0102
london@hhandc.co.uk and Stow-on-the-Wold,
Gloucestershire 01451 870808 stow@hhandc.co.uk ❂

Hedley Wright, Bishop's Stortford, Hertfordshire
01279 465818 sales@hedleywright.co.uk C

Henderson Wines, Edinburgh 0131 447 8580
hendersonwines@btconnect.com

Charles Hennings Vintners, Pulborough, West Sussex
01798 872671 sales@chv-wine.co.uk

Hercules Wines, Sandwich, Kent 01304 617100
mail@herculeswines.co.uk

Hicks & Don, Edington, Wiltshire 01380 831234
mailbox@hicksanddon.co.uk M

George Hill, Loughborough, Leicestershire 01509 212717
andrewh@georgehill.co.uk

Hills Drinks and Oasis Wines, Benfleet, Essex 01268 772611
hillsdrinks@btconnect.com

Hopton Wines, Kidderminster, Shropshire 01299 270734
chris@hoptoncourt.fsnet.co.uk MC

Hoults Wine Merchants, Huddersfield, West
Yorkshire 01484 510700
rob@hoults-winemerchants.co.uk

House of Townend, Kingston upon Hull, East Yorkshire
01482 586582 info@houseoftownend.co.uk ❂

Ian G. Howe, Newark, Nottinghamshire 01636 704366
howe@chablis-burgundy.co.uk

Victor Hugo Wines, St Saviour, Jersey 01534 507977
sales@victor-hugo-wines.com

Inspired Wines, Cleobury Mortimer, Shropshire
01299 270064 sales@inspired-wines.co.uk

Inverarity Vaults, Biggar 01899 308000
info@inverarity-vaults.com ✪
Irvine Robertson, Edinburgh 0131 553 3521
irviner@nildram.co.uk C

Jeroboams (incorporating Laytons Wine Merchants),
London 020 7259 6716 sales@jeroboams.co.uk ✪
Michael Jobling, Newcastle-upon-Tyne 0191 378 4554
info@michaeljoblingwines.com MC
N.D. John, Swansea 01792 644688
nj@ndjohnwinemerchants.co.uk
The Jolly Vintner, Tiverton, Devon 01884 255644
L & F Jones, Radstock near Bath 01761 417117
buying.buying@lfjones.aclm.co.uk
S.H. Jones, Banbury, Oxfordshire 01295 251177
shj@shjones.com ✪
Justerini & Brooks, London 020 7484 6400 ✪F
Just in Case Wine Merchants, Bishop's Waltham,
Hampshire 01489 892969
justincase@bishopswaltham9.fsnet.co.uk

Joseph Keegan & Sons Ltd, Holyhead, Isle of Anglesey
01407 762333 enquiries@josephkeegan.co.uk
Christopher Keiller, Redruth, Cornwall 01209 215706
ghost@gladys.demon.co.uk
John Kelly Wines, Boston Spa, West Yorkshire 01937
842965 john@kellywines.co.uk MC
Kelly of Cults Ltd, Aberdeen 0845 456 1902
Kendalls, Manchester 0161 8323414
Kendrick Wines, Bromley, Kent 020 8467 7524
kmcclem@aol.com
David Kibble Wines, Fontwell, West Sussex 01243 544111
Richard Kihl, Aldeburgh, Suffolk 01728 454455
sales@richardkihl.ltd.uk ✪CF

Laithwaites, Reading, Berkshire 0870 444 8282
orders@laithwaites.co.uk ✪MC

Largs Wine Haven, Largs, Ayrshire 07092 01386
winehaven@tiscali.co.uk

Lay & Wheeler, Holton St Mary, Suffolk 0845 330 1855
sales@laywheeler.com ✪

Laymont & Shaw, Truro, Cornwall 01872 270545
info@laymont-shaw.co.uk ✪MC

Lea & Sandeman, London 020 7244 0522
sales@leaandsandeman.co.uk ✪

O.W. Loeb & Co. Ltd, London 020 7234 0385
finewine@owloeb.com ✪MC

J & H Logan, Edinburgh 0131 667 2855

Longford Wines, Lewes, East Sussex 01273 400012
longfordwines@aol.com MC

Luckins Wine Store, Great Dunmow, Essex 01371 872839
andyfiltness@winebuffs.net

Luvian's Bottle Shop, Cupar, Fife 01334 654820
info@luvians.com ✪

Magnum Wine Company, Swindon, Wiltshire
01793 642569 ✪

Map Wines, Bridgwater, Somerset 01278 459 622
davidpreece@map-wines.freeserve.co.uk

Martinez Wines, Ilkley, West Yorkshire 01943 603241
editor@martinez.co.uk ✪MC

Mason & Mason, West Stoke, West Sussex 01243 535364
sales@masonandmasonwines.co.uk ✪MC

Mill Hill Wines, London 020 8959 6754
laurence@millhillwines.com

Mille Gusti, London 020 8997 3932 millegusti@hotmail.com
✪MC

Mills Whitcombe, Peterchurch, Herefordshire 01981 550028
info@millswhitcombe.co.uk ✪C

Milton Sandford Wines, Knowl Hill, Berkshire 01628
829449 sales@miltonsandfordwines.com ✪MC
Mitchell's Vintners, Sheffield 0114 274 5587
info@mitchellsdirect.com
Montrachet Fine Wines, London 020 7928 1990
charles@montrachetwine.com ✪MC
Moonshine, Bourne, Lincolnshire 01778 421050
andy@moonshine.fsbusiness.co.uk
Moreno Wines, London 020 7960 7161
sales@moreno-wines.co.uk ✪
Moriarty Vintners, Cardiff 029 2022 9996
sales@moriarty-vintners.com
Duncan Murray Wines, Market Harborough, Leicestershire
01858 464935 info@duncanmurraywines.co.uk

Naked Grape, Alresford, Hampshire 0845 226 2550
www.thenakedgrape.co.uk
Nectarous Wines, Cheltenham, Gloucestershire
01242 224466 taste@nectarous.co.uk ✪
The New Pantry, London 020 7602 6964
James Nicholson, Crossgar, Co. Down, Northern Ireland
028 4483 0091 shop@jnwine.com ✪
Nickolls & Perks, Stourbridge, West Midlands 01384 394518
sales@nickollsandperks.co.uk
Nicolas UK of London 20+ stores 020 8944 7514
www.nicolas.co.uk
Nidderdale Fine Wines, Harrogate, North Yorkshire 01423
711703 info@southaustralianwines.com ✪
Noble Rot Wine Warehouse, Bromsgrove, Worcestershire
01527 575606 sales@noble-rot.co.uk ✪
The Nobody Inn, Doddiscombsleigh, Devon 01647 252394
info@nobodyinn.co.uk ✪
Novum Wines, London 020 7820 6720
info@novumwines.com ✪C

Off the Vine, St Albans, Hertfordshire
01727 898290
The Old Forge Wine Cellar, Storrington, West Sussex
01903 744246 enquiry@winelist.net
Oxford Wine Company, Witney, Oxfordshire 01865 301144
info@oxfordwine.co.uk ✪
Oz Wines, London 0845 450 1261 sales@ozwines.co.uk ✪

Page & Sons, Ramsgate, Kent 01843 591214
mail@pageandsons.co.uk
Thomas Panton, Tetbury, Gloucestershire 01666 503088
info@wineimporter.co.uk M
Parfrements, Coventry, West Midlands 024 7650 3646
sales@parfrements.co.uk
Paxton & Whitfield, London 020 7930 0259
sales@cheesemongers.co.uk
Peake Wine Associates, Fareham, Hampshire 01329 822733
roy@farehamwinecellar.co.uk
Thos Peatling, Bury St Edmunds, Suffolk 01284 755948
sales@thospeatling.co.uk
Peckham & Rye, Glasgow 0141 445 4555
alan.rose@peckhams.co.uk ✪
Penistone Court Wine Cellars, Penistone, Sheffield
01226 766037 pcwc@dircon.co.uk ✪MC
Philglas & Swiggot, London 020 7924 4494
wine@philglas-swiggot.co.uk ✪
Laurence Philippe Wines, Chelmsford, Essex 01245 475454
lpwines@lineone.net
Christopher Piper Wines, Ottery St Mary, Devon
01404 814139 sales@christopherpiperwines.co.uk ✪
Plato Harrison, Kirkby Lonsdale, Cumbria 01524 271288
info@platoharrison.com
Terry Platt Wine Merchants, Llandudno, Conwy
01492 874099 info@terryplattwines.co.uk ✪MC

Planet Wine Ltd, Sale, Cheshire 0161 973 1122
sales@planetwine.co.uk MC

Playford Ros, Sowerby, North Yorkshire 01845 526777
sales@playfordros.com MC

Portal, Dingwall & Norris, Emsworth, Hampshire
01243 377883 philip@pdnagencies.com

Portland Wine Co., Sale, Manchester 0161 962 8752
portwineco@aol.com

Premier Cru Fine Wine, Guiseley, Leeds 01943 877004
enquiries@premiercrufinewine.co.uk

Quay West Wines, Stoke Canon, Exeter 01392 841833
sales@quaywestwines.co.uk C

Quellyn Roberts, Chester, Cheshire 01244 310455
sales@qrwines.co.uk

R.S. Wines, Winford, Bath and Northeast Somerset
01275 331 444 sales@rswines.co.uk MC

Arthur Rackham Emporia, Guildford, Surrey 0870 870 1110
info@ar-emporia.com C

Raeburn Fine Wines, Edinburgh 0131 343 1159
sales@raeburnfinewines.com ✪

Ravensbourne Wine, London 020 8692 9655
sales@ravensbournewine.co.uk C

Regency Wines, Exeter, Devon 01392 444123

Reid Wines, Hallatrow, Bristol 01761 452645
reidwines@aol.com ✪MF

Revelstoke Wines, London 020 8545 0077
sales@revelstoke.co.uk ✪MC

Richardson & Sons, Whitehaven, Cumbria 01946 65334
richardsonandsons@btconnect.com

Howard Ripley Ltd, London 020 8877 3065
info@howardripley.com ✪MC

Roberson, London 020 7371 2121 wines@roberson.co.uk ✪

Roberts & Speight, Beverley, East Yorkshire 01482 870717
sales@foodbites.karoo.co.uk

Robert Rolls, London 020 7606 1166 mail@rollswine.com
✪MCF

R & R Fine Wines, Bury, Lancashire 0161 762 0022
info@randrfinewines.co.uk ✪

St Martin Vintners, Brighton, East Sussex 01273 777744
sales@stmartinvintners.co.uk

Sandhams Wine Merchants Ltd, Caistor, Lincolnshire
01472 852118 sales@sandhamswine.co.uk

Scatchard's, Liverpool 0151 922 7346 jon@scatchard.com

Seckford Wines, Woodbridge, Suffolk 01394 446622
sales@seckfordwines.co.uk ✪MCF

Selfridges, London 020 7318 3730 and Manchester
0161 838 0659 wine.club@selfridges.co.uk ✪

Shaftesbury Fine Wines, Shaftesbury, Dorset 01747 850059
prbennett@shafwine.fsnet.co.uk

Shaws of Beaumaris, Isle of Anglesey 01248 810328
wines@shaws.sagehost.co.uk

Edward Sheldon, Shipston-on-Stour, Warwickshire
01608 661409 finewine@edward-sheldon.co.uk

H. Smith, Ashbourne, Derbyshire 01335 342150
horace.smith@tiscali.co.uk

Laurence Smith, Edinburgh 0131 667 3327
info@winesmith.biz MC

Soho Wine Supply, London 020 7636 8490
info@sohowine.co.uk

Sommelier Wine Co. Ltd, St Peter Port, Guernsey
01481 721677 ✪

Springfield Wines, near Huddersfield, West Yorkshire
01484 864929 springfieldwines@aol.com

Frank Stainton Wines, Kendal, Cumbria 01539 731886
admin@stainton-wines.co.uk

Stanton Wine Co., Broadway, Worcestershire 01386 852501
sales@stantonwineco.co.uk
William Stedman, Caerleon, Newport 01633 430055
info@wmstedman.co.uk
Charles Steevenson, Tavistock, Devon 01822 616272
sales@steevensonwines.co.uk MC
Stevens Garnier, Oxford 01865 263303
info@stevensgarnier.co.uk ✪
Stokes Fine Wines, London 020 8944 5979
sales@stokesfinewines.com ✪MC
Stone, Vine & Sun, Winchester, Hampshire 01962 712351
sales@stonevine.co.uk ✪
Stratford's Wine Agencies, Cookham-on-Thames, Berkshire
01628 810606 sales@stratfordwine.co.uk ✪MC
The Sussex Wine Company, Eastbourne, East Sussex
01323 431143 sales@thesussexwinecompany.co.uk ✪
SWIG, London 020 8995 7060
imbibe@swig.co.uk ✪MC

T & W Wines, Brandon, Suffolk 01842 814414
contact@tw-wines.com
Tanners, Shrewsbury, Shropshire 01743 234455
sales@tanners-wines.co.uk ✪
Taurus Wines, Bramley, Surrey 01483 548484
sales@tauruswines.co.uk
ten-acre wines, Welwyn Garden City, Hertfordshire
01707 372760 brian@ten-acre.com ✪
Terroir, Skipton, North Yorkshire 01756 700512
enquiries@terroirlanguedoc.co.uk ✪MC
Thameside Wines, London 020 8878 4752
sales@thamesidewines.com
Theatre of Wine, London 020 8858 6363 ✪
Totnes Wine Co., Totnes, Devon 01803 866357
info@totneswine.co.uk

Trenchermans, Sherborne, Dorset 01935 432857
info@trenchermans.com
Turville Valley Wines, Great Missenden, Buckinghamshire
01494 868818 info@turville-valley-wines.com ✪MCF

Uncorked, London 020 7638 5998 drink@uncorked.co.uk ✪
Unwined Ltd, Sedgebrook, Nottinghamshire 01949 844324
enquiries@unwined.biz

Valvona & Crolla, Edinburgh 0131 556 6066
sales@valvonacrolla.co.uk ✪
Helen Verdcourt, Maidenhead, Berkshire 01628 625577 MC
Veritas Wines, Cambridge 01223 212500
info@veritaswines.co.uk
Veritaus, Alton, Hampshire 020 7353 5385
sales@veritaus.com
Vickbar, London 020 7490 1000
www.vickbarwines.com.uk C
Vicki's Wine Merchants, Chobham, Surrey 01276 858374 ✪
Les Vignerons de St Georges, Windlesham, Surrey 01276
850136 greatfood@the-inn.co.uk
Villeneuve Wines, Peebles, Haddington and Edinburgh
01721 722500 wines@villeneuvewines.com ✪
Vin du Van, Appledore, Kent 01233 758727 ✪MC
Vinceremos, Leeds 0113 244 0002
info@vinceremos.co.uk MC
The Vine Trail, Hotwells, Bristol 0117 921 1770
enquiries@vinetrail.co.uk ✪MC
The Vineyard, Dorking, Surrey 01306 876828
jh@vineyard-direct.co.uk
The Vineyard Cellars, Hungerford, Berkshire 01488 681313
jameshocking@vineyardcellars.com ✪MC
Vino Vino, New Malden, Surrey 07703 436949
vinovino@macunlimited.net MC

The Vintage House, London 020 7437 2592
  vintagehouse.co@virgin.net
Vintage Roots, Arborfield, Berkshire 0118 976 1999
  info@vintageroots.co.uk ✪M
Vintage Wine Cellars, Luton, Bedfordshire 01582 455068
  sales@vintagewinecellars.co.uk

Wadebridge Wines, Wadebridge, Cornwall 01208 812692
  info@wwrw.co.uk
Waterloo Wine, London 020 7403 7967
  sales@waterloowine.co.uk
Waters of Coventry, Heathcote, Warwick 01926 888889
  info@waters-wine-merchants.co.uk
T.B. Watson Ltd, Dumfries, Dumfriesshire 01387 256601
  karen@tbwatson.co.uk
David J. Watt Fine Wines, Austrey, Warwickshire
  01827 830134 fwatt@lineone.net M
Wattisfield Wines, Bury St Edmunds, Suffolk 01359 251260
Peter Watts, Coggeshall, Essex 01376 5661130
  sales@peterwattswines.co.uk
Weavers of Nottingham, Nottingham 0115 958 0922
  weavers@weaverswines.com ✪
Welshpool Wine, Powys 01938 553243
  info@welshpoolwine.com ✪
Wessex Wines, Bridport, Dorset 01308 427177
  wessexwines@amserve.com C
Whitebridge Wines, Stone, Staffordshire 01785 817229
  sales@whitebridgewines.co.uk
Whitesides of Clitheroe, Lancashire 01200 422281
  whitesides.wine@btconnect.com
Whittalls Wines, Walsall, West Midlands 01922 636161
  jrushton@efb.co.uk C
Wicked Wines, Pockthorpe, Kilham, East Yorkshire
  01377 255725

Wilkinson Vintners Ltd, London 020 7616 0404
 wine@wilkinsonvintners.com ✪MCF
James Williams, Narberth, Pembrokeshire
 01834 862200
Wimbledon Wine Cellar, London 020 8540 9979
 enquiries@wimbledonwinecellar.com ✪
Winchcombe Wine Merchants, Winchcombe,
 Gloucestershire 01451 850686
The WineBarn, Dummer, Hampshire 01256 391211
 info@thewinebarn.co.uk ✪
Wine Barrels, London 020 7228 3306
 edwood@scvintners.f9.co.uk
The Wine Cellar, South Croydon, Surrey 020 8657 6936
 winecellarsnd@aol.com
Wine in Cornwall, Penryn, Cornwall 01326 379426
 sales@wineincornwall.co.uk
The Wine Library, London 020 7481 0415
 info@winelibrary.co.uk
The Wineman, Streatley-on-Thames, West Berkshire
 01635 203050 sales@wine-man.com MC
The Wine Mill, Nelson, Lancashire 01282 614618
 enquiries@thewinemill.co.uk ✪
The Wine Portfolio, London 020 7843 1600
 sales@wineportfolio.co.uk
Wine Raks, Aberdeen 01224 311460
 mike@wineraks.co.uk ✪
Wine Society, Stevenage, Hertfordshire 01438 741177
 memberservices@thewinesociety.com ✪MCF
The Wine Treasury, London 020 7793 9999
 bottled@winetreasury.com ✪MC
The Winery, London 020 7286 6475
 info@thewineryuk.com ✪F
Wines of Interest, Ipswich, Suffolk 0870 224 5640
 sales@winesofinterest.co.uk

The Winesmith, Peterborough, Cambridgeshire
 01780 783102 cases@winesmith.co.uk
WineTime, Milnthorpe, Cumbria 01539 562030 **MC**
Worcester Wine Co., Worcestershire 01905 425588
T. Wright, Bolton, Greater Manchester 01204 697805
 wayne.t.wright@fsmill.net
The Wright Wine Company, Skipton, North Yorkshire
 01756 700886 www.wineandwhisky.co.uk ✪
Wrightson & Co., Catterick Garrison, North Yorkshire
 01748 832666 simon@wrightsonwines.co.uk **MC**
Wycombe Wines, High Wycombe, Buckinghamshire
 01494 437228
Peter Wylie Fine Wines, Plymtree, Devon 01884 277555
 peter@wylie-fine-wines.demon.co.uk ✪**F**

Yapp Brothers, Mere, Wiltshire 01747 860423
 sales@yapp.co.uk ✪**MC**
Noel Young Wines, Trumpington, Cambridgeshire
 01223 844744 admin@nywines.co.uk ✪ **F**

AUSTRALIA

Margaret River, WA	2005 2004 2003 2002 2001 2000 1999 1997 1996 1995 1994 1992 1991
Barossa Valley, SA	2005 2004 2003 2002 2001 1998 1997 1996 1994 1993 1992 1991 1990 1988 1986
Clare Valley, SA	2005 2004 2003 2002 2001 1999 1998 1997 1996 1994 1992 1991 1990
Coonawarra, SA	2005 2004 2003 2002 2001 2000 1999 1998 1996 1994 1993 1991 1990
Yarra Valley, VIC	2005 2004 2003 2002 2001 1998 1997 1996 1994
Hunter Valley, NSW	2005 2004 2003 2002 2000 1999 1998 1997 1995 1992 1991 1990

FRANCE

Alsace		2005 2004 2003 2002 2001 2000 1999 1998 1997 1996 1995 1993 1990 1989 1988 1986 1985 1983
Burgundy	Chablis	2005 2004 2003 2002 2000 1999 1998 1997 1996 1995 1992 1990 1989 1988 1986
	Côte d'Or	2005 2004 2003 2002 2001 2000 1999 1998 1997 1996 1995 1992 1990 1989 1988 1986 1985 1983
	Beaujolais	2005 2004 2003 2002 2000 1999 1998 1997 1995 1990 1989 1988

Bordeaux	Left Bank	2005 2004 2003 2001 2000 1999 1998 1996 1995 1990 1989 1988 1986 1985 1983 1982
	Right Bank	2005 2004 2003 2001 2000 1999 1998 1996 1995 1990 1989 1988 1986 1985 1983 1982
	Sauternes	2005 2004 2003 2001 1999 1998 1997 1996 1995 1990 1989 1988 1986 1983
Rhône	Northern	2005 2004 2003 2001 2000 1999 1998 1997 1996 1995 1994 1990 1989 1988 1985 1983
	Southern	2005 2004 2003 2001 2000 1999 1998 1995 1990 1989 1988 1985 1983
Loire	Sweeties	2005 2004 2003 2002 2001 2000 1999 1997 1996 1995 1993 1990 1989 1988 1985 1983 1982
Champagne		2002 2000 1998 1997 1996 1995 1990 1989 1988 1985 1980 1976
Languedoc/ Roussillon		2005 2004 2003 2001 2000 1999 1998 1996 1995 1994 1993 1990 1989 1988 1986 1985
Provence		2005 2004 2003 2001 2000 1999 1998 1997 1996 1995 1993 1991 1990 1989 1988 1985

the best recent vintages

GERMANY
Mosel   2005 2004 2003 2002 2001 1999 1997
                       1996 1995 1994 1993 1992 1990 1989
                       1988 1983

Rheingau   2005 2004 2003 2002 2001 1999 1997
                       1996 1995 1994 1993 1992 1990 1989
                       1988 1983

ITALY
Piedmont   2005 2004 2003 2001 2000 1998 1997
                       1996 1990 1989 1988 1985

Tuscany   2005 2004 2003 2001 1999 1997 1995
                       1993 1990 1988 1985 1983 1982

Veneto   2005 2004 2003 2001 2000 1997 1995
                       1993 1990 1988 1985

NEW ZEALAND
North Island   2005 2004 2003 2002 2001 2000
Hawkes Bay (reds)   1999 1998 1994 1991 1990

South Island   2006 2005 2004 2003 2002 2001
Marlborough (whites)   2000 1999 1998

PORTUGAL
Vintage Port   2003 2000 1997 1995 1994 1992 1991
                       1985 1983 1977 1970 1966 1963

SOUTH AFRICA
                       2005 2004 2003 2002 2001 2000
                       1999 1998 1997 1995

SOUTH AMERICA

Chile	2005 2004 2003 2002 2001 1999 1996 1995
Argentina	2005 2004 2002 2001 1999 1997 1996 1995

SPAIN

Rioja	2004 2003 2002 2001 2000 1999 1998 1996 1995 1994 1991 1990 1987 1982 1981
Ribera del Duero	2004 2003 2001 1999 1998 1996 1995 1994 1990 1987 1986 1983 1982 1981
Penedès/Priorat	2005 2004 2003 2001 2000 1999 1998 1996 1995 1994 1993 1992 1985

USA

North Coast	2004 2003 2002 2001 1999 1998 1997 1996 1995 1994 1992 1991 1990
Napa and Carneros	2004 2003 2002 2001 1999 1997 1995 1994 1992 1991 1990 1987 1986 1985 1984
Central Coast	2004 2003 2002 2001 1999 1998 1997 1996 1995 1994 1993 1992 1991 1990
Oregon/Washington	2004 2003 2002 2001 2000 1999 1998 1996 1994 1992 1990 1989

index 255

TABLE OF ABBREVIATIONS

Asd	Asda
Boo	E. H. Booth & Co
Coo	Co-operative Group (CWS)
M&S	Marks & Spencer
Maj	Majestic Wine Warehouses
Mor	Wm Morrison
Odd	Oddbins
OFW	Oddbins Fine Wine
Sai	Sainsbury's
Som	Somerfield Stores
Tes	Tesco Stores
Thr	Thresher
Wai	Waitrose
WCe	Wine Cellar
WRa	Wine Rack